William Charles Maughan

Rosneath

Past and Present

William Charles Maughan

Rosneath
Past and Present

ISBN/EAN: 9783337077051

Printed in Europe, USA, Canada, Australia, Japan

Cover: Foto ©ninafisch / pixelio.de

More available books at **www.hansebooks.com**

ROSNEATH

ROSNEATH

PAST AND PRESENT

BY

WILLIAM CHARLES MAUGHAN

AUTHOR OF "THE ALPS OF ARABIA," ETC., ETC.

With an Original Poem by the Marquis of Lorne, K.T.

AND

Illustrations by Alex. M'Gibbon, Esq.

ALEXANDER GARDNER
Publisher to Her Majesty the Queen
PAISLEY; AND 26 PATERNOSTER SQUARE, LONDON

1893

To

GEORGE DOUGLAS CAMPBELL,

DUKE OF ARGYLL, K.G., K.T.,

A British Statesman and a Scottish Patriot,

THIS BOOK

IS RESPECTFULLY DEDICATED.

PREFACE.

THE following pages form a modest contribution to those local, secular, and ecclesiastical records of interesting places in our land which are a little removed from the more stirring domains of Scottish history. The author, having resided for over twenty years in the district, has been able to glean his facts from various sources, chiefly the recollections and experiences of aged natives and residents, many of whom have passed away. Much, therefore, of what must irrevocably have been lost is here set down, and it is hoped that the peculiar attractiveness of the beautiful Peninsula, and its inherent poetic and pictorial charms, may render the volume acceptable.

Hardly anything has ever been written about Rosneath, and the tiny rills which it has contributed to the noble stream of Scottish history have but gently meandered on their way. But not a few remarkable men have wandered by its pebbly strand, and inhaled the pure air of its heathery braes, and it is hoped that many may welcome this effort to bring the manifold fascinations of the Peninsula under the notice of a wider circle.

KILARDEN,
ROSNEATH, *12th July, 1893.*

ROSNEATH.

HEIRLOOM of red Flodden's glory! guarded through so many ages,
From thy tranquil, happy story, men may fill enchanted pages—
Tell of Peace as here abiding, when around raged strife and clangour;
Here in peace they dwelt whose guiding led the realm through years of anger;

A.D. 1155. From the times when all these regions heard the shock of Norway's galleys,
And the Maiden Monarch's legions saved the land in yonder valleys;

A.D. 1250. Once again by Haco shaken with invasion's fiery trial,
Till at Largs the challenge taken was repelled with grim denial.
Still, through all, a calm reposes on these woods, and bays, and shallows—
Peace for us in memory closes in the place affection hallows!

Legends tell how noble Wallace here awhile his destined sorrow
Baffled, ere o'er wrong and malice dawned his country's happier morrow.

A.D. 1295. Read the Blind Bard's rough recital! How Rosneath's tall castle slumbered
When he dealt his foes requital, and these shores with dead were cumbered.
It had seen beneath its rafter, king, and soldier, and crusader:
Freed from alien bonds thereafter, never hither came invader.

A.D. 1310. Stoutly from Dunoon Sir Nigel all its English captors hounded,
—Broke with Bruce our nation's vigil—clear our Freedom's trumpet sounded!

A.D. 1430. Hence Sir Duncan bore the treasure, ransom of the King, whose throning
Brought him from fair Windsor's pleasure to the doom of death and moaning.

A.D. 1415. Hence the Chancellor, whose father first as heir this soil had trodden,
Went to meet his fate and gather glory in the van at Flodden.

A.D. 1520. Here too lived, young joy upon her, Margaret Douglas, loved and cherished,
Ere for Covenant and for Honour, earthly good had nobly perished,

A.D. 1661. When the house-dogs howled disaster in the hour the Lord had beckoned,
And Edina saw their master to the martyrs' army reckoned.

A.D. 1685. Yet again these shores were lonely when their bravest went to slaughter,
Fortune's dice were thrown, and only thrown too soon at Cart's dark water!
Still when wars were surging nearer to this Isle in beauty moulded,
It but seemed to Peace the dearer. Here she stood, her white wings folded—

A.D. 1715. Never left the loved green Island—stayed, its watchful, bright defender,
When through Lowland and through Highland rolled the wars of the Pretender.
He who fixed his steadfast gaze on work to bind the realms together
And enrolled within his blazon England's rose with Scotland's heather—
He who rode through Party's phases, borne aloft o'er sneers and slanders
As he rode with poet's praises through the Frenchmen's ranks in Flanders
Long ere ago his fire arrested, when all loves and hates are chastened
Here from war and council rested, here the reign of mercy hastened.

Yes, e'en now, when strokes of hammer on no mailéd forms are ringing,
But with iron tongue and clamour Trade's great song are ever singing,
Peace yet stands, her love unfailing. Here, while Commerce grows around her,
Doth she bless her navies sailing to all lands where men have crowned her.
Here amidst her groves of beeches, pine and fir, and rose and laurel,
Many a memory downward reaches from the days of care and quarrel ;
From the triumph and endeavour that at last in equal measure
Made our Scotland share forever in her foeman's fame and treasure :
When from Cove to Ardencaple flames the western sky, and splendour
Falls on keep, and stream, and chapel, scenes as fair as earth can render,
Speak of deeds, that high and lowly, well may prize as Honour's dower,
In the building, proud and holy, of our ancient Scotland's power !

LORNE.

CONTENTS.

CHAPTER I.
PAST AND PRESENT, - - - - - - - - 1

CHAPTER II.
TOPOGRAPHY OF THE PENINSULA OF ROSNEATH, - - 21

CHAPTER III.
ROSNEATH—A RETROSPECT, - - - - - - 45

CHAPTER IV.
ECCLESIASTICAL ROSNEATH, - - - - - - 92

CHAPTER V.
TRADITIONS, NATURAL HISTORY, AND FOLK LORE, - - 182

CHAPTER VI.
HISTORICAL, ARCHEOLOGICAL, AND MISCELLANEOUS, - - 234

APPENDIX, - - - - - - - - - 264

ROSNEATH.

CHAPTER I.

Past and Present.

THE beautiful Peninsula of Rosneath forms part of the County of Dunbarton, which has been the scene of many stirring episodes in our national history. It was a portion of the ancient territory of Strathclyde, whose capital, Dunbarton, or Dunbritton, figured conspicuously in the story of Roman occupation and throughout the fierce conflicts of the ancient Britons, Picts, and Scots. Amongst the earlier tribes who lived in the country Druidism was the prevailing religion, and it is quite possible that in some of the secluded glens of the Rosneath Peninsula, were beheld, in olden times, many idolatrous and mystic rites. The Britons of Strathclyde had enough to do to protect themselves against plundering inroads of the Picts. About A.D. 508, the famous Prince Arthur, who had been elected ruler or Pendragon by the chiefs, seems, if ancient chronicles can be credited, to have fixed one of his seats of authority at Alcluid, as Dunbarton was styled in those days.

Coming down later in the stream of time we find the Vikings or Northern Sea Kings, who had settled on the Irish coast, crossing the channel and establishing themselves, for a brief period, on the land adjacent to the estuary of the Clyde. They plundered Alcluid and ravaged the neighbouring country in the year 875. When the Britons of Strathclyde, enfeebled by incessant attacks of their enemies, migrated to the vicinity of their kindred in Wales in the year 890, the kingdom they dominated dwindled into anarchy and obscurity, until the Scots of Dalriada finally annexed their territory in the time of Kenneth III.

The Danes, who were such sore scourges to both England and Scotland, afterwards ravaged the shores of the Frith of Clyde, and Dunbritton, or Fort of the Britons, as Dunbarton came to be known, often saw their hostile ships pass her ramparts. Readers of history know that later on, Haco, King of Norway, in the year 1263, set forth to punish the excesses of those whom he considered his unruly subjects in the Western Isles of Scotland. The expedition, which was under Magnus, King of the Isle of Man, proceeded up the waters of Loch Long, which separates the Rosneath Peninsula from the Gareloch. Sailing along its heath-clad mountainous shores to the head of Loch Long, the invaders dragged their boats across the narrow neck of land over to the gravelly strand of the beautiful Loch Lomond. Here they indulged their savage propensities in ravaging the country around the Loch, almost reducing it to a solitude, and further, carried fire and sword far into the confines of Dunbarton and Stirling shires. Vengeance, however, in the wrath of the elements, overtook the marauders, for in retiring with their plunder from Loch Long, a great storm arose and scattered the fleet. Gathering together his forces to their rescue, as well as he could, the Norwegian king subsequently saw his expedition utterly vanquished at the celebrated Battle of Largs.

The County of Dunbarton after this was frequently mixed up with the general course of Scottish history, and the Rosneath Peninsula was from time to time, the scene of striking episodes. It was visited in the course of his romantic career, by the great hero of Scotland, Sir William Wallace. One day, when pursued by his enemies, the hero on his gallant steed leaped from the summit of a lofty rock not far from Rosneath Castle, and, though the horse was killed, his rider gained the shore and swam across the entrance of the Gareloch to the opposite point of Cairndhu, and made good his escape. In "Blind Harry" we read how he sacked Dunbarton, then after burning the Castle of Rosneath, he went to Faslane Castle, near the upper end of the Gareloch, and was received by his friend the Earl of Lennox. As is also well known, another great Scottish hero king, Robert the Bruce, passed many of his latter days within sight of Rosneath Peninsula, in his Castle at Cardross. Enthusiastic votaries of the patriot king go to search for the remains of the royal residence at this spot, but there is hardly any trace now to be found. All fragments of the building have long since disappeared, but the site is generally supposed to be a wooded knoll on the farm of Castlehill, between Cardross and Dunbarton. The King spent a good deal of his leisure time in building pleasure boats, as well as warlike vessels, which he sailed on the placid estuary of the Clyde, and he doubtless often found his way up the landlocked waters of the Gareloch. He lived as became a powerful monarch at Cardross, and handsomely entertained such of the nobility and clergy as came to pay their homage at his court. King Robert died on 7th June, 1329, in the 55th year of his age, lamented by the Scottish nation, whose liberties he had secured. His pathetic charge on his deathbed to Sir James Douglas, the "brave and gentle knight," is well known, and how he told his friend that the dear wish of his heart was to set out for Oriental lands, especially Palestine, to carry on war, in person, against the enemies of his Lord and Saviour. The dying hero enjoined the good knight to take his embalmed heart, accompanied by his devoted followers, to the Church of the Holy Sepulchre at Jerusalem, and there deposit it in the sanctuary. And the story goes on to narrate how the King's faithful friend duly set off on his adventurous journey with a body of chosen companions, and on their way to Jerusalem encountered their Saracen foes. When the enemy's cavalry surrounded the gallant Douglas, and he was about to be borne down by their numbers, he took the silver casket, which with its precious contents, the heart of Bruce, was hung across his neck, and flung it into the serried array of horsemen,

"Pass onward," exclaimed the knight, "as thou was wont, and Douglas will follow thee or die."

Another distinguished name in Scottish history was for long interwoven with the stirring events which have taken place in Rosneath and neighbourhood, namely, the powerful family of the Lennox. Much of the land of the Peninsula and on the shores of the Gareloch was, for centuries, in the possession of the Earls of Lennox, an ancient race. But about the year 1425, the head of the family and various of his near relations were put to death at Stirling. And in 1489, the Earl of Lennox having been engaged in treasonable practices, his lands were confiscated, although as appears from the records of the Scottish Parliament, he was pardoned for the offence. Still the forfeiture of his lands was not withdrawn, for in 1489 the lands of Rosneath were awarded to Colin, first Earl of Argyll. Thus the greatest part of the southern half of the Peninsula was conveyed to the Argyll family, whose genius has so permanently impressed itself upon the history of their country and clan. There were several other properties in Rosneath, such as those of Campbell of Peatoun, Campbell of Mamore, Campbells of Carrick, Cumming of Barremman, some of which only came into possession of the Argylls well on in the eighteenth century.

The estates of Peatoun on Loch Long side, and Barremman on the Gareloch, were never acquired by the Argylls ; the former being still, and for centuries before, owned by a Campbell, no doubt a scion of the powerful "Clan Diarmid." Their holding in the "Island of Rosneath," as the Peninsula was styled in the old title deeds, brought the Argyll family into more immediate connection with the Lowlanders. The Earl of Argyll who first owned Rosneath was a man of some note, sagacious and upright, and he filled several important posts, amongst them Lord High Chancellor of Scotland, and Plenipotentiary at the famous Northampton Conference. It was of much advantage to the district of Rosneath when so powerful a nobleman as the head of the Clan Campbell came to reside on the Gareloch, especially when the fourth Earl of Argyll adopted the Protestant faith. This Earl was the first amongst the Scottish nobility to embrace the reformed religion, and history records the grand stand which his descendants made against the eneroachments of Popery, and in defence of the religion and liberties of their country. At the upper end of the Gareloch, the Rosneath estate is bounded by the ancient property of Faslane, which was once possessed by the distinguished family of Lennox, though, for some time past, this has been the property of Sir James Colquhoun of Luss. The family of Lennox was an old one, the first Earl, Alwyn, being the earliest representative of the race of whom history gives account, and he flourished about the middle of the twelfth century. His descendant, another Alwyn, succeeded to the title and estates; one of his sons, Aulay by name, owning the lands of Faslane. They also possessed an estate near the Castle of Dunbarton, residing often in the Castle. In addition to their other extensive territories, the Lennox family, whose revenues were large, owned land at Balloch at foot of Loch Lomond, besides being judges and lawgivers in the district, when they had feudal jurisdiction. The names are well known in Scottish history, and the collateral branches of the house embraced some distinguished personages, amongst them Napier of Merchiston. But the fortunes of the family gradually dwindled, and the title and estates became merged in the Crown in the sixteenth century by the marriage of Lord Darnley with Mary Queen of Scots.

The family of the Colquhouns of Colquhoun and Luss, whose fine estates dominate the whole of the eastern side of the Gareloch, is one of great antiquity. Its origin is of very remote date, one of the earliest representatives of the race being alleged to be none other than the famous chieftain Galgacus, who contended with the Romans at the battle of the Grampians. In the reign of King David II., Sir Robert Colquhoun of that Ilk married the heiress of the house of Luss, and from that period the name frequently occurs in contemporary records of Scottish history. For a time also the Colquhouns appear to have owned territory in the Rosneath Peninsula. In 1472 the lands of Rosneath seem to have been acquired, through grant from the Crown, by Sir John Colquhoun,—the same who, in the previous year, was made Sheriff-Principal of Dunbartonshire. This Knight was in 1474 raised to the dignity of Grand Chamberlain, and was sent to England with full plenipotentiary powers to arrange a marriage between two of the younger members of the royal families. Though the marriage did not take place, the King was much satisfied with the wisdom displayed by Sir John Colquhoun throughout his mission, and made him governor for life of Dunbarton Castle. As showing how extensive were the possessions of the Colquhoun family at one time, it would appear they held the greater part of the territory of Lennox. They obtained charters under the Great Seal of the lands of Rosneath, Colquhoun, Dumbuck, Garscube, Walton, Dunglass and others, besides grants from the Earls of Lennox of fishings in Loch Lomond, the Leven, and the Gareloch, which were held as separate subjects from their other properties. The 13th head of the Colquhoun family, Sir John, is mentioned in the famous "Casket Letters" which passed between Queen Mary and the Earl of Bothwell. Sir John so far remained friendly to the Queen after Darnley's murder, and refused the call to arms made by the Regent Moray at Maxwellheuch, although at a subsequent date he seems to have forsaken the cause of the hapless Queen and fought against her at Langside. The Colquhouns were supporters of the Royalist cause at the crisis of the great civil war, and their ancient stronghold of Rossdhu was besieged by Cromwell's soldiers, and they were no friends to either nonconformists or covenanters.

Another of the old lords of the soil on the Gareloch was that of Macaulay of Ardencaple, descended from a younger son of Alwyn Earl of Lennox. This family seems to have settled as landowners in the district in the 13th century. Their estates stretched from Cardross on the east, to the head of the Gareloch, and embraced the whole of the land on which the modern town of Helensburgh stands. There were two residences on the estate, one the old ivy-clad castle of Ardencaple, part of which, with some modern additions, still stands amidst fine lofty trees near Cairndhu Point, and the small keep of Faslane near the bay of the same name on the Gareloch. About two hundred years ago the fortunes of the family began to decline, and the then laird, Aulay M'Aulay, had to dispose of his estates to the Colquhouns, and the last of the family died at Row in 1767.

The Argyll family having been so long connected with the Peninsula of Rosneath, it may be well to give a few details regarding this powerful Highland clan. According to the genealogists of the Argyll family, their predecessors, on the female side, were possessors of Lochow, in Argyllshire, as far back as the year 404. In the eleventh century, Archibald Campbell, a gentleman of Anglo-Norman lineage, acquired the lordship of Lochow by marriage with Eva, daughter of the lord of Lochow. Sir Colin Campbell of Lochow, sixth in descent, distinguished himself by his warlike actions, and was knighted by King Alexander the Third in 1280. He was famed for his prowess and added greatly to the possessions of the family, and from him the chief of the Argyll family is styled in Gaelic Mac Chaillan Mor. Sir Colin, who was slain in 1294 in a battle with the Lord of Lorn, and his son, Sir Neil, fought with King Robert the Bruce in most of his great battles. His eldest son, Sir Colin, accompanied the King to Ireland, and married a daughter of the house of Lennox. Passing by his son, Sir Archibald, we come to Sir Duncan Campbell of Lochow, who first assumed the designation of Argyll, and became a lord of Parliament in 1445 under the title of Lord Campbell, and was buried at Kilmun. His grandson, Colin, was first created Earl of Argyll in 1457, and acquired the lands of Rosneath in 1489. He was one of the commissioners for negotiating a truce with King Edward the Fourth of England in 1463, was one of the commissioners sent to France to renew the treaty with that Crown in 1484, and became Lord High Chancellor of Scotland. The Earl died in 1493, and shortly afterwards Archibald, his son, the second Earl, acquired the fine property of Castle Campbell, near Dollar, in 1497, by grant of confirmation by James the Fourth, which remained in the family till 1808, when it was sold. At the fatal battle of Flodden, 9th September, 1513, the Earl of Argyll was killed along with his brother-in-law, the Earl of Lennox, and the flower of the Scottish nobility. Passing by Colin, the third Earl, we come to Archibald, fourth Earl of Argyll, who distinguished himself at the disastrous battle of Pinkie in September 1547, and was the first of the Scottish nobility who embraced the principles of the Reformation. Archibald, the fifth Earl, distinguished himself as one of the most able of the Lords of the Congregation. His name appears in the famous bond subscribed by some of the nobility in favour of Queen Mary's marriage with Bothwell, in which affair he seems to have played a double part. He carried the Sword of State at the coronation of James the Sixth, 29th July 1567, and was appointed Lord High Chancellor in 1572. The first of the family who took a really commanding place in Scottish history and affairs, was Archibald, eighth Earl, and first Marquis of Argyll, who was born in 1598, son of Archibald, seventh Earl, by Lady Anne Douglas, daughter of the Earl of Morton. He attended the famous General Assembly of the Church of Scotland held in Glasgow in 1638, and in 1641, when Charles I. came to Scotland, he was created first Marquis of Argyll. In 1644 Argyll was commissioned by the Convention in Edinburgh to raise an army to oppose the Marquis of Huntly, who had hoisted the Standard of Rebellion. This he did, and throughout the year was engaged in various hostilities in different parts of Scotland, reaching Inverurie, in Aberdeenshire, in October, with an army of 2500 foot and 1200 horsemen, when he found himself close to the camp of Montrose with a much inferior force. Argyll attacked the army of Montrose, and threw the followers of the latter into confusion, but after a time they were rallied and assailed their foes with success, forcing Argyll to draw off his men. In February 1645, Argyll's troops were totally defeated at the battle of Inverlochy by his powerful rival Montrose, when some 1500 of his family and name were killed. Shortly afterwards, at the battle of Kilsyth, his counsel was disadvantageous to the Covenanters, who were signally defeated by Montrose. It was not so much as a warrior that Argyll achieved distinction, but as a statesman and a patriot. Very strongly attached to the Presbyterian party, the Marquis sought to bind Charles II., when he came as a fugitive to Scotland, to support that form of religious observance. At the coronation of the King at Scone in January 1651, Argyll placed the crown on Charles' head, and was the first to swear allegiance to him. His signal services to the royal cause were ill requited by the worthless King, who caused

Argyll to be imprisoned in the Tower for five months, and afterwards sent as a prisoner for trial to Edinburgh. The offence alleged against the Marquis was that he accepted the Protectorate and Government of Cromwell, and was present at the meeting of Privy Council, when the latter was proclaimed Lord Protector. He was beheaded at the Cross of Edinburgh on 27th May 1661, his head being exposed on a spike at the west end of the Tolbooth, and his body buried in the family burying-place at Kilmun. The Marquis met his death with the utmost fortitude and solemnity, behaving on the scaffold with signal courage, and his lofty character and true piety were displayed to the admiration of all who knew him. His eldest son, Archibald, succeeded to the family honours, with the exception of the Marquisate, and had been educated by his father in the true principles of loyalty to the Crown and the Protestant religion. In 1654 he received a commission as lieutenant-general from Charles II., and joined the Earl of Glencairn with the view of taking arms on behalf of the royal cause. In 1657 he was thrown into prison by order of General Monk, and kept in confinement until the restoration of Charles to the throne. During the troubles which befel his father, Lord Lorne endeavoured to save his life, and incurred the displeasure of the Earl of Middleton, Lord High Commissioner, and the sworn foe of the Marquis of Argyll, and afterwards again underwent a long term of imprisonment in the Castle of Edinburgh. Charles becoming sensible of the services which Lord Lorne had rendered him, at last, in 1663, restored him the estates of his father, and the title of Earl of Argyll.

In 1681, when the Duke of York, afterwards James II., went to Scotland, a parliament was summoned at Edinburgh, which established certain oaths and tests to be subscribed by those who possessed offices, civil, military and ecclesiastical, and this test was taken by Argyll. Soon after this he was committed to prison on a charge of high treason, but contrived to make his escape, and fled to Holland, where he resided during the remainder of Charles' reign. On the King's death in 1685, he came over to Scotland with the view of trying to preserve the civil and religious liberties of his country, in concert with the King's nephew, the unfortunate Duke of Monmouth. But the expedition was abortive, and after in vain trying to effect a rising in the West of Scotland, Argyll fled in disguise, and being taken prisoner was carried to Edinburgh, where, in June 1685, he was beheaded. On the scaffold he displayed the same calmness as did his father, and before his death he made a short, serious, religious speech. Thus perished on the scaffold both the father and son, heads of the illustrious house of Argyll, victims of the baseness and ingratitude of two worthless monarchs, who displayed the same cynical indifference to the laws alike of God and man.

The next holder of the title was Archibald, son of the preceding nobleman, who, for certain services performed, but probably more on account of what his father and grandfather had done for the cause of civil and religious liberty, was created in 1701 Duke of Argyll and Marquis of Lorne. His son was the celebrated John Duke of Argyll and Greenwich, a distinguished soldier, who served under Marlborough and contributed to the victories of Ramillies and Malplaquet. In January 1711, he was sent to Spain as ambassador, at the same time being appointed Commander-in-Chief of the English forces in that kingdom. His conduct as regards the Union between Scotland and England was peculiar, for in 1713, though only four years previously he had forwarded that great measure, he supported a motion in the House of Lords for its repeal. For a number of years the Duke held a high position as a patriotic nobleman and a soldier of renown, and the lines of Pope indicate his character—

> "Argyll, the State's whole thunder born to wield.
> And shake alike the Senate and the field."

On his death, without male issue, in 1743, a fine monument was erected to his honour in Westminster Abbey, and he was succeeded in his Scotch title by his brother Archibald, third Duke of Argyll. This Duke also entered the army, and served under Marlborough, being present at the battle of Sheriffmuir, where his elder brother, who was commander of the King's forces, defeated the followers of the Earl of Mar at the Jacobite rising in 1715. He held various important civil appointments—a Lord of Session and Privy Councillor for Scotland, Keeper of the Privy Seal, and Chancellor of the University of Aberdeen. He rebuilt the family seat at Inveraray, and was the confidential friend of Sir Robert Walpole. He had chief management of Scottish national affairs, besides being most attentive in furthering the trade and manufactures of his country.

John, fourth Duke, was the son of the Honourable John Campbell of Mamore, on the Gareloch, and also was an officer in the British army. He was active on the royal side in the rebellion of 1715, and served in the war in Germany in 1744, besides being commander of the forces in the West of Scotland when the rebellion of 1745 broke out. John, fifth Duke, was eldest son of the preceding, and became general in the army in 1778, and field marshal in 1796, and was first President of the Highland Society of Scotland. He married the widow of the Duke of Hamilton, who was one of the three beautiful Miss Gunnings, and their son, George William, became sixth Duke in 1806. Duke George was an amiable, much respected gentleman, and a good landlord, and dying in 1839 was succeeded by his brother, Lord John Campbell, who long resided at Ardencaple Castle, Row. He was thrice married, his second wife, Joan, heiress of John Glassel of Long Niddry, being the mother of the present Duke, George John Douglas Campbell, born in 1823. The Duke married in 1844 Lady Elizabeth, eldest daughter of the Duke of Sutherland, and their son, the Marquis of Lorne, born in 1845, is the heir to the ancient title of Mac Chaillan Mor and head of the house of Argyll.

Some of the heads of the house of Argyll made Rosneath Castle their residence during part of the year, and with one, the famous Marquis, it was a favourite place of abode. Of him a contemporary historian wrote: "He was a man of singular piety, prudence, authority and eloquence; and though he had been much envied and caluminated, yet his death did abundantly vindicate him." His widow continued to reside in the Castle, which he had rebuilt, and long was spared to be a blessing to the locality. Of this good lady it was written : " His noble lady, Lady Margaret Douglas, a lady of singular piety and virtue, bore the sad shock with other both personal and domestic afflictions, with great patience and incredible fortitude, giving herself always to prayer and fasting, and ministering to the necessity of the saints."

Of John Duke of Argyll and Greenwich, Sir Walter Scott, in his novel, "The Heart of Midlothian," wrote with great admiration, "Soaring above the petty distinctions of faction, his voice was raised, whether in office or opposition, for those measures which were at once just and lenient. His high military talents enabled him during the memorable year 1715, to render such services to the House of Hanover, as perhaps, were too great either to be acknowledged or repaid. He had almost by his simple and unassisted talents, stopped the irruption of the banded forces of all the Highland chiefs, and there was little doubt that, with the slightest encouragement, he could put them all in motion and renew the civil war ; and it was well known that the most flattering overtures had been transmitted to the Duke from the Court of St. Germains."

The present holder of this title is too well known to his fellow-countrymen to need much euolgy in a work of this kind. He is the thirty-second Knight of Lochow, and the thirtieth Campbell, in the direct line of descent. From his exalted position as head of the great clan Campbell, from his extensive territorial possessions and above all, from his commanding talents, he is well worthy of taking the highest place in the councils of the nation. From his earliest years he has diligently applied himself to acquire knowledge, and to study the varied and intricate political, social, and scientific problems of the day. Had he not been born heir to one of the most illustrious positions in the British peerage, he would certainly have achieved the highest eminence in whatever department of the public service he entered. As a public man, for over forty years, he has held a great position; he has been intimately connected with the political and legislative movements of his time, and his name is associated with much that is best in our national history for this lengthened term. From his boyhood he showed a remarkable aptitude for business, and displayed those literary graces which have shone conspicuously in later efforts. While Marquis of Lorne, he took an active part in the great controversy relating to patronage in the Presbyterian Church of Scotland, which culminated in the Disruption of 1843. One of his early productions was "On the Duty and Necessity of Immediate Legislative Interposition on Behalf of the Church of Scotland," in which he gave an able *resumé* of Scotch ecclesiastical history. In another pamphlet entitled "A Letter to Rev. Thomas Chalmers, D.D., on the Present Position of Church Affairs in Scotland," he vindicated the right of the Church to legislate for herself. In an essay entitled "Presbytery Examined," published in 1848, the Duke entered upon a critical and historical review of Scottish Church

History since the Reformation, which was most favourably criticised at the time. Since then, his writings upon questions of Church Government, Patronage, and against Disestablishment, have been numerous and important, the part he took, in particular, regarding the abolition of lay patronage being in the highest degree honourable to himself. Amongst the various works of a political, historical, and scientific character which have proceeded from his prolific pen, his "Reign of Law" may perhaps be considered his most original and ambitious effort. In "Scotland as it Was, and as it Is," the Duke treats in an able and exhaustive way the gradual rise of the feudal system of land tenure, and many cognate customs illustrating the modes of dealing with agricultural holdings in Scotland, a valuable contribution to the literature of the great land question. He is a frequent contributor to the magazines of the day, and his articles generally receive the place of honour, while his graphic and pithy letters to the *Times* upon important topics, such as the Land and Labour questions, Home Rule, Education, Disestablishment, and similar topics, command universal attention.

The Duke of Argyll's political career has been long and distinguished. He first accepted office as Lord Privy Seal, under the administration of the Earl of Aberdeen, in December 1852. After Lord Palmerston assumed the office of Prime Minister, he was continued in the same office until, in 1855, he exchanged it for the office of Postmaster-General. In 1859 he again became Lord Privy Seal till 1866; in 1868 was Secretary of State for India till 1874, under Mr. Gladstone's administration. Again, in 1880, he was appointed to his old office of Lord Privy Seal, which he retained till 1881, when he resigned office, and since then has held no post in the Gladstone administration. As is well known, his Grace is a strong opponent of Mr. Gladstone's Irish policy, and he has rendered vast services to the Liberal Unionist cause, not only in Parliament, but by his numerous addresses, letters to the press, and articles in magazines.

In addition to his various hereditary titles, such as Duke and Earl of Argyll, Marquis of Lorne, Earl of Campbell, and Viscount of Lochow and others, the Duke is Knight of the Thistle and of the Garter, Lord Lieutenant of Argyllshire. In 1854 was Lord Rector of Glasgow University. In 1855 he presided over the twenty-fifth meeting of the British Association for the Advancement of Science, held in Glasgow, and on this occasion displayed scientific knowledge and antiquarian research of high capacity, and his remarks upon all the subjects under discussion were listened to with much respect by the eminent savants who were present. His Grace is intimately acquainted with all the details of the management of his extensive estates in Argyllshire and Dunbartonshire, and finds time amidst his multifarious duties and varied correspondence, to reply with his own hand to nearly every letter addressed to him by the humblest tenant on his property. It may safely be affirmed that if there were more noblemen like the Duke of Argyll, who reside upon their properties the greater part of the year, and diligently discharge the responsibilities which Providence has laid upon them, there would be little of the outcry about abolishing the House of Lords, and sweeping away the landed aristocracy, which is put forth by certain demagogues of the day.

CHAPTER II.

Topography of the Peninsula of Rosneath.

THIS diversified Peninsula has long been a favourite place of resort for those who are in search of romantic and salubrious summer quarters. Situated within such easy access from Glasgow, it presents numerous attractions for men of business who seek an entire change of scene after the labours of the day. There is a wondrous charm in the sinuous shores and winding bays of the Frith of Clyde, overlooked as they are by many a heathery mountain slope, across whose breezy heights flit the everchanging shadows on our all too brief summer days. Towards the middle of last century, the scenery of the valley and Frith of Clyde presented an aspect very different from their now luxuriant clothing of well tilled lands and ample plantations of trees. All along the West of Scotland, and the territory bordering on the seaboard, many of the counties presented dreary prospects of moors and poor grass lands, trees were few and far between, and hedgerows were unknown. Even in Ayrshire, the lands were bare and uncivilised, unless in the vicinity of Eglinton Castle, and one or two other noblemen's seats. Anyone sailing down the

Frith of Clyde saw the heather and bracken-clad slopes of the hills, interspersed with glens in which the natural birch and alder trees grew in profusion, but none of the great plantations of larch, spruce, and silver firs, which now are such a feature in the landscape. No doubt in some parts of Scotland, the great indigenous forest trees, the noble old Scotch firs, a few specimens of which, remnants of the old Caledonian forest, are still encountered here and there, the mighty oaks, and venerable yews threw their sombre shade over the turf. But a century ago, even a county, now so rich in forests and well timbered parks as Fife, showed hardly any scanty straggling belts of trees, unless perhaps near Falkland and Mount Melville. Ayrshire then presented to an observer the appearance of an open common, without tree or fence. After the Rebellion of 1745, great changes began to be introduced. Up till then farming was in its elementary state, and was mostly in the hands of small communities of crofters. Scarcely any grass or turnip was sown, and even the potato was little seen, the flocks of scraggy sheep were led out to graze and housed at night. Oxen did most of the ploughing, and the farm produce was carried on creels on horseback. During a great part of the year, except during harvest, the stock roamed about anywhere, and devoured all green vegetation. But, towards the close of the century, forestry got a start, and farmers saw the value of plantations of trees giving shelter to stock. Then it was that the great planting of firs began, which gradually changed the face of the landscape. Some of the grand forests of dark firs which now adorn the slopes of the mountains in the Highlands, and cover the lesser heights in the Lowland counties, took their rise from this period. In Dunbartonshire, on the Colquhoun, Montrose, and Argyll estates, many splendid plantations of dark firs were started, and the Rosneath Peninsula assumed a clothed aspect which gave beauty to its fine outlines.

The Peninsula of Rosneath was indeed, from its delightful situation and vicinity to great centres of population, certain to become a place of resort. Its name has been very fruitful of controversy, being claimed by partisans of English and Gaelic derivations. Undoubtedly the true orthography of the name is *Rossniath*, a Gaelic term, not the modernised and more euphonious *Roseneath*. No doubt the latter mode of spelling is the accepted version by compilers of guide books and railway time tables, but it is scornfully repudiated by natives of the "island," as an unworthy concession to ignorant outsiders. One Gaelic derivation of the word is *Rhosnoeth*, the "bare or unwooded promontory," another, *Ros-na-choich*, the "virgin's promontory," these being the two generally accepted terms which have gradually been corrupted into Rosneath. The latter is most generally accepted, but still another reading gives it as *Rossneveth*, the "promontory of the sanctuary." Now, from time immemorial, there has been a place of worship and of burial in the Peninsula, in the immediate vicinity of the present Church at the Clachan village. A Peninsula, or island, was a favourite spot in ancient times for burying the dead, as securing a place of worship away from the haunts of plundering marauders. Thus the "promontory of the sanctuary" would be an appropriate name for the now populous and frequented parish of Rosneath. Sir Walter Scott, in the "Heart of Midlothian," thus mentions the Peninsula. He is describing the islands of the Frith of Clyde, Arran, Bute and the Cumbraes, and says, "Roseneath, a smaller isle, lies much further up the Frith, and towards its western shore, near the opening of the lake called the Gare-loch, and not far from Loch Long, and Loch Seant, or the Holy Loch, which wind from the mountains of the Western Highlands to join the estuary of the Clyde. The picturesque beauty of the island of Roseneath in particular, had such recommendations, that the Earls and Dukes of Argyll, from an early period, made it their occasional residence, and had their temporary accommodation in a fishing or hunting lodge, which succeeding improvements have since transformed into a palace."

Situated between the peaceful waters of the Gareloch, and the more troubled broad estuary of the Clyde, the Peninsula stretches for about eight and a half miles from the "green isle" point, opposite Greenock, to Portincaple on Loch Long side. Within these limits is embraced a wonderful variety of scenery, in some places all the silence and seclusion of a Highland moor, with its robe of purple heather, feathery bracken, and yielding cushions of velvet moss, in others the sylvan greenery and rich pasture of an agricultural country. The parish consists mainly of one continuous ridge, rising from the wooded point opposite Greenock in gradually increasing lines of elevation to the hill of Tomnahara, the highest point, some eight hundred feet above the sea. With the exception of the level grounds in

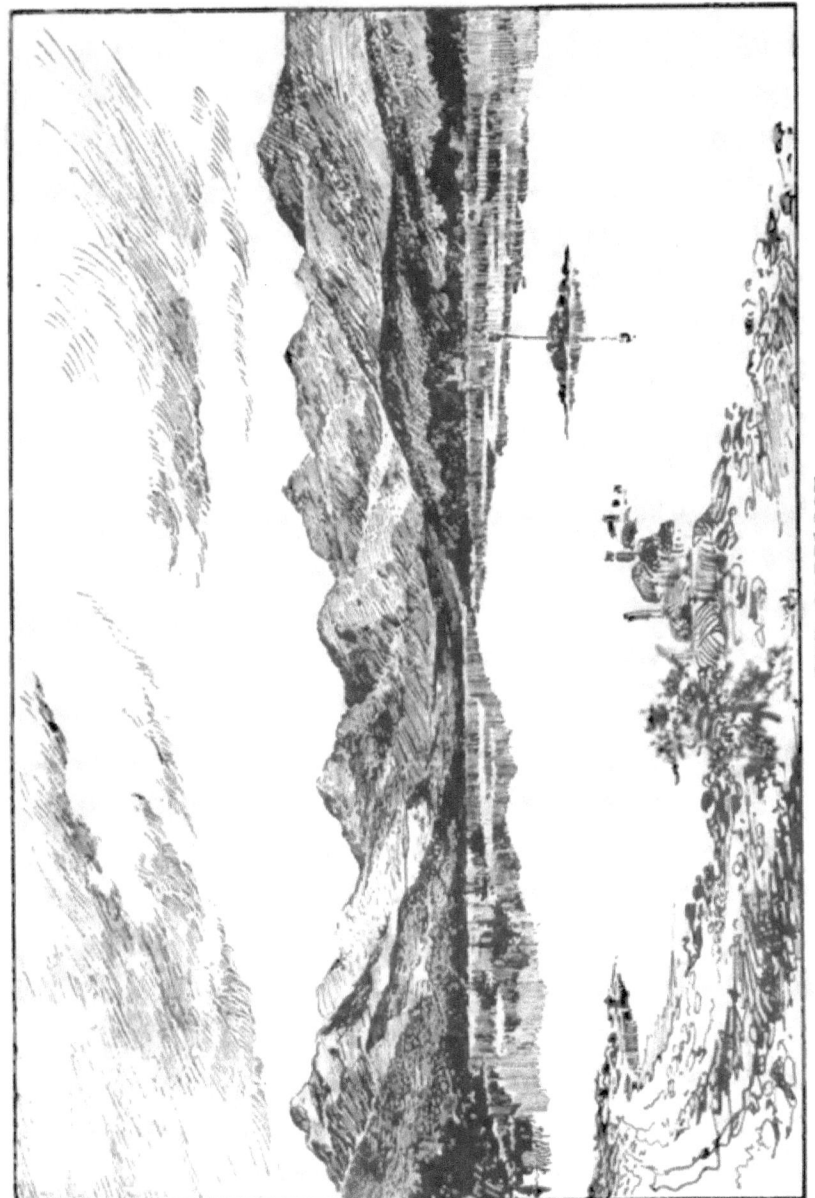

THE GARELOCH.

the vicinity of the Castle and policies, and the fields of the Clachan farm, the cultivated portions of the Peninsula are the slopes on either side rising from the Lochs. The whole of the upper tableland of the ridge is covered with heather or marsh, with many a clear mountain streamlet pursuing its rocky course to the Loch. When a succession of rainy days has filled the burns, they leap down the numerous cascades which break their course, and many a sweet subject for an artist's brush may be encountered by those in search of the picturesque. There is one small fresh water loch in the moor near Tomnahara, its waters are pure, and there is excellent fishing to be had. From Tomnahara there is a grand view, embracing the whole serrated range of the Loch Long mountains, with the dark currents between their slopes and the Peninsula, and the gleaming Loch Goil—

"That dark and stormy water"—

opening to the left, while on the right the Gareloch, with its green fields, embowered villas, and mantling woods, is seen on the other side. Rising above Garelochhead are the swelling outlines of the grassy mountains at the head of Glenfruin, from whence the eye ranges on to Helensburgh and the distant braes above Kilpatrick. Opposite are the uplands of Renfrewshire, the busy ports of Port-Glasgow, Greenock and Gourock, the Cloch Lighthouse, and the long reaches of the Ayrshire coast, and following on you gain fine views of the Cumbraes, Bute, Arran, and the nearer mountains of Argyllshire. On a very clear day it is just possible to descry the far-off noble crest of Ben

Cruachan, and it is surprising what a varied expanse of mountain, moor, craggy fell, and glittering sea, can be gained from this moderate elevation.

Although in summer the view is grand and, lit up with all the sparkle and radiance of that beauteous season, the shadows flitting rapidly across the hill sides, only bringing out into more vivid relief the partially veiled glories of moor, and fell, and gleaming water, still in winter the prospect is one of deep interest and variety. When all around is concealed by one resplendent robe of snow, even the rugged Ben Im, with its majestic double peak, completely mantled with its enveloping shroud, and the soft, wreath-like folds of downy wool resting on the undulating ridges of the Peninsula, then the picture is full of solemn beauty. Each fir plantation and fringe of pine wood is sprinkled with snow that rests lightly on the dark boughs, and, only here and there, on the swelling moor is seen a black protruding speck of rock amid the waste of dazzling white. Then, towards sunset, each lofty peak raising its giant form into the cold, blue air, is pervaded by an exquisite rosy tint, deepening into delicate carmine, and finally the ghostly hue of approaching night, as it settles down upon the landscape, envelopes the whole with the murky pall of midnight gloom. The reservoir which supplies the water for Kilcreggan and Cove covers a good large area of ground near Tomnahara, and gives an ample supply for the wants of the many summer visitors who inhabit the villas which stretch along the shore for miles from Kilcreggan pier to Coulport on Loch Long.

The formation of the shores of the Peninsula adds much to its beauty. Along from the Ferry Inn towards the Rosneath Castle point, the receding line of strand has a semi-circular appearance, the beach of a fine pebbly gravel, takes a graceful curve and then forms the sheltered Campsail Bay, on whose waters may frequently be seen anchored some of the handsome yachts of the different Clyde clubs. This part of the parish is clothed with singularly fine specimens of trees of many varieties, the soil being favourable for their growth, in addition to the indigenous oaks, ash, and birch. Many of the finer garden species, such as the fuchsia, arbutus, myrtle and peach trees, are found scattered along the shores of the Gareloch, and even two good specimens of that valuable genus, the eucalyptus of Australia, are to be seen within the grounds of the Established and Free Church manses. But the trees which seem to attain the finest proportions are those of the fir, beech, and ash tribe, though the severe storms of past years played havoc with many of them, especially the plantation which crowned the brow of the hill above the Clachan Farm. The Gallowhill, between the Castle and Kilcreggan, was covered by a luxuriant growth of firs, but this was cut down nearly forty years ago, and only partially replanted, although there are many fine beeches and firs on the lower slopes of the hill.

Rosneath is a highly salubrious place, as is indicated by the great age to which many of the natives attain. The air is pure, although very moist at times, and the climate is mild, as is evinced by the profusion of ferns and mossy plants, while the rainfall encourages the perennial verdure ever so refreshing to the eye. Being in the vicinity of high mountains, and, from its position, prone to intercept the dense masses of vapour which often roll up the Frith of Clyde, the Peninsula gets an abundant share of moisture. In winter often the mildness of the season is striking, and the rhododendron, laurustinus, jessamine, and other flowering shrubs may be observed in bloom in December. In spring, no doubt, the Gareloch side of the Peninsula often has a continuance of east wind, though, in the Cove and Peatoun districts, the inhabitants are quite sheltered from this unwelcome visitant. Although the upper ridges are in parts marshy, yet no unhealthy exhalations give trouble, and the shores being rocky and gravelly, no unpleasant airs are wafted from long stretches of mud, as you have in other parts of the Clyde. The prevailing winds are the south and south-west, which sometimes blow for days together, the latter often bringing down showers of misty rain, and these are naturally felt in their severity on the Kilcreggan and Cove shores, while, on the Gareloch side, is comparative quiet. Snow does not, as a rule, lie long on the land, which is often entirely free from its presence, while the mainland and mountains beyond are shrouded with a white mantle.

The geological structure of the Peninsula does not require much notice, nearly the whole strata belonging to the primitive class of rocks. The prevailing formation is clay slate, which at times passes into chlorite slate, and occssionally into mica slate. Occasionally beds of conglomerate may be met, as at the old sea cliff near Rosneath

Castle, and one or two other places. On the high ground above Clynder may be observed good examples of chloride slate in the quarries which have been opened up, the direction being from north-west to south-east. On the shore of Loch Long, not very far from Knockderry, there appears a large mass of greenstone lying interposed between the strata. The greenstone is like a dyke from twenty to thirty feet thick, and close to it is more of the chlorite slate rock. Another bed of greenstone is found, nearly half a mile further south. The south-western extremity of the parish is pervaded by conglomerate and coarse sandstone rock, which occurs in beds of considerable thickness. This rock is of similar description to the great sandstone formation which extends along the Renfrew and Ayrshire coasts, and embraces the Cumbraes and a portion of the southern half of Bute. The line of formation between the sandstone and primitive rock of the parish runs along the valley, stretching from Campsail Bay to Kilcreggan. In the slate formation on the Loch Long shore, as well as in the quartz, iron pyrites is found in considerable abundance. It is crystallised in the slate, and in the quartz appears in large irregular masses. In the colour of the slate there is much variety, due to the quantity of oxide of iron pervading the deposits.

Some of the interesting boulders which are to be found throughout the Western Highlands still exist at Rosneath, though it is to be feared that many of them have been destroyed for building purposes. About forty-five years ago, more than one hundred fine boulders of grey granite were found in position on the ridges above the Gareloch, between that and Loch Long, one-third of them exceeding thirty tons in weight. The prevailing rock formation being clay slate, it is possible that the granite boulders came from the north. Probably the boulders had their origin in the great granite mountains, such as Ben Cruachan, more than thirty miles distant, as the crow flies, being transported by the ice across valleys and hills, floating on a sea which may have been over fifteen hundred feet above the present sea level. By the action of ice, large masses of stone have been placed *in situ* on the heights of mountains and in valleys, for there can be little doubt that, in remote ages, glaciers existed in the glens of the Western Highlands. The conclusion which Mr. Charles M'Laren, the eminent Scotch geologist, came to in 1846, regarding these boulders, was that they have come on the sea at a far greater level than now, brought by currents from the north-west. Also, Mr. M'Laren concluded, that local glaciers had at one time existed in all these valleys, as the striations on the rocks were all parallel with the axis of the valley, which generally runs in the direction of N.W. and S.E., and the accumulations of gravel and clay reminded him of the lateral and terminal moraines of Switzerland.

There is a remarkable boulder between the farms of Peatoun and Duchlage, on the Loch Long side of Rosneath. This large boulder rests in the channel of a burn, which runs down to the loch, at a height of 226 feet above the sea. It is of gneiss, resting on the gorge cut by the burn through the clay slate rocks, and has a local name, meaning "house on a knoll." Its dimensions are 24 × 18 × 12 feet, and probably it was transported across Loch Long from the N.W., and came to a stand against the hillside where it remains. It is interesting to note that there is an old sea margin at 45 feet above the present level, near this spot, and another at exactly the same height on the opposite side of the loch. Many of these boulders are encountered in the Rosneath district, and upon the mountains rising out of Loch Long are some fine specimens. On a hill near Loch Goil, about 450 feet above the sea, is a boulder called the "giant's putting stone," from a tradition very common in the Highlands that giants of old used to exercise themselves by throwing these masses of rock across lochs and valleys. Another very remarkable boulder is on the hill above Carrick Castle on Loch Goil; a stone of enormous dimensions, about 1526 feet above the sea. It is called the "stone nicely balanced," and rests on the ledge of a precipitous cliff, over 500 feet high, and must have travelled a long distance. On the farm of Letter, near Peatoun, on Loch Long, there is a gneiss boulder, 12 feet by 8, about 10 feet above high water mark, on the roadside. Numerous other interesting specimens on the Loch Long mountains may be seen; one of them, called Pulag boulder, is near the top of a hill to the west of Ardentinny, almost on the edge of a precipice, 200 feet high, and it could by no possibility have rolled to its present exalted position.

The state of agriculture about a century ago in Dunbartonshire is well described in Forsyth's *Beauties of Scotland*, and much that is said as to the county generally would apply to the conditions of cultivation in Rosneath. Farms, in several instances, were small, consisting of not above twelve or fifteen acres. In order to have their lands ploughed the small farmers were under the necessity of joining with two or three neighbours. Little was laid out in improvements, and so the land gradually became exhausted. Sometimes there were pendicles of a few acres in extent occupied by labourers, and those who wrought at some trade. About this time, however, a considerable rise in the rent of land occurred over what prevailed fifty years before. This was partly because land cultivation was improved, where there were poor black cattle in summer and goats in winter, sheep were placed on the farms. In consequence of the increase in wealth and population in Glasgow and other towns, there was much more demand for butcher meat, and its appreciation in money value. Better farm-houses or *steadings* were being constructed, and, instead of mere thatch coverings, were now being roofed with slate. Sometimes these *steadings* were covered with heath or bracken, which, properly managed, made a tolerably durable roof. This thatch, on the side of the house exposed to the sun, lasted about six or seven years; but when in a northern exposure, might endure well on to thirty years.

Oats was the crop most generally cultivated, bear and barley, owing to cold seasons, were found to be precarious crops. In some parts of the country what was called *blandearded* barley, a mixture, half bear, half barley, was cultivated, and the meal used as bread.

A curious mixture, also, of oats, barley, rye, pease, and beans, was likewise a favourite crop with many, and used for bread. Hardly any wheat was grown in the county, although from the grains of wheat found in a vault under ground at Castlecarry, it would appear to have been cultivated by the Romans. Although turnips were not very much in request, the cultivation of the potato was universal; sometimes where peas and beans were grown, the potato was placed in the same course. Flax was cultivated in many parts of the county where there were clay soils, or flat soils capable of retaining moisture; from eight to ten pecks of Riga seed being sown upon one acre, and the crop, when dressed by the mill, would amount to twenty or even twenty-eight stones. It was found to be of much service in weeding the soil and cleaning the land. The inhabitants of the parishes of Kirkintilloch and Cumbernauld obtained, from the trustees for the improvements in Scotland, large premiums annually for the growth of flax, and it used to be manufactured into yarn by the farmers' wives. Clover and rye grass were much cultivated, white clover being everywhere indigenous to the county.

The common fern, or bracken, grew plentifully in the Peninsula, and was found useful in many ways. No cultivation was needed for ferns, and they grew in the glens and corries, and open fields. While chiefly used for thatch or litter, it was found that horses were not averse to eat them, when well prepared. In the more mountainous and precipitous parts of the county the soil was, to a large extent, marshy and wet, affording poor pasture for sheep. But in many parts of Rosneath there were good natural grasses, and owing to the moist climate they kept verdant throughout the year. Sheep breeding, as a regular business, was introduced into the county by Mr. Campbell of Lagwyne, in 1747, who then resided in the parish of Luss, before which time Dunbartonshire generally was stocked with black cattle, which brought in a poor return.

Considerable quantities of cattle were purchased from Highland graziers, and after being kept for the winter were sold to English graziers, as the Peninsula was, in many respects, suitable for wintering cattle; the food of the animals being chiefly grass, either green or dried, and straw being given to both horses and cows. Clover was much preferred to every other green crop for the cows, as it greatly increased the quantity of the milk and left no bad taste. Horses during winter got their supper of boiled meat often, a mixture of light corn, oat-chaff, and sometimes beans and pease. This was reckoned an excellent food for the animals, enhancing their appearance and maintaining their strength. Cows also, after calving, were nourished with the same mixture, until the grass became plentiful. Very few swine were raised in the district, either for private use or for the market. Cows were universally kept, although the county was not one noted for dairy produce. A good deal of butter was salted for sale in wooden vessels, and what was termed "hung cheese" was extensively made, being so called as the curds were hung, or tied up, in a cloth or net, instead of the whey being extracted as usual by the press.

At that period the enclosing of land throughout the county had made considerable progress. Up till about forty years previously, none of the land was enclosed, with the exception of a few fields adjoining the county residences of the landowners. The enclosures of arable land amounted, as a rule, to about eight or ten acres. One large enclosure of three hundred acres was surrounded by a stone dyke, in the parish of Row, by Sir James Colquhoun of Luss, at a cost of over £300 sterling. That proprietor annually built several thousand roods of dykes, and planted at least thirty thousand young thorns. Hedges faced with stone were not uncommon, and some excellent specimens of this mode of fencing may be seen at present on the road between the Clachan Village and Kilcreggan. The dyke was a couple of feet or thereby in height, built of stone without lime, the thorns and beeches placed in the earth thrown up at the back of the dyke, near the upper course of stones. In the higher parts of the county wooden fences were common, consisting of posts of peeled oak, or branches of elm, or fir trees set upright in the earth, at the distance of a foot and a half from each other, and strongly interwoven with brushwood or brooms. These fences were called "stab and rice."

Lime was used extensively as manure, and allowed to remain some time spread upon the surface before being ploughed down. Sea ware was also profitably used as manure, consisting of two kinds, what was taken off the stones on the shore, and what was driven up by the tides, called "blown wreck." The former was esteemed the richest, as containing a greater proportion of salt. What was cut from the stones grew so rapidly that another crop might be cut in two years; some kinds of sea plants were better than others, the thin, broad-leaved species being little esteemed. The blown wreck needed to be gathered as soon as possible, and was used as top dressing to grass fields, and was sometimes mingled with lime, earth, and ordinary farm manure. Lime and peat moss were in some places spread upon grass lands, for ploughing in the following year; the lime, in powder, being laid on the surface of the ground in autumn, and cartloads of moss overspreading the whole.

At that time the growing woods of Dunbartonshire were noticeable for their extent, the woodlands being computed at about 11,800 acres, of which 6,200 were under natural wood. The natural woods, of which the oak formed a considerable part, were for the sake of the bark, cut every twenty years, only the oak, mountain ash and willow being peeled. The tanners preferred the Highland bark at about twenty years old to others of greater age, and as the price of the timber commonly defrayed the expense of cutting and barking, the profits chiefly arose from the sale of the bark. The mode of cutting wood had much altered in the last few years, it being formerly the universal practice to cut the tree over a few inches above the surface of the ground, the piece left being intended to throw off young shoots of future growth, which, in their turn, were cut off a few inches above the old stock. But it was found that the shoots from the root of the tree were better than those from the "stool," or portion above the ground. The new plants sprang from the root, on a level with the surface of the ground, and acquired new and vigorous roots for themselves. The value of the natural wood was, in many places, considerable, where the oak prevailed it was estimated above £1 per acre, a much higher rent than could be obtained for the same land in any other manner. The county gentlemen seeing how precarious, too often, the grain crops were in a wet ungenial climate, enclosed large portions of their estates for plantation. On the Luss, and Rosneath, and Arden estates, in particular, much planting was encouraged, a single enclosure at Rossdhu containing five hundred acres. It was then seen how foolish had been the improvident and wasteful process by which the ancient forests of the country had been impoverished and destroyed. The yew, holly, rowan, and Dutch myrtle, growing extensively in marshy ground, were amongst the natural woods of the country; in the island of Inch Conachan, on Loch Lomond, there being computed to be several thousand yews, which most probably were planted for the purpose of making bows for the men-at-arms of that period. The famous yew tree avenue of Rosneath will, later on, be described, and there are also some very fine specimens of this species in the policies near Rossdhu. Amongst the notable trees was the decayed ash tree at Bonhill, within the hollowed out trunk of which the proprietor had formed an apartment, nearly nine feet in diameter and ten feet in height. It was lighted by two windows, had a table in the middle, surrounded by seats which could accommodate a considerable number of people.

Limestone was found in different varieties over most of the

county, the first sort containing shells, collaroids and other exuviae of the inhabitants of the ancient ocean, and produced lime of excellent quality. The second kind of lime was called "moor limestone," being commonly situated on the higher grounds, and in strata of various thickness. The surface of the stone was coarse and gritty, owing to the calcareous crystals of which it seemed to be mostly a congeries, and it was destitute of marine productions. Generally it was found in places remote from coal, and sometimes successful attempts were made to burn it with peat. The third kind of limestone was what was termed "canistone," or "glenstone," being met with in the glens of the different parishes. It was of a finer grain, and of a reddish grey colour, but also without any shell or marine remains. It contained a considerable portion of clay, and when exposed to the atmosphere falls down in small pieces. In the parish of Dunbarton natural sections may be seen in the sides of some glens, where over a dozen of thin strata of the limestone are imbedded in the soil. Much of this stone was burnt for manure, and it possessed this peculiar quality, that, when thoroughly burned and while it was red hot, it needed to be slaked in the kiln, for if permitted to cool gradually, it would not afterwards precipitate in powder. For this reason, and that it might be more thoroughly slaked, the kiln was commonly built in the vicinity of a burn. At the Strouel Bay, and other places on the Gareloch side, these kilns were situated; some of them within the recollection of living persons.

It is curious that Forsyth mentions the strange notion that the soil of the Rosneath Peninsula was of deadly quality for rats, and that, if imported, they died within the year. There are other singular details given in this interesting sketch by Forsyth of the county of Dunbarton, its history, and varied products. It was then reckoned to be in the Highlands and, in many parts of the county, especially in the northern portions, the Gaelic language was spoken.

The area of the parish, according to the Blue Book published over twenty years ago, giving particulars of the whole heritable and landed properties in Scotland, amounts to 8,106 acres, the greater portion of which have been brought under cultivation of some sort, though the upper part of the Peninsula is still moorland, and affords excellent grouse shooting. Formerly the arable land was divided into farms of no great size, with the exception of the Home Farm, but several of these have been united into larger holdings. The Home Farm is much the largest in area, and was brought into its present superior condition mainly through the late Mr. Lorne Campbell, the Duke of Argyll's Chamberlain, who was a gentleman of great influence, widely esteemed, and looked up to by every one in the parish. He had succeeded, as factor, Mr. Robert Campbell, who long occupied the Clachan Farm, and the old mansion house at the end of the sombre yew-tree avenue. The latter being an original member of the Highland Society, and encouraged by the then Duke of Argyll, succeeded in inducing the farmers to adopt many improvements in the management of their farms. As showing the great improvements which have taken place in the cultivation of the land, a walk over the

Home or Clachan Farms when the harvest time approaches, will display a sample of crops which it would be difficult to surpass in this part of the county. Most of the soil is peculiarly well adapted for potatoes, and, especially in early varieties, the return is most favourable.

In the statistical account of the parish, drawn up by the Rev. Robert Story, in May 1839, there is a short paragraph upon the agricultural aspect of the district. From this account it appeared that there were over 8,000 acres of uncultivated moorland, although of these it was believed 500 were capable of profitable culture, 520 were under valuable wood plantations of various ages, and 720 of old and natural copse wood. It is further pointed out that the general improvements of husbandry adopted were, chiefly, fencing and draining the fields after the modern system, though there was still much to be desired. Nearly all the fields were enclosed by hedges or stone dykes, and, on several of the farms, much reclaimed land was to be observed. The inferior style of the farm buildings is commented upon, as indicating insufficiency of capital expenditure. There was a steady and regular market for produce of the farm, with easy access, and winter carriage for a constant supply of manures. The ordinary duration of the leases was stated to be nineteen years, on terms favourable to the occupier, and the enclosures were complete, in excellent repair, and more suitable to the purpose of the cultivator than those of any other parish in the district. At that period the old fashioned system of rotation of crops would, no doubt, be maintained, and the primitive modes of reaping the harvest and conducting agricultural operations, then in almost universal use, would curtail the farmer's energies, and sometimes bring about considerable loss.

At that time the average value of land under the plough might be considered about £1 5s. per acre; the charge for grazing a cow £2 10s., and for a sheep 5s., the total rental of the Peninsula being estimated to be somewhat under £3,500. The agricultural labourer received but 1/10, and artisans 2s. 6d. per day, farm servants being hired at £7 and £8 for the half year, with bed, board, and washing. The average yearly value of all sorts of produce, was then about £5,820, which was arrived at as follows—

Value of all kinds of grain,	£2,000
Potatoes and turnips,	1,500
Hay cultivated,	400
Flax,	20
Land in pasture,	1,200
Annual thinings from plantation grounds,	600
Salmon fishing,	100
Together,	£5,820

Sales of produce were effected without difficulty in Glasgow and Greenock. Seed oats were exported to Ireland, and potatoes to the colonies, and there was good home consumption. The common breed of cattle was Ayrshire, and a large portion of the grazing parks were given up to rearing black and West Highland cattle. Facilities for export were found only in one or two parts of the district, but, upon the whole, there was sufficient for the comparatively limited quantity of agricultural produce.

As showing the wonderful change in the value of the lands and farms on the Rosneath estate, the following details from an old rental may be given :—

RENTAL ROSNEATH—Crop 1766.
Feu-duties.

Oursnoch—silver feu-duty, 9s. 3d.—one-half—one half-dozen poultry, 5s.,	£0 14 3½
Blarnachtra,	0 11 6
Barraman. (The Duke was superior),	0 11 4½
Clendroch (Clynder),	0 8 4
	£2 5 6

RENTAL PROPRIETOR'S LANDS.

Parks in Lord Lorne's hands,	£20 0 0	
Meikle Ross—fields beyond the Duke's stables and offices,	28 11 4	
Little Ross—field near Mill bay,	21 11 4	
Part Portkiln—now Gallowhill,	5 0 0	
Total grounds in my Lord's possession,	£75 2 8	
Portkiln farm (Richie's) pays		37 14 9
Little Aiden—John and Andrew Saltyr,		24 16 11

Believed to be descendants of John Balfour of Burley. This tradition fully believed by the late Mr. J. D. Campbell of Peatoun, who lived all his life at Rosneath, as well as by an old Cameronian, the father of the late Mr. Duncan Campbell, local factor on the estate.

Meikle Aiden—Hunters and Halls,	32 10 8
Knockderry—Niven and Marquis,	29 16 3
Together,	£127 4 1

Rental Purchase Lands.

		£	s.	d.
Forward;		127	4	1
Kilcraigan—J. Chalmers,	- - - - -	21	14	8
Hill of Campsail—Mitchell,	- - - - -	20	0	9
Parks, meadows, yards, orchards, of Campsail, and ground-cellar, Miln croft, all possessed by Lady Carrick,	-	12	0	0
Ailie—Chalmers and Brodie,	- - - - -	47	14	10
Mamore, Mambeg, and salmon fishing—R. Campbell and others, same name—				
Rent, - - - - £64 10 0				
18 salmon at 20d. each, - - 1 10 0				
		66	0	0
Feornicarrie—Walker, M'Fun, and D. Campbell,	- -	12	11	4
Duchlaze—small superiority,	- - - - -	2	4	5
Bought by Lord Fredk. Campbell, and left by him to present Duke's father.				
Meal Miln and Lands—				
Duncan M'Neilage—pays 3 dozen poultry, and 4 ells of "linnen,"	- - - - - -	0	13	4
Also 21 bolls meal for mill croft.				
Clachan Farm—				
Easter and Wester Clachan—Hill of Campsail, croft and ferry, possessed by the factor,	- - -	49	7	2
The then factor was Mr. Colin Campbell, father of the late Lorne Campbell, Chamberlain of Argyll. Mr. Campbell was once in the old Black Watch, and died 96 years old.				
Together,	-	£359	10	7
Lands in Proprietor's hands,	- -	75	2	8
Total,	-	£434	13	3

This is a remarkable statement when contrasted with the present rental of the same subjects, giving at least ten times a greater amount of return. There is a great increase in the arable lands' rental, and the feu-duties drawn from the numerous feus at Kilcreggan and Loch Long, and vast improvement has taken place in the general agricultural position of the Peninsula. In the Blue Book the agricultural rental value of the Rosneath estate was stated at £5,170. The rental of Rosneath estate, Whitsunday 1891, exclusive of the castle and shootings, amounted to close upon £8,000, of which sum nearly one-third was derived from the feus along the Kilcreggan and Cove shores. Some years ago the rental was at a higher figure, but abatements had to be made on account of the prevailing depression in agriculture. There is considerable room for increase in feu-duties, if the many admirable sites all the way along above Kilcreggan and Cove are taken into account. The total rental of the Rosneath Peninsula is as follows :—

Cove and Kilcreggan—Burgh,	£11,135
Rosneath—Landward,	10,420
Together,	£21,555

CHAPTER III.

Rosneath—A Retrospect.

THE winding shores of the Peninsula are now adorned by numerous handsome villas and marine residences, where once the mossy turf and springy heather clothed the declivities almost to the shingly strand of the Loch. Fifty years ago, along the sea beach there was an almost unbroken verge of grass or undergrowth, the natural woods spreading close down to the shore about Rahane, Mambeg and Gareloch-head. At Clynder there were one or two villas and thatched houses, and a green, grassy shore, where now there is a continuous row of modern mansions, trim gardens, landing piers, a bowling green, and other indications of teeming summer population. A great charm of the spot was its primitive and secluded air, while the same could be said of the Kilcreggan and Cove sides of the Peninsula. At that time there were no piers for disembarking passengers, and when the steamers came to the head of the Gareloch, those on board had to be landed at their destinations by means of the various ferry boats at Row, Rosneath, Shandon and Gareloch-head.

Previous to this period, communication between Rosneath and

Dunbarton, Glasgow and Greenock, was, at times, difficult and interrupted. Coaches ran on certain days of the week to Dunbarton, Greenock, and other places down the coast; goods being taken by carrier's vans. Connection was kept up with Greenock from the Ferry at Rosneath by a large open wherry, as it was called, which could take a good quantity of farm produce, and a similar one was kept at Kilcreggan, by Mr. M'Farlane the ferryman. These boats carried sheep, cattle, horses, and other domestic animals to Greenock, with perhaps a good many passengers in addition, and generally used sailing power in preference to oars, and, in times of thick fog, were steered by the compass. For the conveyance of the Duke of Argyll and his friends, on the occasion of their visits to the district, his Grace's six-oared, highly emblazoned barge plied between Cairndhu point and the Castle, then occupied by Lord John Campbell. The barge was signalled from Cairndhu point by means of three fires, or smokes, if the Duke and Duchess were to be transported across the channel; two smokes for relatives and friends; and one smoke for those in a humbler position in life; flashes of flame regulating the traffic after dark.

With the advent of steamers, and the gradual opening up of the Gareloch by feuing and building, piers began to be erected at different places. Rosneath and Gareloch-head were the first to be built about 1845, then Row, Kilcreggan, Cove, Clynder, Barremman and Shandon, and one or two others in less frequented sites, such as Balernock on the Shandon side, and Coulport on Loch Long. As far back as 1830, long before the time of the Helensburgh railway, steamers used to ply all the way from the Broomielaw to the Gareloch; such as the old *Caledonian*, which, sixty years ago, used to sail on Saturdays to Gareloch-head, and return to Glasgow on the Monday, the only steamer at that time on the Gareloch. Later on, other steamers anchored off the Ferry Inn, or were attached to buoys in the water, and took in passengers and cargoes from the various farms. The average time occupied was about three and a half-hours, but sometimes, owing to fogs and other adverse circumstances, much longer time was allowed. The old *Waverley*, the *British Queen*, *Oscar*, *Sovereign*, *Monarch*, and others were well known to the Glasgow merchants in their summer peregrinations. The *Duchess of Argyle* left Glasgow at 3 p.m. with its complement of passengers, many of them "kent faces," such as the late eminent Robert Napier of Shandon, formerly a resident on the Gareloch, and others long since gone to their rest. Then some new steamers, known as the "green boats," from their distinguishing colour, were put on, to do the passage in less time. The *Victoria* took over three hours to get to the head of the Loch from Glasgow. Frequently the passengers were landed in the steamer's boats, as the ferry boat might be absent, and, in some cases, a landing was sought where no landing appliances were available. Of the steamers of that period, hardly one is now plying on its route except the old *Inveraray Castle*. Dunbarton, and the other ports on the Clyde, were well served with steamers, such as the *Dunbarton Castle*, which in 1847, with the *Loch Lomond* and *Premier*, made the run every day between Dunbarton, Glasgow and Greenock. Omnibuses also, in connection with steamers, plied between Dunbarton, Vale of Leven, and Balloch, and the goods steamer *Dumbuck* made the voyage daily between Dunbarton and Glasgow. Up till the end of 1890, the old bluff *Balmoral*, known in 1845 as the *Lady Brisbane*, regularly made the passage between Greenock and Gareloch-head, and many regretted the untoward accident which obliged the familiar old specimen of naval architecture to be transformed into a coal hulk. These picturesque vessels were certainly in striking contrast to the graceful steamers, with their yacht-like lines, their spacious saloons, and spick and span appearance, such as the *Gareloch, Lady Clare, Diana Vernon, Galatea*, and others, now placed on the route by the two great railway companies of Scotland. The officers too of the present day are of a different type from the bluff, mottle-faced, weather-beaten salts of yore, whose rough exterior by no means indicated the genuine warmth of heart, and humour, which often characterised those veteran navigators.

In the days of the old ferry boats, and before the era of piers, disembarking was sometimes a work of much difficulty; especially when the north or east wind blew across the Loch, churning its usually peaceful waters into foaming waves. The ferrymen were daring men, ready on an emergency, capital fishermen, although occasionally they displayed, what is but too common in their class, fondness for a dram. It must be confessed that, not unfrequently, they manifested a leniency towards evasion of the excise laws, and were pretty familiar with the persons and ways of smugglers. Few more favourable specimens of the ferryman class could be found than the Macfarlanes of Kilcreggan, the Marquises of Coulport, opposite Ardentinny, who, till 1890, had for a hundred years been tenants of the ferry, and the Macfarlanes of Rahane. The latter ferry is still wrought by John Macfarlane, the third in succession who has handled the oars, and although past the term allotted by the Psalmist, is daily at his post, alert and cheery as of yore. Long may this class of men flourish under the different regime and surroundings which environ us, now that education and social influences are more generally diffused, and we are brought more into contact with those a little below us in the social scale. Hardy, industrious, obliging, ready of wit and kindly in speech, and vigorous in body, may they not lose their individuality and get merged in the undistinguished body of labourers. Even the old fashioned ferry-boat, with its bluff sides and broad seats, is often much more in keeping with the surrounding romantic scenery than the trim built, iron structure, whose slim, spidery-looking formation, with ornamental iron rails, has superseded the venerable, picturesque, and heavy old wooden pier.

On landing from the old *Duchess of Argyle*, fifty years ago, at Rosneath Ferry, the stranger would find himself on a point of land opposite Row, where the tide forms a rapid race at certain periods of its rise and fall. Sometimes, when there is a strong east wind meeting the full force of the ebb tide, the waterway is very rough, and full of breakers; this narrow strip of water constantly changes its aspect, and, according to the atmospheric phases and iridescence of the sky, the colouring of the waves is strangely varied. A beautiful expanse of water stretches away from the point beyond the Ferry Inn. Undoubtedly the shores of the loch, at one time, were much more extensive, and there was an ample carpet of turf. Some seventy years ago, there stood a lime kiln in the middle of the grassy verge of the loch at this place, but the gradual encroachment of the tide has long since carried every vestige away. The view up the loch on a calm day, with the shadows of the mountain slopes reflected in the transparent water, and the fine, rugged, outline of the "Argyle Bowling Green" bounding the prospect, is one of the most beautiful which can be imagined. Sometimes, on a very still night, though the loch may be in perfect repose, the rushing sound of the tide within the narrows is audible for a great distance, and has a curious effect at the silent hour, when all nature around is hushed in midnight slumber.

As you disembarked on the shore half a century ago, the only house visible was the little Ferry Inn, which has stood in its present situation for about one hundred years. During the occupancy of Mrs. Whyte, the present tenant, it has been thrice enlarged; the first modest building having only one window in the second storey above the door, and the old stable was below at the corner of the road. Most of the stones of which the inn is built were brought from the remains of the old mansion, belonging to the Campbells of Carrick, which stood close to the celebrated silver firs, known as the "Big Trees," within the Campsail Woods. The former hostelry, a humble, thatched, single-storied house, stood a little further up, facing the castle and bay, and the ancient road to the ferry followed the bend of the shore from Strouel Bay, and skirted the beach all the way along to the Mill Bay. Just beyond the inn is a pretty glen, shaded with trees of considerable size, through which the Clachan burn meanders, until it enters the loch close beside the little one-storeyed cottage, built at the beginning of the century by old Neil Fletcher, who tenanted the salmon fishing there. Mr. Fletcher came from the island of Mull, and long resided at Rosneath, and helped to plant the wood full of umbrageous trees between his house and the Clachan village. For a short time previous to Mr. John Dodds being appointed schoolmaster, Fletcher conducted a small school at the Hill of Campsail. Some of the old stakes which supported the salmon nets are still to be seen on the shore. His widow, who lived to the patriarchal age of 96, and was much respected, resided here until a few years ago. There is now a rising boat building establishment located at the entrance of the burn, started by Mr. John M'Lean, and managed by his son Peter, an energetic young native of Rosneath, and some of their four and five tonners have been very successful as racing craft.

A short distance up the road is the Clachan of Rosneath, which, even now, is a picturesque-looking row of houses, and has interesting features fast passing away. Before the erection of the new schoolhouse and grocer's shop adjoining, the row of cottages were whitewashed old structures, with thatched roofs, or red tiled ones, mellow with age, and overgrown with moss and lichens. The cottage adjoining the post office, with the roof partly open, was, in its day, thought a handsome one, and was put up by the two brothers of Mr. Lorne Campbell for the widow of the Rev. Mr. Macfarlane, minister of Arrochar. Now only three or four cottages have tile roofs, the others being slated, and the interpolation of a newly constructed stone house detracts considerably from the air of antiquity once so pleasing. The end cottage was long a noted public house, kept by Mr. M'Wattie, one of the six which were in existence when the Rev. Robert Story was minister of the parish. The old house with its gable to the road, and facing the Churchyard, was long used as the village school, and the schoolmaster occupied the upper storey. It was for many years tenanted by the late respected Mr. John Dodds, who, for fifty years, taught the youth of the parish, and died in 1870. Here assembled not only the sturdy, chubby-faced, young children of the farmers and their labourers, but the families of the resident gentry were glad to enjoy the privilege of the admirable tuition dispensed by Mr. Dodds. In addition to the ordinary branches of knowledge imparted in the parish schools of Scotland, Mr. Dodds taught the higher departments of mathematics, land-surveying, and navigation, and gave competent instruction in French. Many of his pupils achieved distinction in various walks in life, and remembered long, with kindly affection, the thorough grounding in education acquired at the Rosneath school. Mr. Dodds filled other posts in connection with the parish and Church, and for twenty years was kind enough to act as postmaster, upon most inadequate remuneration. The letters were posted at a small slit in the wall near the door of the house, which can still be traced in the surface of the plaster, while they were given out at a square window, which used to be in the little brick building formerly annexed to the house.* Dr. James Dodds, the esteemed parish minister of Corstorphine, is a son of the worthy old schoolmaster of Rosneath.

At that time there was some fine old trees surrounding the Churchyard, one specially admired chestnut tree being right opposite the schoolhouse, and a low broken dyke, covered with turf, bounded the burying ground. The public road to the Clachan and old Church opened on to the village opposite to the new post office, and on the right hand side, not far from the manse, there was a thatch-roofed public-house, with its gable on to the road, which has long since disappeared. All the fields about the Clachan Village had their names, and those are now well-nigh forgotten, except by some of the older inhabitants. The field between the Yew Avenue and the Clachan Braes was known as the "Enclosure," the corresponding one on the other side of the Avenue was "Barn park." The park near which the new schoolhouse stands is "Tom-a-Mhoid," the "field of justice." This is a name common in the Highlands, there is a similar one at Balernock on the Shandon side of the loch. The field in front of

---

* By a recent alteration a stair leads to the upper part of the house, thus forming a second tenement.

the new schoolhouse was called "Callum Crubach," or in English, "Cripple Malcolm." The new Church stands on what was known as the "Manse Croft," and that on the right hand, as you go to the Ferry Inn, is the "Ferry Park." The one beyond it again has long been known as "The Moyachs," which term, in Gaelic, signifies "a hare." The piece of ground partly occupied by Tigh-na-mara villa, and Kenmure Cottage, above the Strouel Well, was known as the "Strouel Acre." The "North" and "South" parks are those near Mr. Howie's new Clachan Farm, and other local names may still be recalled by those who knew the district before it lost its primitive character.

One of the admired features of Rosneath is the fine avenue of yew trees, which extends from the little wooden bridge over the Clachan burn, up to the old mansion at the other end, which long was used as a sort of dower house of the Argyll family. It is not easy to ascertain the exact age of these stately yews, but it certainly must be well on to two hundred years. In the very hottest day in summer, there is ever a grateful shade under their mantling boughs, which are, at many points, interlaced together, and form an appropriate avenue to the ancient resting-place of the dead. Sometimes the light breezes play amidst their sombre sprays, with a subdued murmuring sound, like the hollow voice of the ocean. Many generations of Clachan children have gambolled under the branches of these venerable trees, their merry cries resounding throughout the bosky glade. This is a favourite subject for artists, and in summer they

THE YEW-TREE AVENUE.

may often be observed depicting this rich sylvan scene. When the moon is full, and shining right down on the hoary yews, the soft shadows lie sleeping on the sward below, and the vista is one full of still, impressive beauty. Beyond the yews are two rows of spreading lime trees, which give shelter to the avenue, and whose boughs in summer resound with the hum of many bees, as they gather their fragrant harvest, and "flee hame wi' lades o' treasure."

Conjecture has been busy as to the meaning of this yew avenue, and the moss grown mansion house. It would seem that two massive stone pillars once formed the entrance, at the spot where the wooden bridge over the Clachan burn now stands. Their foundations were seen, not long ago, by the village joiner when making some repairs. There was a tradition that a monastery had once existed where the Clachan House is placed, and when the tenant of the farm was making a drain he came upon a quantity of massive stones, all solidly located, and forming a firm foundation for a large building. The existing house has been erected at different dates, the oldest portion being next the avenue, and was once of much greater extent,—a large wing having been pulled down forty years ago. John Campbell, of Mamore, an ancestor of the Duke of Argyll, lived in this house in the last century, and, since then, it was long occupied by Mr. Robert Campbell, the Duke's factor; by his son, the late John Douglas Campbell of Peatoun; and by Mr. Howie, tenant of the Clachan farm. It is now partly tenanted by several families, and is falling considerably out of repair, in many parts, but forms an appropriate and picturesque termination to the yew avenue. The old garden beside it is of some size, and in the park behind are several large plane and ash trees. One of the finest plane trees in this part of Scotland is to be seen on the left hand of the yew avenue, near the Churchyard, overhanging the burn. This noble sycamore has a grand appearance, its gigantic limbs springing from a massive bole, which, at three feet from the ground, is fourteen feet, three inches, in circumference. There is a most useful bed of sand, admirably suitable for building purposes, in front of the Clachan House near the public road.

A little distance from the old house, along the road, you come to the Strouel Well, which is a running stream of water that has only been known to fail on very rare occasions of extreme drought. The old road to the ferry used to run along the shore between the beach and the row of venerable ash trees which now overhang the Strand, and, one by one, are succumbing to the fury of the wintry blasts.* Early in this century the road had diminished to a mere track, and has long been wholly obliterated. No doubt this was the ancient road from Glasgow to the Western Highlands by which pilgrims journeyed to Iona. It was a continuation of the "Highlandman's Road" at Row, and led along the Loch side as far as the Hatton-burn at Barremman, and then crossed the field in an oblique

---

* The straight road from the Mill Bay across the field in front of the Church, along the end of the Clachan Village to Strouel Bay, was made by John Duke of Argyle about the year 1770. It ran all the way from the Castle of Rosneath to the head of Loch Long. See Appendix.

direction, near Barremman House, over the moor, and down upon Coulport, Loch Long. The loch has made gradual incursions upon the existing road, and, in front of the houses at Strouel, where now only a narrow strip of turf two or three feet wide extends, there was, sixty years ago, sufficient space for the boys to play at shinty. About that time there was an old drying kiln, just below the cottage a little way from the Strouel Well, to which the farmers brought their grain. There is another of the splendid plane trees which flourish so well in this Peninsula, just below the cottage, and its great twisted, gnarled, roots are exposed to view, as the soil is gradually becoming washed away.

We now are at the commencement of the various feus which have been taken off the Barremman estate, which joins the Duke's land at the small burn beyond the Strouel well. Feuing commenced in the year 1825, previously to which date the shore, from this point to Gareloch-head, presented an unbroken slope of green fields and bracken-clad braes, with the exception of some thatched cottages at rare intervals. Indeed, Mr. James Campbell, Strouel Cottage, whose father tenanted Strouel farm, has ploughed along the whole shore up to Barremman pier, where now is a continuous row of handsome villas. The first feu, taken about 1825, from Barremman estate, and subsequently entirely bought up, was the villa now known as Achnashie, "Field of Peace," where the Rev. Dr. M'Leod Campbell died.* Mr.

---

* The small villa, known as "Strouel Cottage," was also feued in 1825.

Angus, who was the feuar, verbally arranged with Mr. Cumming, the proprietor of the estate, that he should have the shore-land as far as low-water mark, but this was afterwards disputed by the laird. Upon taking the matter to the Court of Session, it was agreed that the feu should extend as far into the loch as a man on horseback could ride, starting at low water. The house erected by Mr. Angus, and left to his two daughters, was known as "The Chateau," until Dr. Campbell selected the more appropriate Gaelic name of Achnashie, and was an unpretending, solid, stone structure, with heavy overhanging eaves. The square house, close to the road within the grounds, is called "Gareloch House," and was also built by Mr. Angus. Nearly opposite is the small rocky island, which is entirely submerged at high water, known as *Carrick-na-raon*, or "Rock of the Seal." This shows that seals used to frequent the Gareloch before the advent of steamers.

Passing by Achnashie and the little cluster of houses at Strouel, which were erected about the same time, we come to Strouel Lodge, a comfortable-looking old-fashioned mansion, erected in 1829 by the late Mr. William Robertson of Greenock, a noted yachtsman in his time, his old cutter, *The Gipsy*, being a great success in the early days of pleasure cruising on the Clyde. Mr. Robertson, a quaint gentleman of the old school, was one of the last who practised the classical pastime of hawking, and might often be seen on the Rosneath roads and uplands, the hawk on his wrist, pursuing his favourite calling. His son, the late Mr. George Robertson, for more than fifty years resided at Strouel, whose familiar and respected figure was well-known in the parish, died in 1887. The next feu taken off Barremman was "Whitelea," in the year 1829, when Mr. Stenhouse built the substantial square house, which he occupied himself, and then left to his nieces. Another large feu taken shortly afterwards was by Mr Monteith, who built Clynder House, and several smaller houses, with their gable ends on to the road. This was long a favourite spot with summer visitors, who used to land from the steamer in a small boat kept by James Campbell, Crossowen, the old ferryman, until, in 1866, Clynder pier was built by Mr. Archibald Chalmers, a native of Rosneath. This pier has now been acquired by Mr. Thom of Barremman, and is in process of gradual demolition, as he considers the requirements of the district are amply met by Barremman pier. Up till 1866 the shores of the loch had a sweet secluded aspect, which was lost when the hotel and buildings, and the lofty tenement known as Victoria Place, were subsequently erected by Mr. Robert Turner, another native of the parish.

Before the erection of the villas and shops at Clynder, there were a few rough stone houses, with thatched roofs, (one row a little way above the spot on which the small iron Church now stands), and their gables to the loch, which have been pulled down. Also at Crossowen, near where Barremman pier is placed, there was the small, old thatched farm house and buildings, and another similar cottage at Hattonburn. Going along the shore, you now come to Barremman House, a plain mansion, of moderate size, facing the loch. The estate was for more than a century and a half in possession of the Cumming family, who had long been connected with the district. In 1871, Barremman was sold by its late proprietor, Mr. Robert Crawford Cumming, and acquired by its present owner, Mr. Robert Thom of Glasgow, who is also proprietor of the Island of Canna in the West Highlands. Barremman House has been three times added to, the original mansion having been a humble structure with the door between two windows, and three others above. About 1840, Mr. Cumming made an addition of some rooms, and a porch facing the south, and when Mr. Thom acquired the property, he doubled the accommodation by a large increase to the west.

A little to the north of the present house, the old mansion stands where the Cummings resided in former days, a very simple, rough-cast house of two storeys. Part of the house is antique, the lower portion having been originally built with unhewn stones, taken from the shore, interspersed with clay, and it had a thatched roof. An extra storey of more substantial architecture was added, and a slate roof substituted. Over the door the following names are cut in the stone :—

PATRICK CUMING, 1730.

MARY M'FARLANE.

The whole has a venerable aspect, and in olden times, with its shelter of ash and plane trees, and the wimpling burn behind rushing in sparkling cascades down to the loch, it must have shown a pleasing display of sylvan rusticity. From the windows of the mansion house there is a fine prospect of the entire range of the Gareloch, and, towards the south-east, you see the long stretch of Row Point, with the headlands of Cairndhu and the Ardmore promontory in the distance. Towards the north end of the loch, there is the noble outline of the Loch Long range of mountains, and those on the opposite shore of Shandon above the Glenfruin valley, near Loch Lomond.*

On the left, up the hillside, are seen the two farms of Little Rahane and Meikle Rahane, with their dwelling houses and steadings, some way above the loch. It needs all the patience and energy which the farmers possess to enable them to overcome the unremunerative nature of their working in such exposed positions. But it is interesting to note what has been done to develop the natural capabilities of the bare hillside, and good stock has been reared on those Gareloch farms. The small village of Rahane consists of a few humble cottages, and three or four villas of some pretensions; a primitive looking place altogether, but in summer much frequented by visitors.

Passengers from the steamers are landed at Rahane by ferry-boat, and the veteran John M'Farlane, whose patriarchal aspect is well known to the frequenters of the Gareloch, does the honours of his humble craft. The third in descent of his family who has occupied

---

* The Loch Long ranges of mountains form the great feature of the scenery of the Gareloch, and have various Gaelic names, more or less unpronounceable by Lowland tongues. From Cruachash, at Ardentinny, to Tullich Hill, Ben Breack, Ben Vorlich, Ben Vannach, Ben Im, "The Cobbler," and others, some over 3000 feet high, they make a fine picture.

a cottage at Rahane, the worthy ferryman can give interesting reminiscences of the past. His white cottage, built fifty years ago, occupies the site of two older thatched structures which stood on to the road. A few years since, three other contiguous cottages on the roadside were pulled down. These were originally malt houses for the distillery, which stood a hundred yards, or so, back from the ferryman's cottage, and he remembers the ruins of that building when he was a boy, but no trace of them are now to be seen. The malt mill was a little nearer the shore, on the border of the burn, into which the water wheel projected, and delighted the village boys with its gyrations. Several red tiled cottages were in front of the distillery, which were pulled down twenty years ago, and only their site can be traced. He remembers that there used to be a small crofter settlement in a field near the farmhouse of Mamore, above Rahane, but no vestige now remains of this. Honest John is a skilled fisherman, and still nets large quantities of herring in the season, one favourable night, in 1891, yielding him the handsome return of 4500 herrings from the head of the Loch. From this to Gareloch-head the road is well shaded by the trees which grow down to the water's edge, some of them fine old specimens of oaks and ashes. In spring, these woods and all the fields which slope down to the road, are thickly covered with a luxuriant, beautiful growth of primroses, and the pale yellow flower also decks the mossy banks of the burns which bound down to the Loch past many a shady nook. A plantation of young birch, rowan, hazel, beech, fir, and other varieties of trees, clothes the hillside near Mambeg, and every few years it is thinned for the bark. A mile beyond this, the houses of Gareloch-head open to view, and the end of the parish is reached at the burn which flows down the hill from the heights above Whistlefield.

Gareloch-head extends on the right in a semi-circular form; a number of commodious villas, with grounds well stocked with flowering shrubs and larger trees, nearly the whole of which have been built within the last forty-five years. Little more than that time has passed since there were not above half a dozen slated houses in the whole village, one of them being Fernicarry, where the Campbell family lived, who were so noted at the time of the strange excitement regarding the supposed gift of "tongues," Bendarroch, built by Mr. Bennett Browne, and also the old school-house, which occupied a site close to where the present post-office stands. At the back of Fernicarry, up the hill side, is a small cave known as M'William's cave, from a tradition that, long ago, a man of that name found shelter there, for a considerable time, after a murder committed in the neighbourhood.

Returning to the Clachan of Rosneath, and proceeding in the direction of the Castle, the visitor will notice the fine old trees, chiefly of the plane and ash species, which adorn the landscape. The hedgerows also are deserving of notice, so thickly grown and well kept, evidently of considerable age; the one on the road to the Mill Bay being over a hundred years old. The Mill, or as it is sometimes called Campsail Bay, is seen now, gleaming through the trees, one of the most beautiful inlets of water in all the Frith of Clyde. The trees all along the shore here literally shed their leaves into the sea at high water, and this is a favourite anchorage for yachts of various sizes, when laid up for the winter. Last century there was a mill which stood in the Castle grounds, a little way from the low bridge admitting to the policies, hence the origin of the name of the Bay. No trace of the mill now exists, but the ruined cottage near the bridge was known as the "burnt mill," and was occupied by the miller, and later on by the forester.

Near the middle of the bay, an ancient-looking avenue gate points the way to where Campsail House once stood, that was possessed by a branch of the Campbell family. The gate posts are covered with beautiful grey lichens, and one of them has an ornamented top in the form of an acorn, its fellow having long since disappeared. The wood beyond is a sylvan scene of rare beauty, many of the trees being old, and casting a sombre shade from their mantling branches. Oaks, beeches, walnuts, Spanish chestnuts, planes, and straight, lofty silver firs, all combine to impress the spectator with a feeling of peace and solitude, as in some lonely forest far from the haunts of men. The bracken and ferns which clothe the ground, mingled with periwinkle, wild sorrel, and other creepers, harmonise with the verdant retreat, and the shining leaves of holly bushes and ivy, thickly clustering round the rugged trunks, gleam amid the slanting sunrays. A short walk from the old avenue gate brings the visitor in front of the two peerless silver firs, which are the special glory of Rosneath,

THE CELEBRATED SILVER FIRS.

whose fame has endured for many generations. These are two grand specimens of the fir tribe, their huge trunks, gnarled and massive, having all the solidity and seeming indestructibility of the granite rock, their great roots deeply fixed in the mossy soil. Probably not in Europe are there to be seen two such magnificent and venerable silver firs as these celebrated "big trees" of Rosneath. Thousands of visitors have been attracted to the Peninsula, many from America and the colonies, to behold these two monarchs of the forest, which for centuries have flourished in the secluded woods of Campsail. Nearly twenty-five feet in circumference, and one hundred and thirty in height, with immense branches, themselves respectable trees, springing from the great, grey seamed stem, hoar with age and clad with lichen as the rock—these twin giants lift their verdant crests above their companions of the grove. What a tale could they tell of the many visitors, of all ranks in life, who have stood in their majestic presence, and gazed upon the spreading boughs which so long have wrestled with the wintry tempest! *

---

* The following notice of these firs appeared in *Gardening Illustrated*, Feby., 1891 :—Silver firs are in almost every district of Great Britain. Many range from 100 to 130 feet high. Loudon says the species was introduced in 1603. On the Duke of Argyll's property at Rosneath are many fine old trees of silver fir species, from 100 to 130 feet in height, with clean stems, and girth 20 feet at a yard from the ground. Especially there are two fine old silvers, called Adam and Eve. First named has few equals in this or any other country. They were planted over 200 years ago, and are now respectively 130 and 1.4 feet high. The cubic contents of the two trees are computed to be 2500 feet. Eve rises 124 feet, and girths at 3 and 5 feet, 22 feet 8 inches, and 21 feet 8 inches, respectively.

Close beside the great firs may be observed the foundations of the old mansion of Campsail, once belonging to the Campbells of Carrick, and where their representative, the sister of Duke John of Argyll, known as Lady Carrick by the Rosneath people, long lived, and was beloved for her good deeds. A sweet spot it must have been, with fine mossy sward around the ancient pile, which had a peep, through the trees, of the seaside town of Helensburgh. Even now the terraced formation of the turf indicates where the pleasure grounds had been; the old well still offers a cool draught of limpid water, and the well worn flag-stones of the courtyard speak of days of "auld lang syne." In the earlier part of the century the stones of the old dwelling were partly removed to build the inn at Ardencaple, near Row, and to add to the accommodation of the Ferry Inn, Rosneath. There are several other splendid firs of the silver species in these woods, which would be accounted noble specimens anywhere, but are eclipsed by their colossal neighbours in the vicinity of the ruined house of Campsail.

Emerging from the wood by a wicket gate, between two very lofty silver firs, the road by the shore is regained, and the visitor sees before him the low bridge which forms the very modest entrance into the castle grounds and woods. Turning to the left hand and passing some old beech trees overhanging the water, there is now a

---

At 1 foot from ground Adam girths 28 feet 10 inches size of stem, and is 130 feet high. There is one silver fir, near the New Forest, which is 130 feet high, but only 14 feet in girth.

long stretch of avenue with a border of fine luxuriant rhododendron bushes which, in their season, present a splendid blaze of rich colour. Lifting their dark bushy heads above the surrounding trees are several old picturesque Scotch firs, with rugged, red bark which glows in the rays of the setting sun, and harmonises well with the prevailing colouring around. There are various walks and roads opening out as the wood is explored, and a full growth of rhododendron and holly bushes covers the ground, while ivy closely twines round many a tree of stately girth. Beautiful peeps of the loch and distant hills are gained as the visitor skirts the winding reaches of the shingly strand, and on the other side some old beech trees spread their umbrageous boughs over the sward. It will be noticed that the beech trees are more venerable in their aspect than those hitherto seen, and especially those near the old sea-wall of conglomerate rock, at the spot known as "Wallace's Leap." It was here that the hero leaped down with his gallant steed from the summit of the rock, and made good his escape across the loch to Cairndhu point. This took place somewhere about the year 1297, when Wallace was contending against King Edward of England. After his escape from his foes at Rosneath, it is probable that Wallace proceeded to Dunbarton Castle, then in possession of the English, and went to an inn to lodge. His enemies got word of his being in the town, and sent twenty-four men and an officer to apprehend Wallace, who however leapt out of the window, and proceeded to assault the soldiers outside. With one or two sweeps of his terrible two-handed sword, he cut down the com-

mander of the party and a dozen of his men, while the rest fled precipitately to the castle for refuge. Some high fir and beech trees grow right on the verge of this rocky precipice, and hang over the avenue along which you pass towards the castle. A little way from Wallace's Leap there is seen the old garden, now in a neglected condition, but all the more picturesque in its disarray. The crumbling wall which surrounds it, is constructed of stones which, from their appearance, seem to have been gathered on the shore, large irregular rounded boulders. All the upper part of the wall seems to have been pulled down, along a great part of its course, but enough is left to form a substantial fence. In many parts it is overgrown with sheltering ivy, which is a great resort for birds at the breeding season. At one end of the garden there is a range of buildings, now used as stables and workshops, but which, it is surmised, were for the use of the large number of workmen required when the castle was building, although the Marquis of Lorne considers they may have formed part of the old castle outhouses. On the grassy plateau opposite them stood, about forty years ago, an old house, which was then pulled down, and of which the only portion remaining is a stone, with the date upon it, 1638.*
From this place the ground slopes down to the lawn surrounding the

---

* This house was probably the dwelling of the valiant Captain of Knockdunder, mentioned in the *Heart of Midlothian*. Other authorities will have it that the distinguished officer dwelt in a house built on the Cove side of the Peninsula, the site of which is occupied by Knockderry Castle.

castle, a noble building of massive construction, the work of an Italian architect, Bonomi of London, and begun in 1803. The site is a fine one, at a greater distance from the shore than the old castle, which was destroyed by fire. This former residence of the chieftains of the Clan Campbell long rested upon the promontory of land opposite Ardencaple Castle. It does not seem to have been a building of any special importance or architectural merit, but, about the year 1630, it was enlarged and embellished by the famous Marquis of Argyll. This mansion remained until about the beginning of the present century, when it was nearly all burnt to the ground. Upon this occasion the old Duke of Argyll, a pious man, calmly viewed the conflagration from his castle of Ardencaple, opposite, and expressed his gratitude by saying, "I thank my God, I have another house to go to!" The uninjured part of the castle was for a considerable period rented by the late Mr. Smith of Jordanhill, grandfather of the respected Member of Parliament for Partick, who was an enthusiastic yachting man. His well known yacht the "Orion" used to lie at her moorings just below the Castle Point, and Mr. Smith could hail his skipper from the drawing-room window, when giving his sailing orders. Two old ash trees, still standing on the grassy headland, mark where the entrance to the castle was, its foundation being on the rocky beach, not far from the point. An existing range of buildings, known as the "Low barracks," formed part of the castle outhouses, and were used as servants' accommodation. They are of solid construction, vaulted in some parts, and have an appearance of considerable antiquity, and are partly covered with old ivy. A flight of stairs from the outside of the main building communicated with the "barracks," and when the former was demolished, the stones were utilised in constructing some of the offices at the Home Farm.

In 1803, the present castle, as it is styled, though palace would be the more correct term, was begun upon a site a good distance from the point, but commanding a noble prospect. Its architecture, in the Italian style, is massive and imposing, the splendid Ionic portico, with its lofty stone pillars, being the chief feature, and may be considered almost unequalled in Scotland. The castle is 184 feet long and 121 in breadth, with two very handsome fronts, each adorned with fine Ionic columns. From the high circular tower in the centre of the building there is a grand panorama of wood, water, lawn and moor, which affords an endless enjoyment to the beholder. You look right up the estuary of the Clyde, far beyond Dunbarton, and down the river as far as Bute in another direction, and towards the rugged range of the Argyllshire hills to the North. The castle forms a parallelogram, and, had it been finished, would have been a truly imposing building, but the Duke of Argyll who started it found himself in the position of the man in the parable who began to build without counting the cost. The stone is of the finest freestone, from the famous Garscube quarry, near Glasgow, and is hewn into imposing blocks. All round the building it was intended to erect a range of the same noble pillars which adorn the portico, and over them a course of elaborate capitals, a finely moulded balustrade surmounting all. Each

ROSNEATH CASTLE.

door and window is of stately proportions, and the interior is on the same scale of classical, sculptured adornment. A spacious corridor extends from one end of the building to the other, off which the large public rooms open, from each of which there is a beautiful view. The rooms are very lofty and handsomely proportioned, and have decorated freizes on the upper portions of the walls and ceilings. One exceedingly elegant room is the circular library under the tower, with stone walls, and classic ceiling decorations—a finely designed apartment. Down stairs, the kitchen is of great size, with various other vaulted halls and rooms; several of those at the east end of the castle being unfinished and used for storing plants, containing also a considerable portion of the stone balustrades and other ornaments of the exterior. The upper part of the castle has a number of large bedrooms, all plainly fitted up, for there is little splendour in any of the internal furnishings. A few family portraits—one recently added, a full-length picture of the Marquis of Lorne, and an engraving of the beautiful Miss Gunning, adorn the public rooms, and two handsome alabaster vases in the library will attract attention. But want of funds compelled the abandonment of the original design, and only the north part of the castle was completed according to the architect's plan.

Bordering the avenue are some grand old beech trees, their huge branches sweeping the ground, and numerous lofty trees of the silver and Scotch fir species adorn the woods. All along the lawn, near the castle, in the spring there is a profusion of cowslips and primroses, while the songs of the mavis, the blackbird and chaffinch, resound through the thicket. The walks extend through the dense groves of rhododendrons in all directions, affording sweet glimpses of the shore and sea, with the most perfect retirement. One charming feature is the delightful old-fashioned garden at the back of the castle, with its long stretches of mossy turf and quaint arrangement of laurel and heath plants, groups of flowering shrubs and old-fashioned bushes, trimly kept walks with heavy box border, all vastly superior to the formal arrangements now in vogue. The mossy soft walks seem to allure you to stroll along, and to enjoy the scent of wallflowers, sweet peas, and mignonette. There are quiet, retired nooks, in which you may sit quite secluded from observation, and listen to the cooing of the wood pigeons or the warbling of the mavis from the adjoining wood, while the songs of infancy steal over the senses, or the day dreams of mature years enrapture the mind with the soft languor of thrilling remembrance. Beyond the castle garden the plantations extend all along the shore, until you reach the point opposite Greenock. Near the old buildings known as the "Low barracks" are some very fine specimens of Scotch firs, their gnarled red trunks and umbrageous tops standing out amid the lesser trees. In many cases the largest trees are tightly encircled by ivy, thus sapping all their strength and rendering them all the surer victims to the wintry storm.

The Heronry is situated in the thick woods about a mile beyond the castle, close to what is known as the "Green Isle Point," at the extreme end of the Peninsula. It is singular that a bird that is so solitary in its habits and, as a rule, avoiding the haunts of man, should have selected, for its breeding place, a spot only separated from the busy town of Greenock by about three miles of water. But there are so many secluded bays in the Peninsula, and quiet nooks on the shingly shore, such as this shy bird loves, that he finds a sufficient attraction to linger long in these parts. There are many heronries scattered about the West of Scotland, not always in lofty trees, though this is the usual nesting place selected. On the point of Ardnamurchan, for instance, where the rocks are steep, and covered ivy and shrubs, there is an extensive colony of herons.

The Rosneath Heronry is in the midst of a wood of lofty silver fir trees, surrounded by a belt of thick plantation. This is a spot of still beauty, forming a retreat of sylvan repose, which the visitor would scarcely expect to meet in this locality. The screen of spruce, larch, and silver firs intervenes between glassy glades, and stretches of turf decked in spring with a perfect carpet of wild hyacinths. But a little distance beyond is the busy, seething, world of toil and commerce, with the manifold wheels of industry in ceaseless hum, while here is all the seclusion of the forest. In the spring, however, the woods resound with the harsh cries of the herons, who are engaged in the important work of rearing their young. The nests are great unshapely masses of dried twigs, with a few tufts of coarse grass inside, and there are generally four eggs in each, of a pale green colour. Sometimes the bird will courageously defend itself, if surprised by an intruder while sitting on its eggs, and a blow from the sharp, horny bill is sufficiently severe. There are some sixty or seventy nests, and, as you walk below the lofty trees, when the breeding season is in full swing, there is much commotion above. The herons fly to and fro, crashing amid the boughs with their long bodies and immense wings, many of them carrying fish between their bills to satisfy the clamours of their nestlings. The visitor will find much to interest him, not only in the study of the herons and their ways, but in observing various other aquatic birds which congregate in numbers along the shallow bays and shingly strands that indent the end of the Peninsula.

There are several large fields beyond the Castle of shingly, light soil, famed for potatoe crops. Here may often be seen the welcome and friendly peesweep, skimming lightly over the ground with its quick flight, and uttering its shrill, cheery cry. This bird, and the equally familiar curlew, abounds in many parts of the Peninsula, the latter being met with in the sandy shoals of the Mill Bay, as well as on the confines of the moor. The pewits are often seen in considerable numbers, their graceful evolutions as they turn on the wing, bringing the white of their breasts into view, and often a continuous clamour arises, as they seem to chide the intruders who invade their haunts. While walking along the plantations near the shore, the pedestrian will hear the long drawn, curious cry of the curlews which frequent this place. At evening time, sometimes, the ear will be startled by their strangely varied notes of surprise or alarm, and, if it is the nesting season, the bird will wheel rapidly overhead, screaming as it flies.

Proceeding now across the fields at the back of the Castle, the visitor sees the extensive pile of buildings, known locally as "The Steeple," forming the range of steadings of the Home Farm. The buildings are about 280 feet in length, and were once ornamented by a fine tower, 90 feet in height, designed by Nasmyth of Edinburgh, but which, after the fire, was curtailed of its lofty proportions. Its name very probably was given on account of the tall spire that formed the centre portion of the building, and which was even higher before the great fire, which forty years ago, consumed the interior of the steading. Originally, these buildings were intended to have been the Castle stables, but were either found too expensive or too far from the Castle, so they were made into a farm steading. Owing to their massive construction, the walls were little injured by the fire, which raged for many hours with little check, and there is ample room for the requirements of the large farm. Returning by the Home Farm road, the visitor again finds himself at the entrance to the Castle grounds at the Mill Bay, and turns his steps along the road to Kilcreggan.

On the left hand is the Gallowhill, which once was completely covered with a fine plantation of fir trees, but, more than thirty years ago, these were cut down by the proprietor. The view from the summit of the hill is extensive, and gives a striking idea of the diversified scenery of the Frith of Clyde. Looking towards the north, the whole of the upper part of the Peninsula is seen, a mass of purple heather and feathery bracken, while the dark mass of mountains above Loch

Long, and the distant peaks are faintly shrouded in blue haze. Many burns seam the sides of the hills round the Gareloch, whose waters reflect the fringe of trees along its shore, amid which nestle numerous handsome villas, and the green fields above join on to the moors. The russet brown of autumn spreads its mantle over the uplands, and the plantations on both sides are glowing with yellow and rosy tints. In the full blaze of mellow sunshine, which, on an autumn day, bathes the whole loch and surrounding mountains, beautiful effects are gained by the delicate blending of the warm tints of moor, glen, and swelling upland. While the edge of the nearer rugged mountain outline is sharply defined against the sides of the far off peaks which reflect the sun with more brilliant lustre; a lovely, soft, haze envelopes the horizon, although the immediate foreground is strongly coloured with the purple loch and dark green of the pine plantations. A white line of strand marks the upper reaches of the loch, and the tawny coloured streaks of spreading bracken give variety of tints to the picture. Some of the old beech trees are seen in the Castle woods, their foliage flaming with yellow and purple, and their shining, grey trunks intervening between the red Scotch firs and spreading oaks—all presenting a variegated, sylvan scene of vivid beauty. Turning round, the broad estuary of the Clyde extends between Helensburgh and Greenock; many a stately steamer lying at anchor, and smaller craft plying their busy way up and down the river. Beyond the spacious heather-clad summit on which you stand, the Castle and roads around it come into view, with the mass of fine old Scotch and silver firs where the Heronry is situated, near the Green Isle point. Casting the eye over Helensburgh, the distant hills in the neighbourhood of Stirling are descried, while opposite Dunbarton rock the Renfrewshire hills close in the scene, and, following the bend of the Clyde, you trace the animated panorama of towns, harbours, quays, villas, and shipping, until the misty outlines of Bute and Arran bound the view. Your solitude is undisturbed, for there is a considerable extent of moor all round the summit of the Gallowhill, and it is difficult to realise, at certain points of the landscape, that you are so near the great bustling world of commercial enterprise of which Glasgow is the centre.

The lower slopes of the hill are covered with wood, embracing many varieties of deciduous trees, the oak and beech predominating, and many fine specimens of each will be noticed. A good carriage drive once existed, winding round the base of the hill, but it is completely grass grown and rarely used. Spreading all round in the leafy recesses of the wood is the luxuriant undergrowth of vegetation which flourishes so abundantly in the district. The carefully trimmed hedgerows of beech, and hawthorn, and holly, will be noticed on both sides of the road here; indeed the hedges in all this part of the Argyll estate are particularly healthy and well kept. Some of them are considerably over a hundred years old, and while the unpicturesque wire fence is so rapidly gaining ground in our land, it is a pleasure to see the perfectly tended hedgerows of Rosneath.

An old saw mill is now passed on the left hand, within the wood, which is of some interest. The shed, open on one side, farthest away from the road, and covered over with mouldering, moss-grown, red tiles, was the place where the Free Church congregation of Rosneath first found shelter after the Disruption. Here the distinguished leader of the Free Church, Principal Rainy, preached his first sermon. Of those who worshipped in that retired spot, only a few survive in the Peninsula, but there are several who can recall all the stirring incidents, and somewhat painful memories, of that period of strife. Under a wooden shed beside the mill there stood, for many years, a curious old barouche of the Argyll family, belonging to the former Duke, and emblazoned with their proud coat of arms. It had done duty for generations, not only in this country, but on the Continent, and its great C. springs and ponderous leather straps attached to them, were curiosities in their way. Many a journey, to and from Inveraray, had the Dukes of Argyll made in the lumbering old vehicle.

A little beyond this, the small hamlet of the Mill of Campsail is reached. The old meal mill is a picturesque building, and has been a prominent feature in many an artist's sketch. It is an undershot mill, the water descending on the near side of the wheel in place of being precipitated over it, and it has features of interest for those conversant with such structures. There is the date, 1752, on the lintel stone of the door, low down, indicating likely the date of its construction, and another date, 1777, is cut on the stone projection at one end of the roof. The building is of rubble work, "harled" over, but has long lost its pristine whiteness, and, in many places, is thickly covered with soft mossy growth, like green velvet. A rich mantle of lichens covers the roof, and thick layers of the downy moss overspread the stone work and cornice, while ferns have obtained a lodgment in many parts, and hung their graceful fronds over the old walls. Even, in one or two places, sapling trees have obtained a foothold, and add to the picturesqueness of the fabric. But most of the pictorial aspect of the mill is marred, by the fact that the door is used as a medium for communicating to the public the incomparable merits of sundry soaps, and "matchless cleansers," and placards of rival lines of ocean steamers repose, side by side, on the same friendly board. The old wheel, with its water trough, down which generally trickles a tiny streamlet, forms an appropriate subject for the pencil. Inside the mill are some massive oak beams, and the machinery, though antiquated, is fit for its work, the axle beam of the wheel, of good oak, being a hundred years old. At the back is the drying kiln for preparing the grain, and this, too, is a building of considerable antiquity, the roof showing ominous symptoms of giving way. The genial miller, Peter M'Neilage, is the descendant of a long line of tenants of the mill and adjacent farm, and will be found ever ready to welcome a visitor. He deplores the lack of custom from which he suffers, the requirements of the farmers in the district being but small, and whereas, in 1850, his father milled perhaps 1250 bolls of meal, in the year past he only sent out 150 bolls. So the world goes on, and the miller philosophically remarks upon the uncertainty of all sublunary things, and the unreasonable competition of America, which sorely affects his business.

There are a few cottages on the hillside at the back of the mill, of no special interest, and, showing through the belt of trees behind is the Free Church manse, having a fine situation, and a pleasant prospect of Helensburgh and Ardmore point, with Rosneath Castle and grounds in the foreground. The church is on the roadside, just beyond the miller's house, and is of very plain architecture, but of ample size for the requirements of the district. Some notable men have preached within its walls, one of the most highly honoured being the well known, and beloved, Dr. John Wilson of Bombay. The eloquent Gavazzi has, more than once, thundered within the walls of this place of worship, and many an honoured divine has proclaimed peace and salvation to men in this unpretending building. The present minister, the Rev. John MacEwan, has laboured faithfully here for the long period of thirty-seven years, and has seen many changes during his incumbency.

Above the Free Church, on the hill-side, not far from the pond which supplies water to the mill, may be discerned the remains of one or two cottages, a scene recalling some of the features in the "Deserted Village." This once was a hamlet called Millbrae, and here long lived Donald Campbell, the Duke of Argyll's gamekeeper, whose son still survives at Kilcreggan. Forty years ago, this presented a sweet and beautiful aspect of rural repose and quiet seclusion. There was a path, leading over the gorse-clad, rocky brae, where the sheep wandered at will. A pretty garden, with fruit trees and rustic flowers, was carefully tended by the cottagers, and still some of the trees remain, with broken branches and severed stems. Truly a peaceful spot, from which the visitor could survey the opening of the Gareloch, with the villas of Row beyond, embowered amid trees, and the ridge of hills above the sorrowful Glenfruin bounding the view.

Returning to the road, the traveller opens up the broad estuary of the Clyde, with its purple waters ploughed by many a passing vessel, and the white tower of the Cloch Lighthouse on the opposite headland. After dark, especially on a clear frosty night, when the atmosphere is clear and free from smoke, a remarkable display of lights is seen for miles, all along the opposite strand from Port Glasgow to the Cloch. Dunoon, Kirn, Innellan, and the Cowal hills form the right hand of the picture, by day, with the low lands of Bute and the swelling mountain outlines of Arran on the horizon. Coming down the road, the visitor now sees on his left the little row of old thatched houses known as Old Kilcreggan. This primitive little hamlet remains pretty much as it was fifty years ago, when there was not a slated house on all the shore between Kilcreggan and Coulport. Poor, roughly constructed dwellings they are, but they are a type of most of the cottages on the land in this part of the country. In former years they had a very picturesque appearance, as they faced the rippling burn which falls into the sea near the old pier, but the addition of one or two new slated houses have rather injured the ancient look of the village. The road between the Mill of Campsail and Kilcreggan is as badly engineered as could well be, and culminates in a very steep descent upon the iron church and Kilcreggan pier. At the foot of the road stands an old cottage embowered in flowers where the Macfarlane family have long lived. Mrs. Macfarlane, widow of the former ferryman who, for many years, plied his ferry-boat between Kilcreggan and Gourock, still survives in serene old age, a link between the past and present. Her pretty abode, with its little plot of soft turf in front, and roses, jasmine, clematis and other flowering plants, is a model of tidiness inside and out. Long ago it was a public-house, one of the numerous places for the sale of drink which, happily for the morals of the district, were suppressed under the energetic crusade of Mr. Story. Mrs. Macfarlane's father and grandfather both served the Dukes of Argyll, and her husband long was the ferryman here, and started his large commodious wherry, or open boat, from the old pier, whose massive stones are still in their places, a little to the east of the existing wooden pier. This old boat took all sorts of produce, sheep, cattle and horses over the firth, and brought back coals and other necessaries for the inhabitants of the Peninsula. Sometimes great risk was run in the violent gales which prevailed, and, at other times, the compass had to be used when the thick fogs enveloped the entire channel. How different now is the crossing in four or five minutes in the swift steamers of the Railway Companies!

On the opposite side of the road is the iron church, whose belfry is seen above the trees which surround the simple building. For more than a quarter of a century it has stood there, and, in summer, it is filled by a congregation largely drawn from the visitors who throng this favourite resort. Old sheds and boat houses, on the shore below, indicate the scene of Mr. M'Laren's boat-building yard, and many a smart little craft has he turned out. On examining the low pier close by, it will be seen that some of the larger stones, at the end next the sea, have been dislodged, and it is strange that nothing has been done to repair this good, massive structure. A few still living on the shores here can remember when Macfarlane's smack transported themselves and their goods across to Greenock, and the uncertainties which prevailed regarding their return.

The road which leads along the shore is only for the special use of the Home Farm, but it commands a fine view of the firth, with its numerous steam and sailing vessels plying their busy trade with Glasgow and the various river ports. In some places it is sustained by a sea wall of massive stones which, in the course of many wintry gales, have been much displaced. The ground rises sharply in the direction of the Gallowhill, forming a sort of natural terrace which might afford sites for palatial villas that would enjoy splendid views of the opposite coast, and the Loch Long and Holy Loch ranges of hills. Proceeding along the shore, you come to Meikleross Bay, and presently the lofty tower of the Home Farm is seen, with the two wings at either side, surmounted by two circular towers, the whole façade pierced with regular Gothic windows, in a style of architecture quite superior to an ordinary farm-house. A belt of old beech trees extends from the building to the shore, joining on to the fir woods in which the Heronry is situated.

Returning to Kilcreggan, it is difficult to realise that where there is now a continuous row of handsome villas, all along the shore for four miles, sixty years ago there was nothing but the hillside of turf, bracken, and heather, sloping down to the rugged shore. From Mrs. Macfarlane's cottage, until you come to what is now Cove pier there was only a small thatched cottage at Craigrownie, and one or two similar structures below the rocky face of the cliff above Cove. One of these, which was a public-house, was occupied by the father of Mr. John M'Lean, Clachan of Rosneath, who also acted as ferryman to the opposite hamlet of Blairmore. Going past these, and crossing the Dhualt burn, which falls into the small bay of the same name, there was nothing on the shore road until the Peatoun house and one or two cottages beyond were reached; an unbroken stretch extending from Letter farm until you come to Coulport Ferry. On the high road there were the various farms of Meikle and Little Aiden, near Kilcreggan, North and South Ailey, Knockderry, and Barbour, besides some others now no longer existing. About this time the Duke of Argyll caused a carriage drive to be made along the shore, with an occasional circular space for turning the carriage. This took the place of the old track, which was only suitable for rough carts, as it was rudely constructed, overgrown with brambles, and obstructing stones and portions of rock protruding above ground. After the old thatched house at Cove pier, the first one built was another cottage, which still forms one of the range of buildings near the post office, Cove.

Proceeding along the shore road past Cove pier, a fine prospect is opened up of Loch Long, with the dark, swelling forms of the mountains rising from its deep waters, prominent amongst them being Cruahash, above the little village of Ardentinny. The new cemetery constructed for those resident in the Peninsula, who have no right of burial at Rosneath, occupies a fine site on the Barbour farm, and already a good many graves mark the last resting place of inhabitants of Cove and Kilcreggan. A tasteful monument has been erected to the memory of Dr. Mackenzie, well remembered and much beloved for his generosity to the poor, who died, in the spring of 1880, at Dax in the south of France. It is a peaceful spot, where nature has put forth her gentle hand to soothe the sorrows of those who mourn departed friends taken to their heavenly home.

> "There servants, masters, small and great,
> Partake the same repose;
> And there, in peace, the ashes mix,
> Of those who once were foes."

From the winding walks of this secluded resting-place of so many loved ones "gone before," you have beautiful views up and down Loch Long, with the fir clad slopes of the Cowal mountains opposite. The bold headland of Knockderry stands out above the shore, and is interesting from its being the site of an ancient Danish or Norwegian fort, little trace of which now remains. It probably was built about the time of the battle of Largs, and it commands a wide range of observation along the narrow arm of Loch Long, and far away to the Cumbrae islands. From this point we may conceive the Danish invaders sailing along the calm loch as far as Arrochar, wondering if any inhabitants dwelt on those heath-clad, seemingly deserted mountain slopes, until their unsuspected abodes were discovered in the islands of the romantic Loch Lomond. There is a double row of villas at certain parts of the Loch Long side of the Peninsula, some of them of lofty proportions and highly ornate architecture, with well kept gardens, trees, shrubs, glass houses, and the usual accessories of sea-side residences on the Clyde. After passing Knockderry, these become fewer in number, until the old mansion house of Peatoun is reached, close beside Camloch burn, when they again commence, the last being near the pier of Coulport. From this point, across to Ardentinny, on the opposite coast of Argyllshire, there is a royal ferry, which has, by law, to be kept up by the proprietors on both sides. This was an important mode of communication in olden times, and it was by this ferry, and the roads connected with it in Argyllshire and Dunbartonshire, that the regular journey was made between Glasgow, Inveraray, and the district beyond. In stormy weather, accommodation was provided for travellers in the small inn which used to be at Coulport, and the old road from thence, across Letter farm and Peatoun, was a most important means of transit, although now it has been suffered to relapse almost into a state of nature. Few finer views are to be found in this part of the country, than are gained here by crossing the moor and taking this time honoured route to Coulport ferry. There was another ferry, more than fifty years ago, from Cove across to Strone point near Blairmore. The ferry-man, Macfarlane by name, lived in an old cottage on the shore, nearly opposite to where Hartfield House now stands, but the ferry-house was pulled down over forty years ago, and the steamers now do the work of the humble sailing craft.

The feuing on the Rosneath Peninsula has indeed been a source of much wealth to the proprietors, and it has greatly changed the appearance of the loch side. More than fifty years ago, the whole Peninsula had a population of not above 700 souls, who were scattered over the district in the various small hamlets of thatched houses. In the Statistical Account of last century, the population was then stated to be only 394, but the gradual spread of agricultural improvements, and consequent increase of labourers, account for the difference. At the present time, the last census showed that the population of the Gareloch side of the Peninsula, reckoning as far as Kilcreggan pier, was 894, an increase of 27 since 1881. On the Kilcreggan and Cove sides the total population was 1,165, an increase since last census of 47. In 1755 the total population of the parish was 521, in 1790 it had sunk as low as 394, and, in 1801, had risen again to 632, of whom 297 were employed in agriculture, and only 29 in ordinary trades. Where there used to be 25 farms in the Peninsula, there are at present only 14 or 15,—the remains of some of the farm steadings of former days, that are now amalgamated with others may be traced on the high road between Kilcreggan and Peatoun. Commencing at Coulport, on Loch Long side, sixty years ago there was a small farm with two or three fields attached to the Ferry. Then came Duchlage, Letter farm, and Peatoun mansion, and farm. There used to be two thatched cottages between Peatoun and the sea, and then you came to Barbour farm, and Knockderry, Blairnachtra, and Cursnoch; the three latter are now all included in the one farm of Knockderry. Next came North and South Ailey, and Meikle Aiden, and Little Aiden. At Barbour farm there were two rows of thatched cottages, near the road side, and about fifty families altogether lived on the farm, which was let in four parts to different tenants, and amongst them were twenty cows and four horses. Blairnachtra was divided into two such farms, let to different tenants, and many of the farmers and servants were connected through marriages. Now the farmers have good, commodious, steadings, and well kept fences, and excellent crops are raised from the soil, which is of a light description, suitable for potato and turnip cultivation.

All along the shores of the Peninsula there are numerous splendid sites for feuing villas, and these have largely been taken advantage of by Glasgow and Greenock gentlemen, who have erected palatial residences both on the Loch Long and Gareloch sides. A good many natives of Rosneath, still living, can remember the time when no houses were on the Kilcreggan shore between the old ferry house and Cove, at which place there stood against the rock an old thatched house that was formerly a public house, and beyond this there was no dwelling till you came to Peatoun. The Duke of Argyll improved the old cart track along the shore, and made it passable for his stately old chariot, with C springs, which used to roll along the road. About sixty years ago, another small house was erected at Cove, close to the existing post-office, which Mr. M'Lean, the present Post-master at Clachan, helped to build and thatch. At that time many of the old houses on the farms were miserable hovels, built of unhewn rough stones and thatched, no fireplace in the wall, only the fire kindled upon a large flat stone in the centre of the floor, and peat, burnt heather, and other fuel, kept up heat within. About 1840, the house called Glendhu, near which stands the new pier of Kilcreggan, was built on a 99 years' lease, and the daughter of the builder occupies it, at a very advanced age. The Duke promised the man who raised it a regular feu contract on certain terms, and since then the lengthened ranges of villas have arisen along the Kilcreggan shore. When most of the shore feus were taken up, the Duke made the excellent road on the high ground, commanding splendid views of the Frith of Clyde, and distant islands of Bute and Arran, and various feus have been taken at its commencement. It opens up fine prospects of the Frith and surrounding swelling hills and dark mountains, the villa covered slopes of the heights at Kirn, Dunoon, and Innellan, Rothesay bay and the uplands of Bute, with the Arran mountains in the background. Few more eligible building sites could be found than those along this road, and the pure breezes from the noble estuary of the Clyde temper the warmth of the sultry days of summer. Now that the rival railway companies have got their own fast steamers running in connection with the express trains from Glasgow, great facilities for rapid transit are afforded to the business man, who, in little over an hour, is transported from the centre of Glasgow to the heath-clad slopes of the beautiful Rosneath Peninsula.

The walks in Rosneath are not numerous, but there are many beautiful scenes to be met that would delight the artist. All through the woods round the Castle, and in those where the two giant silver firs are, there will be found any number of lovely sylvan pictures. From the higher ground at the back of the Clachan farm, or from the slate quarry above Clynder, a splendid prospect is gained of the entire Gareloch and the estuary of the Clyde, beyond Helensburgh and Ardmore point. For a fine breezy walk, the road past the Home farm, away down to the shore, and so on to Kilcreggan, can hardly be surpassed, and though this is not a public road, permission can easily be got from the tenant. Then the walk along the high road, starting from old Kilcreggan and along the upper ridge of the Peninsula until you reach Peatoun, and thence over the moor to Rahane, commands fine views down the Frith of Clyde. At first you have the stretch of water opposite Greenock and Gourock, with the Cloch Lighthouse, and all the fields and farms beyond, till the moors of Renfrewshire are reached. In the other direction your eye ranges over the Helensburgh and Dunbarton shores of the Frith, with the braes above Kilpatrick in the distance. Going further on, Loch Long opens up on the right, with the Holy Loch and mountains beyond, and the lines of pretty villas at Blairmore, reaching on to the dark woods near Ardentinny. Fields and plantations stretch away down to the shore on the left hand, and on the right is the moor, with its purple slopes of heather, from whence is heard the harsh cry of the black cock, as he skims past in rapid flight. As you approach Barbour farm the view grows wilder, and Loch Long assumes the appearance of an inland lake, seemingly surrounded with hills, those in the foreground bearing signs of cultivation, while the mountains on the opposite shores of the loch rise steep and rugged, clothed with bracken and birchwood near the water's edge. Ascending the hill after crossing the Camloch burn, there is a broad expanse of moor, the distant swelling outlines of the ridges beyond Loch Goil now coming into view, and the serrated peaks of the Argyll Bowling Green forming an appropriate background. Turning round, your eye ranges away over the glistening Frith of Clyde, until Toward point and Bute are descried, with the Cumbraes beyond, and in the distant horizon the grand mountain summits of Arran.

CHAPTER IV.

Ecclesiastical Rosneath.

In ancient times the parish of Rosneath used to extend to much greater proportions than now, and it used to be styled in the Presbytery and other records, "the parochin without and within the isle." It is now contained in the Peninsula alone, with the small portion in the parishes of Cardross and Row, a change which was effected in the year 1635. Much difficulty was experienced in erecting the new parish of Row, but in time a presentee was inducted with the proviso that, when the measure was matured, it should first receive his sanction, and that he would be willing to alienate a portion of the tiends to provide a competent living for the minister. The Laird of Ardencaple only agreed to his admission on condition of his preaching alternately in the new church of Row.

The date of erection of the first church in Rosneath is not known, but it is mentioned in the charter conferred by Alwyn, second Earl of Lennox, at the end of the twelfth century. Alwyn's second son, Amelec, granted the church of Rosneath, with all its pertinents, to the monastery of Paisley, which grant was confirmed by Amelec's elder brother, and afterwards by King Alexander III. Amelec also conferred on the monks the gift of a salt-pan on his lands of Rosneath. Further, it was arranged between the Bishop of Glasgow and the Abbot of Paisley, in 1227, that the church of Rosneath should belong to the monks and be exempted from the payment of procurations, on condition of their presenting to the church a proper secular chaplain. The church continued in possession of the monks of Paisley, who drew all the revenues till the Reformation, a curate being employed in preaching and performing divine service. At the Reformation the revenue was let by the Abbot for £146 13s. 4d., and in 1587 the patronage and titles, which then were held for life by Lord Claud Hamilton, were granted to him and his heirs for ever. Subsequently the patronage of the church was acquired by the Argyll family, who retained it till the abolition of patronage in the Church of Scotland.

The Church of Rosneath was dedicated to St. Modan, who lived in the sixth century, and is supposed to have set out from Iona on a mission of Christianity towards Loch Etive, near which he dwelt for a considerable period, and established a chapel. He dwelt for a time on the shores of the Kyles of Bute.

The author is indebted to the kindness of Lady Elisabeth Clough Taylor, of the Argyll family, for the following beautiful and appropriate lines bearing upon the legends of the life of the patron saint of Rosneath, which may fitly be inserted here:—

THE BELL OF ST. MODAN'S CHAPEL.*

A LEGEND.

In good St. Modan's ruin'd shrine
  Once hung a golden bell—
And still Loch Etive's fishers gray
  Its strange, sweet story tell—
How, in the days of other years,
  Its healing pow'rs were blest,
And many throng'd from distant isles
  In simply trustful quest—
And none unanswer'd turn'd away,
  But all found health and rest.

How, when from restless fever'd couch
  The sick man could not rise
Nor knew, in wild delirium's dreams,
  His lov'd one's tearful eyes—
When watching long by cradled babe
  The mother's anguish sore
Yearn'd o'er the little wasted hands
  That sought her own no more—
They came with long procession slow
  And bare the sacred bell.

With prayer and praise their anthems rais'd
  In wood or lonely dell,
Till Death's dark Angel spread his wings,
  And the strong man once more
Went forth to toil—the fair-hair'd child
  To laugh by rock and shore,
With falt'ring joy of baby-steps
  And lilt of broken words,
Sweeter than rhythmic movements all
  Or notes of woodland birds.

---

* Patron Saint of Rosneath.

But if too long in careless mood
    The healing bell they left
Far from the chapel of the saint,
    Aloft it soar'd, and cleft
With wings invisible the air,
    While wond'rous music swell'd
In tender strains that coldest hearts
    To reverence impell'd.

Far o'er Loch Etive's waters dark
    At morning's pearly dawn,
The boatmen laid aside their oar
    And left their net undrawn,
When, ringing sweet in highest heav'n,
    Those notes unearthly clear
Peal'd forth a message of such love
    As hush'd to sleep all fear.

And oft at summer eventide,
    When sunset's crimson glow
Lit up each rugged peak and scaur
    And the dark firs below—
Oft when the full moon's radiance soft
    Made fair the northern night,
Waking lone depths of mountain tarn
    To laugh in tremulous light—
The glorious melodies that told
    Of love-assuagëd pain
Rous'd many a late despairing heart
    To hope and trust again.

. . . . . .

But soon there came a day of grief—
    Dalriada's proud king
To ancient Scone's embattled walls
    The golden bell bade bring,
Then mourn'd bereft Balmhaodan's shrine
    That saintly hands had rear'd,
Voiceless and sad the fair glen lay,
    By no soft music cheer'd.

Lo ! scarce the second day had dawn'd
  When once again the bell
By priest and peasant welcom'd back,
  Return'd its tale to tell.
No longer now with sacred awe
  The list'ners bent the knee,
To clangour loud and discord harsh
  Were chang'd, ah woe is me !

The weird, sweet harmonies that erst,
  Dear messengers of health,
To weary frame and breaking heart,
  Were more than mine of wealth.
For now, alas ! in place of chant
  That angels might have sung,
It utter'd heartless words and cold—
  In ceaseless dangers rung
Thro' every path of life where self
  Engross'd in loveless cares,
Scorns the deep joy each heart may know
  Another's load that bears.

A curse lay on the golden bell
  And marr'd its magic tone,
Nor might the peasant e'er again
  Its healing virtue own,
Or the good priest with earnest faith
  Watch thro' the sleepless night,
Speeding the Messenger of Love
  And praying for the light.

. . . . . .

Fair is the spot St. Modan chose
  Wherein to work and pray—
The slumb'rous gloom of purple hills
  O'ershadow creek and bay,
And far and wide, from yon green glen,
  Upon the wanderer's sight
Rises the mountain range of Mull
  In everchanging light.

While fierce and free by Brandir's pass
   In eddying rapids wild,
The foaming Awe leaps headlong forth
   From waters many isl'd.

And at his feet the ancient well,
   Awaking tender thought,
Of all the weary suffering souls
   Its healing charm that sought,
Still feeds from never-failing depths
   The murmuring mountain burn,
That low-voic'd wooes to fleeting kiss
   The drooping sprays of fern. . . .
But greener woods, more smiling shores,
   Wash'd by a gentler tide,
Where Cruachash and his brethren guard
   The fertile vale of Clyde,
Welcom'd the aged saint's worn feet
   To haven of repose.

And there, in memory of his name
   And long life's peaceful close,
His followers rais'd the cloister'd aisles
   That Fancy's feet alone
May tread again with rapt delight
   In day-dreams all her own.
Her eyes alone see 'neath sad years,
   With measur'd footsteps walk
Rossneveth's * cowled monks of yore
   In grave and earnest talk.

The records of those ancient saints, who have left many interesting traces of their remarkable personality, are of importance in considering the state of enlightenment and religion of Scotland in early Christian days. About the year 410 A.D.,

---

* The old way of spelling Rosneath.

the Romans finally quitted our country, and for a long time afterwards, we are left in obscurity, with little historic light or reliable information. For centuries after this there was but scant intercourse between Britain and the continent of Europe, and the former came to be considered a gloomy, barbarous and mysterious land, far from human ken. Meanwhile, races of men, new to our shores, were ravaging England and Scotland; Jutes, Angles, Saxons, the Picts from the northern part of Caledonia, and the Scots from Ireland. The early Church in Scotland was very much independent of Rome, and its ministers looked more to direct guidance from heaven and the word of God than from any earthly bishop or Roman pontiff. Druidism, with its horrid cruelties and superstitious rites, after enthralling the poor simple natives with its vile fetters, had largely passed away, although in many parts its customs lingered long. Ninian is one of the early saints whose name is perpetuated in various districts throughout Scotland, and his godly life and precepts did much to commend the religion he taught and to speed the light of Christianity. He dwelt and taught amidst the sterile lands of Galloway and other parts of the south of Scotland, and instituted a system of monasticism that did not seek seclusion and holy isolation from mankind, but endeavoured to leaven the mass of heathendom by mingling in all ranks of the people. The church and school which Ninian founded at Candida Casa, on the bare Promontory of Whithorn in Galloway, long afforded shelter and instruction to those who sought to enter the ranks of the ministry.

Another, but less known name, is that of Palladius, who was sent from Rome by Pope Celestine, in the year 430, and was the first regular bishop commended to those who professed Christianity in Scotland and Ireland. In an old "Life of St. Kentigern," it is stated, "The venerable Palladius, the first bishop of the Scots, who was sent, in the year of the incarnation, 430, by Pope Celestine, as the first bishop to the Scots who believed." Finding that the Irish Christians, who had received little else from Rome than strife and persecutions, were not willing to bow to his authority, Palladius sought a more congenial sphere of labour in Scotland. Here, after wandering about for a time, and the records of his life and works are so vague and shadowy that much uncertainty prevails, he found a haven of rest in the sequestered Vale of Fordoun, at the foot of the Grampians in Kincardineshire. In the old church yard of Fordoun, beside the murmuring stream which passes through the village of Auchenblae close to the church, there is still standing, overhung by venerable ash trees, the small, ancient building known as the chapel of St. Palladius. Here it is supposed the bones of the good bishop rest, amidst the pleasant surroundings so much in keeping with his character and work.

A more distinguished personage than either Modan, Ninian or Palladius, is that of Patrick, the great apostle of the Irish, whose name is such a tower of strength in that distracted land. Dunbartonshire can lay good claim to be the birthplace of this true evangelist, for it is believed that he was born at Alcluid, the capital of the British kingdom of Strathclyde. Indeed, the name of the village near Dunbarton, Kilpatrick, would seem to point to that district as the one where first he saw the light. The story of his life and labours is well known, how he was made prisoner by a band of sea-robbers, who had crossed the Irish Sea in their piratical craft from the North of Ireland, and made a sudden descent upon the defenceless shores of the Clyde at Dunbarton. Amongst others whom they found watching with unsuspicious eye the roving vessel, was the young man afterwards known as St. Patrick, and whom they carried away with his companions and sold to a chieftain in the wilds of Antrim. Left to wrestle alone on the mountain side with his doubts and spiritual foes, Patrick emerged victorious from the conflict, and became a changed man, full of burning zeal to spread the gospel. After his escape from captivity in Ireland, Patrick returned to the shores of the Clyde, where he laboured for some years in his parents' dwelling house near Dunbarton, until an irresistible impulse carried him over again to Ireland. From this time forward he went about preaching and teaching the people everywhere to repent of their sins. Familiar with their dialect, he was able to reach the masses and tell to them the simple meaning of the cross, till the faith began to spread. Thus matters went on till his death about the year 465, verging upon fourscore years, during the latter portion of which he had succeeded in planting in different parts of his adopted country no less than three hundred and sixty-five churches, and earning for himself the title of the "Apostle of Ireland."

No such power or marvellous success attended the life work of Modan, the Saint of Rosneath. After his residence on the Kyles of Bute he made his way slowly over the mountainous district of Cowal, halting for a time at some of the scattered hamlets of Argyllshire, until he reached the rugged shores of Loch Long. Crossing its deep and dark waters, he found before him the heathery peninsula of Rosneath, from whose summit he could descry afar off some of the mountain peaks in the vicinity of his early home. In imagination he could travel still further away, until he reached the shell-girt strand of that strange lone island of Iona, where the lamp of Christianity so long burned in solitary brightness, illuminating the heathen darkness around. After a sojourn at Rosneath, St. Modan turned his steps over the narrow neck of water which surges through the deep entrance to the Gareloch, and made a sort of a missionary tour along by Dunbarton, the sweet Vale of Leven, Loch Lomond, the grandest of Scottish lakes, along the valley of the Endrick, until he reached "Grey Stirling, bulwark of the North." After a time he visited Falkirk, and evangelised the country between that district and the Clyde, with occasional visits to his early home on Loch Etive, but Rosneath would seem to have been his favourite abode, and there, wasted and worn with his labours, he turned his steps to die. In the *Breviary of Aberdeen* there is a notice of St. Modan, in which is recorded how he passed his early days in poverty and obedience. Casting aside the adventitious advantages of riches and royal descent he lived in frugality, content with bread and water from the spring, never using wine or flesh, till he became a model of life in ways of truth, virtue and holiness. In his later days, after labouring all round Stirling and Falkirk, where churches were called after his name, he retired to a sequestered spot (meaning Rosneath) not far from Dunbarton and the Gareloch. The *Breviary* closes its record of the Saint by narrating that, "after many wonderful miracles he fell asleep in the Lord in the place where the Parish Church of Rosneath stands, dedicated to his honour. His most sacred relics rest in a certain chapel of the cemetery of the same church, and are held in the highest veneration."

Christianity indeed made distinct progress throughout the ancient Kingdom of Strathclyde, until it became gradually impregnated into the domain of Scotland. For centuries it was established in Dunbartonshire, and Kentigern, the patron Saint of Glasgow, for a time took up his abode at Dunbarton, until he excited the jealousy of the King of the Britons of Strathclyde, and fled to Wales. After the extinction of the monarchy of Strathclyde the ecclesiastical rule, which had been established on the lines laid down by Columba and Kentigern, was further consolidated by the Culdees. The Culdees derive their name according to some authorities from the Welsh *cêl*, a hiding place, while others prefer the Gaelic derivation, *Culdee*, a monk, or *ceile-de*, a servant of God. Though the form of the Church government is much disputed, whether episcopal or presbyterian, they were largely free from the prevailing errors and corruptions of the Church of Rome. But after having lasted nearly four centuries, this simple mission church excited the ill-will of both secular and ecclesiastical powers, and it was suppressed early in the twelfth century.

By this time the Celtic Church was everywhere in a disturbed or dying state. The greater part of the rich endowments of the monasteries was held by laymen who assumed the name of Abbot, while the ecclesiastical duties were handed over to a Prior, who presided over twelve Culdees. The church lands were secularised, and the lay abbots were often men of extensive influence and wealth. Gradually the distinctive character of the Scottish Church was lost, as through the policy of Margaret the English Princess, niece of the Confessor, and wife of Malcolm, King of Scotland, it became assimilated to the Anglican model. The remodelling of the Scottish Church was effected by the establishment of Parishes, the initiation of Diocesan Episcopacy, and the monastic orders of the Romish Church.

The various storms which from time to time agitated the ecclesiastical atmosphere, in the west of Scotland, had but small effect in a secluded parish like Rosneath. After the Reformation the patronage of the living was in the hands of the Argyll family, and a succession of ministers unknown to fame attended to the spiritual requirements of the parish. One of them, in the year 1709, was the Rev. Neil Campbell, who was afterwards Principal of the University of Glasgow. In 1722 the minister was the Rev. James Anderson, father of the founder of the Andersonian College of Glasgow. Matthew Stewart, who was minister in 1745, was subsequently Professor of

Mathematics in Edinburgh, and the father of the famous Professor Dugald Stewart. On 1st May 1766, the Rev. George Drummond, preacher of the Gospel, was ordained minister of the parish by the Rev. John Freebairn, minister at Dunbarton, and was unanimously received by the heritors, elders, and people. Mr. Drummond continued minister of the parish until the year 1818, when his increasing infirmities compelled him to accept, as assistant and successor, the Rev. Robert Story. During Mr. Drummond's long ministry, the affairs of the parish were conducted in the quiet way usual in rural districts, and the session records afford an insight into the morals and manners of the neighbourhood. In June 1766, the Kirk Session seems to have consisted of the minister, Mr. Colin Campbell, factor of Rosneath, Mr. Campbell of Peatown, heritor, Patrick Cuming of Baremman, heritor and elder, and John Paton, Duncan Ritchie, Alexander Mitchell, Duncan Turner, and Alexander Campbell, elders. Session Clerk, Thomas Sharp, schoolmaster. At that date the sum paid for support of the poor was £59 8s. The following inventory of utensils was taken as the property of the Session:—"Two silver cups for the Communion, four Communion tablecloths, big and small, two pewter flagons, a big pewter plate, a pewter basin for baptism, two mortcloths, one large, one small. The Session appoints that the large mortcloth be let out within the parish for 2s. 6d., and the small one for 1s. 6d. sterling."

The school fees were appointed as follows:—"For such as read English only, 1s. 6d. for each quarter. For those who read and write only, 1s. 6d. for each quarter. For those who learn English, writing, and arithmetic, 2s. 6d. for each quarter. For Latin, 2s. 6d. Fees to be paid regularly at the beginning of each quarter. Schoolmaster shall have 6s. yearly for acting as session-clerk and precentor. For every baptism, 6d. to the session-clerk and 4d. to the 'beddal.' For every marriage, 1s. to the precentor and 6d. to the beddal, with 20 pence to the poor when proclaimed on three several Sabbaths. If on two Sabbaths 3s. 4d., and if on one Sabbath, 10s. 6d." There were pretty frequent cases of discipline in connection with members of the congregation, and the offenders had to submit to a solemn rebuke administered before the congregation, in addition to being fined. One of the Heritors seems to have given cause for rebuke, whose fine was sometimes four or even five guineas, but those lower in the social scale were let off with a payment of five shillings. The school appears to have hitherto been held in the church, but in October, 1766, it was reported that " the school could not be kept longer in the Kirk on account of the coldness of the weather, and the Session appoint the house formerly possessed by David Guthrie to be cleared and the school kept there."

On 20th December, same year, D. M'W. appeared before the Presbytery and was rebuked, and remitted back to make his profession of repentance before the congregation. At the same time, the Heritor before alluded to, was reported to have " behaved himself to their satisfaction, and also in regard that their poor funds are at present low, and the poor in great straits, the majority of the Session were therefore of opinion that it would be more beneficial to dismiss P. with a Sessional rebuke and an extraordinary fine, for these reasons they do approve the said P. to pay a fine of four guineas, and their moderator to rebuke and absolve him in presence of the Session, as soon as the said fine is paid." The officer being ordered to summon P. to attend the Session, on 15th March, 1767, D. M'W. having now appeared and been rebuked for five several Sabbaths before the congregation, the Session are of opinion "that his making any further appearances will neither tend to his own reformation or to the edification of others." On 30th April, 1767, the Session Funds for the Poor were found to be £13 17s. 4¾d. P. appeared, and was "rebuked, exhorted, and absolved."

On 29th May, 1769, new communion tables were ordered at a cost of 30s. sterling, and likewise the "Tent" was to be repaired. On 12th November of that year, the school, on the other side of the parish, for children from six to ten years old, was to be kept at the Barber during the winter quarter. The schoolmaster to be paid five shillings, the sum usually given by the Session.

On 6th December, 1772, new elders were chosen, namely, Donald Campbell of Peatoun; Archibald Marquis and Archibald Niven, both in Knockderry; Archibald Chalmers in Blairnaughter, John Campbell in Milnbrae, John Walker in Meikle Rahane. The session "now send their officer to the most patent door of the church to call upon the congregation three several times to offer their objections, if any, they had to the life, faith and conversation of the above mentioned persons. The officer having returned, and no objection offered, the Session unanimously resolve that the foresaid persons be this day ordained elders in presence of the congregation."

On 10th November, 1773, it is stated that the "Bason made use of in baptisms almost wore out, Treasurer to get it exchanged and pay the balance." Duke of Argyll had ordered gates to be made for different entries into the churchyard.

Meeting, 26th May, 1775. "Considering that the old poor's box is slight and insufficient, the Session hereby appoint the Moderator to get a new one made with two locks and two keys, one key to be kept by the minister, and another by the schoolmaster, and said box to be lodged with the schoolmaster in his house."

On 16th November, 1775, Archibald Niven is appointed Treasurer, and the following entry occurs, "No person has yet cast up to take the £20 appointed by the Session to be lent out." Money in poor box, £27 7s. 7d.

8th May, 1776. "The Session, considering that they have more of the poors' money on hand than they choose to keep by them without bearing interest, and as no private person of good security can be found to take it, they therefore unanimously resolve to put £120 into any one of the banks of Glasgow, and for that purpose they now lodge the money with their Moderator, hereby appointing him to lay it out as above, as soon as convenient."

An overture from presbyteries as to ruling elders was considered and agreed to be made a standing act. The General Assembly hereby enacts : 1. That no person shall be ordained an elder of this church before he is 21 years of age complete. 2. That all Presbytery elders shall be selected within two months after the sitting of Synod to attend the Presbytery and ensuing Synod of that bounds. 3. That any elder so chosen shall produce an extract of election under the hand of the Session-Clerk, before he be received on the roll of either Presbytery or Synod.

2nd May, 1783. List of funds on hand :—

Money in the Box,	£18 16 0
Auchan's and Glenfalloch's Bond,	120 0 0
Taylor & M'Auslan's Bill,	20 0 0
	£158 16 0

22nd November, 1784. Of this date there is an entry regarding a case of discipline against one of the Kirk Session, who resigns his eldership, and is rebuked and fined £2 2s., which was duly paid.

12th June, 1790. The following irregularity occurred, resulting in that Donald Campbell of Peatoun, and Isobel Drummond, sister to the minister of the parish, appeared before the Session and interrogated. They acknowledged that they were married at Edinburgh, 31st May last, and produced a certificate of marriage, signed by themselves and the person who married them, and by two witnesses. In presence of the Session they now owned each other as man and wife, declared their living together in that relation, and promised adherence. The Session fined them, and they, after paying the fine and Kirk dues, were, by appointment of the Session, rebuked for an irregular marriage and absolved.

4th May, 1806. The following were ordained elders: Robert Campbell, factor, Rosneath Castle; John Mackenzie, Cursnoch; James Chalmers in Barbour; Duncan M'Lellan, Strouel.

From this date there seems to be a blank in the record of proceedings of the Kirk Session for a good many years, during which the old minister, Dr. Drummond, grew more and more feeble and unfit for duty. No special cases of importance came up for adjudication, and the affairs of the parish proceeded on an even way. Dr. Drummond seems to have been one of the old "moderate" ministers of the Church of Scotland, and he added to his modest stipend by farming the Strouel Farm, with the aid of two men and horses. For some time he had been tutor to the laird of Luss, and through his influence with the Duke of Argyll, the tutor in time became minister of Rosneath. One or two of the old inhabitants of the parish remember Dr. Drummond, who got into his dotage at the last. He married a widow possessed of some property on the water of Endrick, who appears to have been of a managing turn. On one occasion she reminded the servants at Strouel Farm that the men on farms near the Endrick were accustomed to work in the dark, thatching stacks with candles in their bonnets, but the hint was not taken, as the minister's labourers thought their hours long enough. Mrs. Drummond had a nephew in the army, rather inclined to be a fast youth, whom she kept well supplied with money. The laird of Peatoun,

Donald Campbell, had, as we have seen, contracted an irregular marriage with the sister of the minister of Rosneath, and as there was no family, and the estate not entailed, Mrs. Drummond thought the laird could not do better than leave Peatoun to his wife's nephew. The old gentleman, however, grew very angry, and solemnly declared there never should be a Drummond inherit Peatoun as long as there was a Campbell on the face of the earth.

On one occasion, at a rent collection at Luss, Dr. Drummond happened to be present, along with Sir Humphrey Colquhoun, and the Sheriff of Dunbarton. The party were at dinner, when on a sudden, three men, with blackened faces, having overcome the resistance of the servants, rushed into the room and attacked the astonished gentlemen. Evidently they hoped, in the excitement following this unwelcome intrusion, to secure the rent money which lay loose in a paper inside the press. However, the minister of Rosneath made a valiant defence, first laying hold of a chair and then the poker, with which he struck one of the robbers violently on the head. The wound inflicted was the means of identifying the man, John Gray by name, and he was subsequently convicted for his crime at Dunbarton. Owing to loss of blood from a wound he received in the struggle, Dr. Drummond was long an invalid, and in the closing years of his ministry the duties of parish minister were almost entirely performed by assistants. Some of those were decidedly insufficient, and the parish had got into a sadly disorganised state, the influence of the church was weakened, and its public services neglected.

As shewing the melancholy condition of affairs in Rosneath, in the year 1815, the following extract from a letter of the Duke of Argyll's local factor, the respected Mr. Robert Campbell, a fine specimen of the typical, kindly Highland gentleman, is of interest. Writing in July to Lord John Campbell, father of the present Duke of Argyll, Mr. Campbell says, "The poor infirm body Brown, who assisted Dr. Drummond, died on Friday last. The old Doctor, whose mind is almost gone, has entered into some engagement with our idiotical schoolmaster, Graham, to make him his assistant, although he wants two years of his divinity studies, and was on that account refused a license by the Presbytery of Dunbarton."

In the autumn of 1815, however, an offer was made to the Rev. Robert Story, who had recently received license as a preacher from the Presbytery of Haddington, to become assistant to old Dr. Drummond, which was accepted. Thus the name of Story first became connected with Rosneath, and continued between father and son, both ministers in the parish, down to the year 1887.

Robert Story, for over forty years minister of Rosneath, was born in the village of Yetholm, a few miles from Kelso, in March, 1790. His father, George Story, taught the parish school, besides acting as factor or agent for Mr. Wauchope of Niddrie, his mother being Margaret Herbert, of a Northumbrian family. In November, 1805, he left home and entered the University of Edinburgh, long considered one of the most famous and learned in Europe, and her *alumni* have made the fount from whence their erudition was drawn renowned throughout the world. At that time the celebrated Dugald Stewart, son of a former minister of Rosneath, was one of the Professors, many of whose students have achieved high distinction in literature and philosophy. After fulfilling three sessions at the University, Mr. Story agreed to superintend the education of the only son of Baron Hume of the Exchequer, and continued in the family for three years, at the same time carrying on his own studies. He appears to have early imbibed a taste for poetry and rhetoric, and paid assiduous court to the muses, in which he was encouraged by various friends, amongst them the well known Dr. Thomas Brown and Dr. John Barclay. Two closely written manuscript volumes of five hundred pages attested to his devotion to the muse, but they never achieved the dignity of print. His pupil, young Hume, evidently regarded him with warm affection, and kept up a close correspondence with Mr. Story, and some of his letters gave interesting details of the social life and ways, as well as sketches of the notabilities of the Scottish metropolis.

In July, 1811, Mr. Story left Edinburgh for Ballindalloch, in Morayshire, to fill the situation of tutor in the family of Mr. Macpherson Grant. This neighbourhood is full of romantic beauty, and has many stirring historical attractions, and here the youthful enthusiast could give vent to his poetic fancy, fired by the charms of rural and mountain scenery. He writes to a friend, "I sometimes sigh over the days that are past, and the friends of my youth that I have left at a distance. I bless, however, my God, that my lines are yet cast into a pleasant place." His young charge was an amiable and kindly boy, and he received every consideration from his father and mother. In describing his new home he says his room has a beautiful view, it "looks into a garden, and I might pluck the wall-fruit which is spread round it; beyond this garden is a lawn, which is bounded by the oblique winding of the river." During a considerable part of his residence at Ballindalloch, Mr. Story passed through a period of painful doubts and uncertainties upon the eternal verities of religious belief, and agnostic difficulties dimmed the happiness and depressed the spirits of the youthful student. Finally, partly influenced by the failing health of his father, and more probably by the mental distress under which he laboured, though even then he had some thoughts of venturing upon a literary life, he relinquished the position which he held in the kind family at Ballindalloch.

For nearly a year he remained at home, but in April, 1813, Mr. Story accepted the situation of tutor in the family of Mr. Burton Grieve, who lived at Fishwick Mains, on the Tweed, opposite Norham Castle. Though brought up as a Presbyterian, he had sometimes thought of taking orders in the Church of England, in spite of the fact that the curriculum of study he had hitherto pursued was that prescribed for licentiates of the Church of Scotland. About this time he came under the influence of Mr. Morton, subsequently vicar of Holbeach in Lincolnshire, who had almost persuaded him to join the English Church and apply for ordination to the Bishop of Durham. But the strong remonstrance of his parents, and his sense of filial duty and affection overcame his nascent inclination for Episcopacy, though he ever retained some ecclesiastical bias in that direction. As showing the bent of his mind at this time, the following extract from a letter to his friend Pringle is of much interest: "My present residence is a monument of ancient hopes; consider it as a token of the complete abandonment of those vain and unsatisfactory schemes which I impiously framed, and which I elevated against the Highest. What is a name or immortality? Before I desire that of genius, I have resolved to secure that of virtue. When I am good, then shall I be great."

Soon after this he entered upon one of the happiest periods of his life, having been appointed tutor in the family of the Earl of Dalhousie. His youthful charges, Lord Ramsay and the Hon. Charles Ramsay, were interesting boys of amiable dispositions, and their father and mother showed the utmost courtesy in their treatment of Mr. Story. An increasing number of correspondents now occupied the attention of his pen, amongst them Mr. Pringle of the Register Office in Edinburgh, Mr. Thomas Cannan, afterwards minister of Carsphairn, and the famous Edward Irving, then Rector of Kirkcaldy Academy. Eager to distinguish himself, and sensitively in earnest in perfecting his Christian character, with fastidious taste and lofty ambitions, Mr. Story still had much distrust of the manner in which his duties were performed. His studies were all this time going on for the ministry of the Church of Scotland, and he was growing somewhat anxious as to his Presbyterial examinations, being apprehensive lest his religious difficulties and doubts should raise the censure of the Divinity Hall. Indeed, the criticism of one of the reverend Professors upon Mr. Story's prelections and discourses very distinctly pointed to an absence of evangelical fervour in the young Divinity student. However, the Presbytery of Haddington, to whom he applied for license, found Mr. Story thoroughly qualified to fulfil the position of a minister of the Gospel, and, in July, 1815, he was licensed to preach in connection with the Church of Scotland, and shortly afterwards was appointed assistant to the Rev. Dr. Drummond, minister of Rosneath.

At that time the spiritual condition of the Parish was at a very low ebb. Where there are now seven places of worship, belonging to the different denominations, there was the old church in the churchyard of the Clachan of Rosneath. Of course, at that period, besides the various farm houses and cottages attached, and with the exception of the Clachan, Clynder and Rahane, where a few poor thatched cottages stood, there were hardly any residences in the parish. None of the numerous handsome villas, extending for more than four miles on the Loch Long side of the Peninsula, which now form such a feature in the landscape, were then in existence. On a Sabbath morning the farmers and their servants, and the humble cottagers, might be seen crossing the moor by the various pathways which led to the House of God from the different farmhouses. And in simple rustic finery, the women would be seen sitting along the Clachan burn, washing their bare feet in its limpid water, and donning their stockings and shoes, which had up to that point, been carried in their hands. The service was lengthened, two homilies being frequently rolled into one, and the devotional part of the worship was full and deliberate. The Sacrament was administered, in this and the neighbouring parishes, but once in the year, and on this occasion, all the churches near contributed to swell the congregation, the services lasting from eleven in the forenoon until the evening. And on the Monday a dinner was given to the officiating ministers and elders who had taken part in the solemn commemorative service, which too often partook of the nature of a carouse. At this festivity there was much drinking of healths, and honouring of sundry appropriate and inappropriate toasts the whole evening, a most unseemly climax and finish to a significant and holy ordinance of the Church.

Mr. Story was introduced to his charge by Dr. Thomas Chalmers, who was his warm friend and a frequent visitor at the manse, sometimes accompanied by the brilliant but erratic Edward Irving, along with others subsequently known to fame. The young minister set to work with great energy to reform many of the abuses prevailing in the parish, of which drinking and smuggling were two of the worst. There were seven public houses in the Peninsula, and a considerable amount of drinking resulted, especially on the occasion of marriages and funerals. It was no uncommon thing for newly married couples and their friends, after attending Divine Service at the Church, to adjourn to the tavern in the Clachan, kept by a character M'Wattie, and indulge in a carouse, with little regard for the sanctity of the day.

Smuggling, too, was very general, several of the glens along the Loch side affording favourable cover, particularly the one near the famous Strouel Well. The young minister soon gained the affections of his people, and he was enabled to effect a radical reform in many of the customs which prevailed that were injurious to the morals of the community.

During Mr. Story's long ministry of forty-two years, he saw many changes from the days when, as a young minister of the Gospel, he first took up his charge on the peaceful shores of the Gareloch. He was fearless in the discharge of his duty, bravely encountering dangers, whether from ill-disposed parishioners who resented his vigorous denunciations of their drinking and smuggling propensities, or from the occasional malignant diseases which might affect the neighbourhood. A touching prayer is recorded in which, before visiting a case of specially virulent fever, against the advice of the doctor attending the case, he commits his family to the care of God, and asks that, in doing what he recognises as his duty, no evil may befall him, "the unworthy servant of the most High God, and follower of Him who went about doing good."

Mr. Story was a minister of ardent piety and enthusiastic temperament, whose spiritual life, after it had, by the grace of God, been aroused and quickened, was, though outwardly subdued, yet of a warm type. One of his parishioners was the once well known Isabella Campbell, the memoir of whose life was written by her minister. She lived at Fernicarry, near the head of the Gareloch, with the other members of the family, in one of the more commodious residences on the verge of the Loch. Isabella was a favourite with her minister, her fine countenance early acquired a cast of pensive, almost heavenly expression, and she showed much aptitude in acquiring Bible knowledge. After passing through the Sabbath School and minister's Bible Class, she was received into full communion, but ere long fell into a decline, and soon the fatal seeds of consumption showed their baleful fruit. Her short life was a blameless and beautiful one, and those who were privileged to see the dying girl could testify that her "life was hid with Christ in God." She had been so much in communion with her Maker, that many stories were repeated of the marvellous spiritual insight which she possessed, and her influence was profound with those who had been in attendance on the sufferer, or were admitted to her friendship. The quiet secluded spot is still shewn where the pious Isabella was wont to resort for prayer, but a short distance up the hill side, at the back of Fernicarry, and a brief inscription on a stone marks the place. Mr. Story's memoir of Isabella Campbell was largely read, and several editions were published and extensively circulated, not only in Scotland, but also in England and America.

Another of the same family, Mary Campbell, a sister of Isabella's, became, about this time, well known in connection with the singular development of religious belief which led many to credit that the gifts of tongues and miracles were again vouchsafed to those who had sufficient faith. Mary was young and beautiful, and being in delicate health, she had a highly susceptible, nervous temperament, and numbers of visitors, attracted by the fame of her saintly sister, came to Fernicarry. One Sabbath evening in March 1830, Mary Campbell, in the presence of a few friends, began to utter strange sounds which she believed to have resemblance to the tongues spoken by the disciples in Jerusalem on the day of Pentecost. This language she affirmed to be that spoken in a group of islands in the Southern Pacific Ocean, and imagined it was a manifestation of the power of the Holy Spirit, and an invitation to her to proceed as a missionary to these remote parts of the earth. Soon after this, Mary Campbell, after a surprising, or, as she affirmed, a "miraculous" recovery, was married to a young man of the name of Caird, who had been attracted to Fernicarry by reading her sister's memoir. She was taken up by the gifted Edward Irving, who had full confidence in her manifestations and "tongues," and was introduced through him to various people of fashion and title, eager, like the Athenians of old, for some "new thing." But in their society her piety and fervour began rapidly to deteriorate, her missionary zeal cooled, and the temporary excitement caused by her reputed sanctity soon passed away.

Dr. Chalmers wrote to Mr. Story on 24th April 1830, on the subject of the so-called miraculous gift of "tongues" in the following terms: "Do give me, if you can with pleasure to yourself, your information and views about the gift of tongues, said to be now descending on people in the West. Could you transmit a copy of the handwriting by Mary Campbell alleged to be in an unknown language. I have written to Mr. Campbell (of Row) on the same subject." The specimen with which Dr. Chalmers was furnished he submitted to the inspection of Sir George Staunton, the eminent Oriental scholar, whose opinion of it coincided with that of Dr. Lee, of Cambridge, who wrote, "my opinion is, that it contains neither character nor language known in any region under the sun." Mr. Story wrote to Dr. Chalmers as follows :—" For several days I have been just upon the point of writing you about the memorable things that are passing before me, so that you may conclude I very willingly answer your letter. Often I have visited and spoken to Mary Campbell as a dying believer, and every medical man that saw her declared that she could not possibly recover. Even still, Dr. Bryce, who has been in attendance upon her and her brother, persists in denying that she is well; and in proof of what he conceives to be a true judgment of her case, said to me the other day, that he has known hectic patients rally and manifest extraordinary strength even the very day before their death. He is quite sure she will kill herself. For three or four months she had been somewhat convalescent, during which period she was persuaded that God was to raise her up, and for a purpose which, from the very first days of her divine life, was uppermost in her mind, the speaking about the Gospel among the heathen. You observe I do not use the word *preaching*, as she would not use it in our sense herself, but in so far as it implied that she witnessed for God and His truth, which all believing people as well as ministers, women as well as men, are called upon to do. The *history* of the case you will soon have an opportunity of scrutinizing: and the greater jealousy manifested by you and others, who, from your station, are much in the eye of the Church, the more will you serve the interests of truth, and the more I am persuaded will you be prepared to conclude that these things are of God and not of men. If a delusion, it is one of the most cunning Satan ever devised. Many here say it is of the Devil, while even some impartial people of the world, I have heard observe: 'It is not like his way of working, for every word these people speak is obviously for the glory of God.'

"But I know you are waiting impatiently for some testimony regarding the gift of tongues. I shall tell you all I know. I did not myself, until Monday morning, witness what is of necessity attracting attention everywhere. I had said to her, as upon former occasions, that I had no feeling of curiosity in the matter, but that I was applied to from so many quarters, that I felt it to be a matter of some importance that I should be able to testify regarding a subject of such deep interest. 1 desired her to retire from the company, and make it a subject of prayer that, before we separated, she should be able to make manifest before me the power of God. I had just taken her by the hand to bid her adieu, when, obviously possessed by some irresistible power, she uttered, for I should suppose nearly an hour, sounds altogether new to my ear, but which seemed certainly to be language. She knows when the languages change, and the articulations are obviously different—some of them exceedingly musical— others not so. Sometimes she has an impression that what she is uttering is the language of a particular people. One she has often conceived to be Turkish; one of them she spoke in my presence she cried out she knew to be the language of the Pelew Islanders.

"She seemed greatly oppressed in spirit that the power of interpretation was not given. It has been occasionally given to some of those present. On Saturday last, Lady C—— G—— was constrained to interpret various sentences. M'Donald, who commanded her to rise, was at first very sceptical regarding the gift which he heard Mary had received; but now the same power rests on him and his brother, and they mutually interpret. I read your letter to Mary, and she told me that she felt as if she would write in a little the characters of some language. She describes it as being a very different kind of influence, and, as I understand her, she does not always see the characters of the language she is speaking. I have stated to you all that I can rightly testify regarding the matter; and my testimony is simply this—these sounds *do seem* to be language. Mary and the M'Donalds themselves believe they are language.

"The individuals who thus testify are very holy persons. Should the gift be conclusively ascertained, I see only, for my own part, what would to me be in perfect accordance with the past manifestations of God's power. Ever since Mary Campbell became a Christian, her desire has been to make known the Gospel; for six years such has been the passion of this holy young woman. Many others have imbibed the same spirit; and if some can scarcely see the scriptural authority for such a movement as her going forth on this errand, yet such a gift (of tongues) would obviously annihilate all objection from preconceived opinions; and the fact of a numerous band of young persons, of both sexes, going forth with the Gospel *so sanctioned*, is well fitted to reprove our dead church. But while many considerations conspire in my mind, to efface any obstacle to the willing belief of what is alleged as having been, and still is, manifested by God in Mary and others, I feel that I am called upon to be especially jealous in my scrutiny, seeing that it involves such weighty and important consequences. I am very anxious to have the matter fully and thoroughly investigated; and with this view I was just on the point of writing you, as well as Drs. Gordon and Thomson, when your letter arrived. If a delusion, the more speedily it is given to the winds the better. If it be a reality, this one conclusion I know you will at once feel to be utterly unavoidable. Before I conclude, I have the prospect of seeing Mary, and of receiving the *characters* you are naturally so desirous to see. For my own part, I recognise in none I have seen the signs of any language I know, and therefore, to me, they are not evidence; but many have seen her note them down, and it is with inconceivable rapidity, and as if she herself were unconscious of the exertion. Both in speaking and writing she describes her words and movements as in every respect independent of her own volition." This would indicate a belief, on Mr. Story's part, to a certain extent, that the strange manifestations were something more than the outcome of an excited, hysterical disposition; but he soon had ample reason to distrust the new religious movement, because he had cause to lose confidence in those who were taking a prominent part in its direction.

After the first enthusiasm for spiritual work as a pastor settled in a new parish, had, in the course of some years, begun to abate, Mr. Story seemed to feel the solitude of his secluded parish somewhat irksome, and entered a good deal into the society of friends in various parts of the country. His exceedingly handsome and striking appearance, his cultured mind and agreeable manners, made the young minister to be courted by the wealthy and even titled in the land. Not being restrained at this time by the higher standard of religious walk and conversation to which he subsequently attained, he allowed his time to be too much engrossed by these social blandishments. During the winter of 1826-7, his health became seriously impaired, owing to exposure to severe weather in visiting the more remote portions of the parish, and in the summer of 1827, he sought change of climate, and relief, by a visit to England. While in Liverpool, and afterwards in Buxton, he improved considerably, and was able to do ministerial work; a goodly number of the health-seekers in the latter well known resort being attracted by the earnest pleadings of the youthful Presbyterian preacher. From Buxton he proceeded to London, visiting, amongst others, Edward Irving. With this friend he attended the so-called "Prophetical Conference," held at Albury Park, under the auspices of the well known and eccentric Henry Drummond, afterwards a personage of some note in the political world, when member of Parliament, and the chartered humourist of the House of Commons. Of this gentleman, Irving wrote, in the dedication of one of his works, "Who hath taken us poor despised interpreters of prophecy under your wings, and made the halls of your house like unto the ancient schools of the prophets."

During his residence in England, Mr. Story's religious belief underwent a certain change, which more or less influenced his subsequent pulpit teaching, and his conception of what a minister owed to the flock committed to his charge became proportionately higher. In a letter to his valued friend, Mr. Robert Campbell of Rosneath, about this time, the following passages occur: "You seem to think that my recovery has been retarded by plunging into the haunts of fanatics and enthusiasts, and thereby exerting myself beyond my power. It is not, however, so. I did attend, as you know, the Albury conference in November, but change of air and other inducements combined to render it of no inconsiderable importance that I should be there. The great evil is, that immortal beings, who must all stand before the judgment seat of Christ, will resort to any occupation and any amusement rather than deeply and seriously consider what preparation ought to be made for that fatal trial, upon which depend everlasting and irrevocable issues. I look back upon the past, and it seems to me that in what most would call, and what I myself thought pastoral fidelity, I discover very little indeed of that apostolical devotedness which, whosoever does not imitate, is chargeable with the guilt of neglecting the souls of his people."

Shortly after his return, the rumours regarding erroneous doctrine held by the young and saintly minister of the Row, opposite to Rosneath, the Rev. John Macleod Campbell, began to attract much notice to the ecclesiastical surroundings of the Gareloch. Various correspondents wrote in terms of kindly monition to Mr. Story, who was known to sympathise largely in the views of his clerical neighbour and friend. Amongst these was Dr. Thomas Chalmers, who thus expressed himself: "It is more for the purpose of doing justice to my own emotions than for anything else, that I now write you, and to assure you of the unabated regard of one, who looks back with pleasing and tender recollections on all the intercourse he had with you in other days. And it has served greatly to confirm and augment that regard, to have heard of your growing interest in the great work of your Lord and Master. I will not enter into the peculiarities of that doctrine which I have heard ascribed to you, but I rejoice in the devotedness which you manifest to the best and greatest of causes, and I accept of this as one of the most hopeful symptoms that all is, or will be, right. 'If thine eye be single, thy whole body shall be full of light.'" And so the good minister of Rosneath went on with his pastoral work, his zeal quickened and his feelings stirred by the impulses of divine grace, and seeing the work of the Lord prosper in his hands.

Some time after his return from England, Mr. Story was happily united in marriage to Miss Helen Boyle Dunlop, one of a numerous family, her father, Mr. Dunlop of Keppoch, near Helensburgh, being a respected banker in Greenock. Some of the sons achieved distinction in different parts of the world; the eldest, John Dunlop, being the father of the temperance cause in Scotland, and his name is held in high honour amongst the friends of that great movement. Mr. Story's friend, Edward Irving, would fain have him pay his addresses to a lady of his acquaintance, whom he believed would have made him an admirable help-mate—a special recommendation being, "She knows more of the mystery of the Papacy than any woman in England, except my wife." Mrs. Story, a clever, practical and energetic lady, was long spared to be a comfort to her husband, and soothed him in his last lingering illness, and died at Rosneath in 1882, greatly regretted by her many friends.

Years rolled on, and four children enlivened the quiet Rosneath Manse by their infantine prattle, though two of them were early removed from the scene, flowerets plucked from the stem by an unseen but resistless hand. One of the sons lived to succeed his father as minister of the parish, and to make a name in the world and in the Church, the well known Robert Herbert Story, now Professor of Church History in the University of Glasgow. The Row heresy case continued to drag on its weary length, giving rise to angry and painful recriminations, and Mr. Story warmly supported the talented and amiable minister, who, however, was deposed from the ministry in May, 1831. The proceedings, through which Mr. Campbell, subsequently better known as Dr. John Macleod Campbell, had his reputation greatly extended, originated in certain doctrines regarding the Atonement held by him, which were considered to be opposed to the standards of the Church of Scotland. No one disputed the earnest and lofty character of Mr. Campbell, and his ability and originality as a thinker, while his parishioners were devotedly attached to their minister. After the sentence of the General Assembly, he left the shores of the Gareloch for a number of years, but afterwards returned to Rosneath. He purchased a residence not far from the Clachan village, to which he gave the Gaelic name of Achnashie, "Field of Peace," and there he died in 1872, and his remains rest close to the old ruined church in which his eloquent voice had so often been uplifted in solemn accents of affectionate exhortation.

In August, 1839, another beloved child was taken away, and keenly did Mr. Story feel this second afflicting dispensation from his Heavenly Father. In a letter to a friend, he wrote of "the sacrifice that God's fatherly heart made and felt when He gave up His Son to die. He knows, exclaimed I, what I feel; He once had a dead Son. The Infinite from that blessed moment seemed to be in my presence, actuated by fatherly sympathies, swathed as it were in a human heart, afflicted in my affliction; the incomprehensible Jehovah manifest to me indeed in flesh, the fountain of my Father's nature, and bathing, so to speak, my fatherly sufferings in His fatherly sympathies." All through life Mr. Story had shown exceeding tenderness in his home circle, and the milk of human kindness in him overflowed even to casual strangers whom he met by the wayside, and would invite to the manse to partake of Christian hospitality.

During the time of his peaceful ministry in his quiet vineyard, Mr.

Story ever kept a watchful eye upon the movements and ecclesiastical controversies which agitated the seething world outside. For years the Church of Scotland was the arena of angry contentions and bitter strife, the "Moderate" and "Evangelical" parties gradually becoming more estranged from one another, and more intolerant of any interference with their freedom of opinions and actions. The story of these wrathful years has been over and over told with all the amplitude of detail becoming a struggle of national importance, in which men of great intellect and profound theological acquirements displayed oratorical graces and gladiatorial skill of surpassing interest. Many ponderous volumes have been indited giving full particulars of the battles in Church and Law Courts.

After the Revolution of 1688 the Church of Scotland was constituted on its present basis, the mode of election of ministers to vacant charges being by joint suffrages of the heritors and elders of the parish. But in 1712 the system of Lay Patronage was brought back, and thus was unhappily restored a fruitful source of many unseemly struggles within and without the Church. The public standards, embodying her views of Christian doctrine and duty, continue unchanged since first they were adopted for the guidance of her ministers and people. When she became an Established Church, her Confession of Faith and Directory of Worship were ratified by the State, and to alter those without mutual consent would have been a violation of compact. The vexed question of Lay Patronage remained, and caused many disputed settlements, outbursts of embittered feelings and wranglings in Church Courts, and the agitation for Reform precipitated on the political world by the Bill of 1832 communicated itself to ecclesiastical circles. To give effect, as far as practicable, to the just wishes of the people, without infringing on the rights of the patron, the popular and evangelical portion of the General Assembly passed, in 1834, what was known as the "Veto Law." The same Assembly admitted ministers of Chapels "*quoad sacra*," to the full status and functions of parish ministers. The Veto Act bore the approval of very high legal authority, and was supported by the irresistible eloquence of Dr. Chalmers and the famous band of Divines who constituted afterwards the leaders of the Free Church. But by the final decision of the House of Lords, in May 1839, the Veto Act was declared illegal, in the famous Auchterarder case, and thus the Church's action was overturned by the highest tribunal in the land. Happily, the painful controversies in the Church of Scotland, which still continued through the action of the law of patronage, were brought to a close by the abolition of that law in 1874. A Bill to abolish patronage and repeal the Act of Queen Anne, was introduced into the House of Lords by the Duke of Richmond, and supported by the eloquence and great influence of the Duke of Argyll. The House of Lords, by the tone of its discussion of the measure proved that it desired to uphold the true principles of the Church of Scotland, and conserve the rights of the people. After certain judicious amendments, the act passed into law, by which patronage was vested in the congregation, due compensation being offered to the patron should he care to claim it, and the Church itself was left to define who were the members and adherents in each particular congregation.

During all these long and painful scenes in the Church Courts, Mr. Story took but little part in the struggle, his sympathies largely going with the evangelical party, though he considered their action as endangering some of the best interests of the Church. He stated from the pulpit of Rosneath Church that it would now be needful, on account of the heavy responsibility involved in "vetoing" the presentee, that the strictest investigation would need to be exercised in admitting candidates to the full position of communicants. It must be remembered that the veto law gave to a majority of male heads of families, in any parish—being communicants—the absolute right to reject the presentee, without any reason being required to be offered.

Prior to the great and painful act of Disruption on the memorable 18th of May 1843, when 451 ministers left the Church of their fathers, the popular majority of the Assembly had been taking measures to promulgate their views upon ecclesiastical government throughout the length and breadth of the land. At the same time they were to endeavour to gather together all material resources, from subscriptions and otherwise, available during the struggle which was impending. Deputies, consisting of fiery and impassioned orators of the popular party were sent to many a rural parish to enlist the support and sympathies of those who shunned the idea of "Erastianism." Amongst other favoured places, Rosneath was not neglected, although in many parishes the deputies were not permitted to address the congregation from the pulpit of the parish church. Mr. Story, however, with characteristic magnanimity, not only gave the two deputies full leave to speak, but hospitably entertained them at the Manse, though well aware that 'much pain might thereby be entailed upon himself. One of his old parishioners did not take quite the same kindly view of the errand of the worthy deputies, for on being asked to contribute to the fund for the ministers who might secede from the Church, she replied, "I hae heard e' some that went oot langsyne, but they were tell't no to tak purse or scrip wi' them, but ye're a hantle wiser—ye send the purse and the scrip afore ye."

After the Disruption, and Mr. Story had returned home from the General Assembly of 1843, he found his hitherto happy and undivided parish in the full throes of the painful excitement of that memorable time. On the Sabbath mornings, instead of the crowds streaming down the heathery braes and bracken-clad slopes above the parish church, a full half of the cottagers turned their faces towards the new and temporary place of worship in the school house on Loch Long side. Party spirit in the district ran very high, angry controversy ensued, but the good minister of Rosneath charitably wrote: "If the agitation shall lead to the conversion of any from the error of their ways, I shall be thankful for it all." Some of the reasons given by the humble parishioners for quitting the old church were diverting from their simplicity, and the peculiar frame of mind indicated. One indignantly enquired, "Div ye think I'll stay in a kirk where I'm tell't that if I dinna believe the Almighty's my father, I'm nae Christian?" Another worthy, the coachman of a local gentleman of great influence, who drew with him not a few of those who looked to him as a guide and friend, gave, probably, a unique reason for his joining the ranks of the Secessionists. A friend meeting the impressionable charioteer, said to him, "And what will you do John?" to which query came the ready response, "I'll gang whar' the horse gangs." Even on the Lord's Day the new formed antipathies were apt to burst into open conflict. In speaking to a gentleman about some jeering remark uttered by a seceder to his quondam neighbour in the Establishment, as they met one Sabbath, the latter said, "Was it no a mercy it was the Sabbath day, and a borrow't umbrella in my hand, or as sure's death I wad hae felled him."

On the first Communion after the Disruption, Mr. Story alluded to that event in an address from the pulpit. "At our Communion in May, we all met, the whole body of Sacramental worshippers in the parish at the table of the Lord; now we are divided. Regarding those who have gone, I have nothing to say, to their own Master they must stand or fall, and I desire not to judge them. My heart's desire and prayer for them is that they may be saved; and God is my record how earnestly I longed after them in the Gospel, how willingly I would spend and be spent in their service, but they desired it should be otherwise. This act of separation was theirs, not mine, and now our accounts as minister and people are closed until we stand together before the judgment seat of God—I to give account of what I have said and done—they to answer for all they have seen and heard. Since they have chosen another to be set over them, I feel it is not consistent with the purposes of good order that I should interfere with his ministry, though I shall willingly cooperate with him in every good work." In this kindly way did he express himself towards those who had felt constrained to forsake the parish church, and he was quite as willing to labour and spend his strength amongst those who sought his assistance, whether amongst the seceders or those of his own flock. In not a few cases, in their last illness, and on a dying bed, some of his former congregation called for the attendance of their old friend and minister, nor was the call ever made in vain. At any hour of the night, and in any illness, no matter how dangerous and deadly, Mr. Story would cheerfully seek the sufferer's bedside.

> " Beside the bed, where parting life was laid,
> And sorrow, guilt, and pain by turns dismay'd,
> The reverend champion stood. At his control
> Despair and anguish fled the struggling soul."

Towards the close of the year 1849, symptoms of failing health began to manifest themselves in Mr. Story, whose upright form, dark kindling eye, and long, flowing, white hair, attracted observation wherever he moved. He found he was unequal even to the task of mounting to the summit of the beautiful braes at the back of the church without an undue palpitation of the heart. After consulting two doctors in Edinburgh, the decision was come to that it would not be advisable to preach out of his own pulpit, as he was suffering from a species of heart disease, rendering all loud speaking or violent exercise highly dangerous. Though thus stricken with an insidious malady, while apparently in the full vigour of life, with all his mental faculties unimpaired, he meekly submitted to the will of his Heavenly Father. Though unable himself for much sustained exertion, he was ever ready to forward any plans of rural excursions or exploration of the sylvan and heathery beauties of the Peninsula, that might be projected by the circle of youthful friends or relatives who often enjoyed the hospitality of the Manse. He also kept up a regular correspondence with a wide number of attached friends, some of them men who have left their mark on the intellectual history of our time. The tendency of his devotional reading was towards the works of authors such as Erskine of Linlathen, the Hares, Robertson of Brighton, and Maurice, though with many of the views of the later works of the last-named divine he could not sympathise.

Soon after this the circumstances of the parish began to make another place of worship on the Loch Long side of the Peninsula desirable, and Mr. Story himself undertook the chief work of raising the necessary subscriptions. The Duke of Argyll having willingly granted a site on a beautiful and commanding position above the rapidly rising summer resort of Cove, the foundation-stone of the new edifice was laid on 31st July, 1852. It remains an enduring memorial of Mr. Story's self-denying labours and vigilance for the spiritual welfare of his people, and there can be little doubt that the exertions he made, in many ways, in raising the necessary funds, told considerably upon his enfeebled frame. By this time he was obliged to have the aid of assistants in the carrying on of his ministerial work, though he rarely delegated to them his beloved duties of visiting the sick, or such occupations as demanded but little exertion of voice or strength. He greatly enjoyed also his visits to relatives in Edinburgh, Bridge of Earn, and also for several summers to Ireland, where he had some very attached friends whose society afforded him especial delight.

As the years of 1858 and 1859 gradually passed away, it became evident that the days of the much loved pastor of Rosneath were drawing to a close. Many of his dearest friends came to the Manse, so suggestive of joyous memories of the past, in order to see once more its honoured head, and have a few farewell words of communion and fellowship. For friends and parishioners alike he ever had the same winning smile and kindly welcome, and the blessing, though sometimes well nigh inaudible, was hardly ever omitted. His son and successor in the ministry, who was doing work in a church in Montreal, was hurriedly summoned across the Atlantic, but arrived too late to take farewell of his beloved father. He died on the 22nd of November, 1859, after much uncomplaining suffering, for there had come over him great weakness, inability to move, and oppression in breathing. His spirit was calm and his intellect unclouded, and, as one wrote regarding him, "when seated in his chair, it was hard to realize that one whose mind was so active, and whose interest in others was so great, could be rapidly hastening to his grave."

> " All that live must die,
> Passing through nature to eternity."

A chaste and simple monument, in the form of a tablet and medallion on the wall inside the parish church, from the design of the late William Brodie, R.S.A., was raised to his memory. The medallion portrait of Mr. Story, in white marble, forming part of the monument, is by the same eminent sculptor. The inscription is as follows:—

DEDICATED
BY
HIS PARISHIONERS AND FRIENDS
TO
THE REVERED MEMORY OF
ROBERT STORY,
FOR FORTY-TWO YEARS
THE FAITHFUL AND BELOVED MINISTER
OF THE CHURCH AND PARISH OF ROSNEATH.
ON EARTH HIS EARNEST AIM WAS TO SHEW FORTH BY WORD AND LIFE THE GOOD AND PERFECT WAY WHEREIN HIS GREAT MASTER WALKED; IN HEAVEN THERE ARE MANY WITH HIM TO TESTIFY THAT HE DID NOT LABOUR IN VAIN, NOR SPEND HIS STRENGTH FOR NOUGHT.
BORN 3RD MARCH, 1790.
ORDAINED 26TH MARCH, 1818.
DIED 22ND NOVEMBER, 1859.

The brief summary given of the life and character of the life of Robert Story will suffice to show what manner of man he was, and to testify the affectionate regard in which he was held by those who knew his worth. While he was its ruling spirit, the manse of Rosneath was ever open to such as sought it, whose character and circumstances would justify the kindly hospitality ever readily offered even to the veriest stranger. All and sundry were made welcome, many of the visitors being in comparatively humble walks in life, though not a few were among the titled magnates of the land. Of his own contemporaries in the ministry were several of those who had charges in the immediate neighbourhood,—two very dear and close friends, the Rev. J. Macleod Campbell of Row, and his successor, the Rev. John Laurie Fogo, as also the Rev. William Dunn of Cardross, both of them ministers of those parishes for about fifty years, honoured and faithful workers in the Master's vineyard. With Dr. Chalmers he long enjoyed warm friendship, having, as before mentioned, been first introduced to his charge by that celebrated divine. At one time, Chalmers had been inclined to propose that his friend should become assistant minister of the Tron Church in Glasgow, but the idea was not carried out. On one occasion, when Dr. Chalmers accompanied by Edward Irving, then his assistant, visited Rosneath, an entertainment was given in their honour by Miss Helen Campbell at her bower, or sylvan retreat, above the little fall known as "Helen's Linn," in the Clachan glen. The rustic bower was in a retired and sweet spot in the romantic glen, where a dense and dark shade cools the visitor even on a hot summer day, the overhanging old oak and fir trees, twined round with clinging woodbine, scenting the air, and mantled with glistening ivy leaves. The large and happy party from the Manse and Clachan House partook of breakfast in the bower, after doing justice to which, one of the gentlemen played an inspiring reel tune on the violin, and no less decorous a reveller than the celebrated Irving danced the Highland fling, with astonishing vigour. After the entertainment was over, and the friends returned to the Manse, Mr. Story enquired, "What shall we do now?" when Dr. Chalmers, in his characteristic way, exclaimed, "Come and let us abandon ourselves to miscellaneous impulses!"

The gifted and eloquent Edward Irving was a frequent visitor at the Manse, and he tried hard to persuade his friend to join the Catholic apostolic body. Sometimes on sacramental occasions at Rosneath, he used to address the large congregation assembled in the church-yard from the wooden "tent," which stood near the Manse, and astonished those present by his weird and dramatic oratory. He warmly espoused the claims of Mary Campbell to supernatural gifts and manifestations of the "tongues," and the series of extraordinary scenes and blasphemous utterances of the excited spiritualists, which occurred in Regent Square Church, resulted in his deposition from the Church of Scotland. Irving made various attempts to induce Mr. Story to join the prophetic band of demented enthusiasts. "Oh Story," he wrote in 1832, "thou hast grievously sinned in standing afar off from the work of the Lord, scorning it like a sceptic, instead of proving it like a spiritual man." Meanwhile Irving had been removed from the pastorate of Regent Square Church by the Presbytery of London in May, 1832, and was deposed by the Presbytery of

Annan in March, 1833, on a charge of heresy regarding the humanity of Our Lord Jesus Christ. "Ah, brother," he said again, "you have seen the shortcomings of the brethren in private, but I have heard the voice of the Eternal Spirit in the midst of the great congregation." This gifted, though mystical, preacher died in December, 1834, and was buried in the solemn and gloomy crypt of Glasgow Cathedral, and it is recorded that a band of his devoted followers stood around the grave expecting their honoured master to rise from the dead.

Among many friends who came to visit Mr. Story at Rosneath were various ministers of his own Church, such as Dr. Chalmers, Dr. Robert Gordon, afterwards of the Free High Church, Edinburgh, Rev. David Landsborough of Saltcoats, afterwards F.C. minister at Stevenston, a special and beloved associate, whose writings upon natural history and his account of Arran are well known, Rev. Alexander Young of Mochrum, Dr. Wylie, long minister of Carluke, a gentleman of the old courtly school of manners, Rev. Robert Paisley of St. Ninians, besides dignitaries of the Episcopal Church, as the venerable Archdeacon Goold of Raphoe, and the Rev. David Ker, of the body long known as "Irvingites." All of these and many others, besides a host of friends and acquaintances of the laity, were made welcome at the kindly board of the greatly loved pastor of Rosneath, who was also on most friendly terms with three Dukes of Argyll, the Earl of Shaftesbury, Lord John Russell, and others of that class in the social scale, who enjoyed his cultured conversation.

On the parish becoming vacant, through the lamented death of Mr. Story, the then patron of the living, the Duke of Argyll, appointed his son, the Rev. Robert Herbert Story, to the church and parish of Rosneath. This appointment gave much satisfaction to the congregation and inhabitants of the district generally, the young minister having been born and brought up in their midst, and inheriting many of the qualities which had made his father so greatly beloved. On his return from Montreal, in Canada, where he had been labouring for some eighteen months, Mr. Robert Herbert Story at once commenced to do duty as parish minister early in 1860, and was warmly welcomed by the congregation. The following sketch of his career appeared in an interesting volume about the ministers and churches of Helensburgh and neighbourhood, published in Helensburgh in 1889:

"Robert Herbert Story received the presentation to the parish, rendered vacant by the death of his father, early in the year 1860. The patron, the Duke of Argyll, did not need formally to consult the parishioners as to the appointment. He knew that to them it would be acceptable. The presentee had been brought up amongst them; he was beloved for his father's sake; they were proud of him for his own. His career at Edinburgh University had been a distinguished one; he had made his mark in Montreal, where he had officiated for eighteen months as assistant minister in the Presbyterian Church of St. Andrew. The appointment, which thus commended itself to the parishioners at the time it was made, was fully justified by its subsequent results. The young minister proved himself a successor worthy of his father. The methods of 1816 were scarcely suitable to 1860. The pastor's relations to his flock were changed; a different style of preaching had come into vogue; the entire Service of the Sanctuary was conducted under new forms. But though the new minister worked by methods unknown to the old, he worked in a kindred spirit. He was equally faithful in his ministrations to the sick and the afflicted; he was equally earnest in his efforts to cultivate among his people practical godliness; he preached with like freedom and courage the gospel of the grace of God. By temperament the younger Story was less impulsive and less frank than the older. But though to strangers he might thus be less accessible, his parishioners soon learned that beneath the more frigid exterior there was a heart not less warm and true. He was regarded by them accordingly, before he had been many years their pastor, with scarcely less of esteem and affection than that which had been accorded to his venerable father. Even those who esteemed the father, most recognised in the son, if not a more faithful and earnest, a more effective preacher. His preaching from the first was fresh in thought, devout in tone, graceful and poetic in diction. As he grew in knowledge and experience, it became richer, wiser, and more spiritual. The high-toned preaching of the young minister and the orderly and dignified devotional service which he conducted, soon made the parish church of Rosneath a centre of spiritual attraction to the surrounding district. In the summer season the church was over-crowded, and it became necessary to add transepts, containing nearly two hundred sittings, to the original building. By this time, about 1867, the battle of the organ had been fought and won, and an organ, with the unanimous, or all but unanimous, assent of the parishioners was placed in the north transept of the enlarged parish church. Not long afterwards the Scottish Hymnal received the sanction of the General Assembly, and was of course adopted by the congregation of Rosneath. The enriched service of praise, and the beauty of the enlarged church, into which two fine stained glass windows—one of them the gift of the gifted authoress of the *Chronicles of Carlingford* —had been introduced, made the Sanctuary by the shores of the Gareloch more attractive than ever to residents in the district. Larger congregations went up with gladness to the House of the Lord, and worshipped Him there in the beauty of holiness. The manse, as well as the church, was in its own way a centre of attraction. Mr. Story had married in 1863 Miss Maughan, a lady well known in the Edinburgh society of the period. This lady, with ready adaptability, suited herself at once to the life of a Scottish manse. She had the social gifts which enabled her to be at ease with persons of all ranks and conditions, and to set them at ease with herself and with one another. She consequently became a great favourite in the parish. The society of Rosneath during the incumbency of the younger Story was, of course, other than it had been during that of the older. Barremman, Peatoun, and Portkill, were tenanted by new occupants. The families at Strouel Lodge, and at the Mansion House of the Clachan, were greatly reduced by death or by emigration. The only survivor of the former, Mr. George Robertson, and one of the two survivors of the latter, Mr. John Campbell, were members of Dr. Story's Kirk Session, and were always welcome visitors at the Manse, to whose inmates they were attached with a loyalty that was touching. Another family associated with the older period had settled in the parish. It was that of Dr. John M'Leod Campbell, now honoured in the land, though not restored to his status in the Church. At Achnashie (the "field of peace") the last years of that man of God were peacefully spent, and these years were gladdened for him by the society of the son of his old friend at the Manse, and by that of his old friend's widow at Kenmure Cottage, where she, with her daughter and grand-daughter, had settled. Such was the society of permanent residenters at Rosneath during the early years of Dr. Story's ministry. The Castle from time to time was occupied by the ducal family, whose relations with the minister and his household were always of the pleasantest. Sometimes, too, the summers brought congenial sojourners to the villa residenters in the district. More transient visitors to the hospitable Manse itself were frequent, not to say incessant. Among these were many of the most notable divines in Scotland—Dr Robert Lee-Principal Caird, Principal Tulloch, Principal Tulloch's successor—Dr. Cunningham, and Bishop Ewing. The sweet-souled Dean of Westminster also was a guest beneath Dr. Story's roof-tree, and a preacher from his pulpit.

Dr. Story, during the twenty-seven years of his residence at Rosneath, was a diligent worker. He was methodical in the arrangement of his time, and thus, in addition to the faithful discharge of his pastoral duties, he accomplished a considerable amount of literary work. He published, in 1862, the memoir of his father, a biography which in respect of literary grace and graphic interest, will bear comparison with Stanley's graceful tribute to the memory of Arnold. In 1870, Dr. Story again appeared before the public as a biographer. In that year his *Life and Remains of Dr. Robert Lee*, his friend and teacher, was published. In respect of literary excellence, this book is perhaps scarcely on a level with the author's previous effort, but it tells effectively, though here and there with unnecessary bitterness, the story of Dr. Lee's contendings for improved worship and emancipated thought. Subsequently to the publication of the life of Dr. Lee, Dr. Story published a *Life of Principal Carstairs*, from whom, through the Dunlops, he was collaterally descended. The preparation of this volume involved a considerable amount of research and the study of documents bearing upon the somewhat obscure history of the "Resolutioners and Protesters," and of the period which succeeded the Revolution of 1688. The book is painstaking and accurate, and though the story of the party warfare referred to is somewhat dry, that of Carstairs' earlier trials and of his relations to William of Orange, is graphic and interesting. In addition to these more laborious literary efforts, Dr. Story published a volume of sermons entitled *Creed and Conduct*, a monograph on *S. Modan*, and a little volume on the health resorts of the Riviera. A rumour, it may also be mentioned, to which credence we notice is given in the sketch of Dr. Story in *Men of the Time*, attributes to him the *Nugæ Ecclesiasticæ of Dr. Moses Peerie*, edited by Jabez Gilead. The *Nugæ* are made up of dramatic fragments, humourously descriptive of incidents in recent ecclesiastical history, and of rhymes in which the characteristics of leading ecclesiastics are happily hit off.

Dr. Story for the last fifteen years has taken an active part in the work of Church Courts. He first came forward in the General Assembly, somewhat in the character of a free lance, and fluttered considerably those who occupied its chief seats around the table. His sarcasm, in that earlier period, was often over-bitter. He has mellowed, however, with years, and if he be satirical still, his satire —except when as in the Hastie case, he speaks under strong provocation—is for the most part kindly. The Presbytery of Dunbarton, recognising his power as a debater and his ability as a man of business, has elected him annually as one of its representatives in the venerable Assembly. The wisdom of this departure from custom in the matter of representation has been proved by the position to which Dr. Story has risen in the great council of the Church. Through his frequent attendances in the Assembly he has become familiar with its forms of procedure, and well qualified to take a leading part in its debates, and to assist in conducting its business as junior clerk. The long struggle for improved worship in which Dr. Lee had fallen was at an end before Dr. Story took a prominent part in the proceedings of the courts of the Church. By no other controversy of equal interest has the Church been agitated subsequently to Dr. Story's appearance on the arena. Party conflicts there have been, such as that in regard to elders' subscription, and to the "guerilla erastianism," as Dr. Wallace used to call it, of the Baird Trust Deed. In these controversies Dr. Story, as might have been anticipated, fought on the liberal side, along with Principal Tulloch, Dr. Wallace, and Dr. Cunningham. Of late years, thanks to the attacks of the liberationists, party distinctions in the Church of Scotland have been well nigh obliterated. The Church is now of one party, that which exists for the defence of an institution, with the continued existence of which she believes that much that is best in the nation's life is bound up. Of this great party Dr. Story is recognised as one of the most able and influential members. He did not spare himself at Church defence meetings during the crisis of 1885. It will be in the recollection of most of our readers, also, how manfully he rebuked certain utterances of Lord Aberdeen and the Marquis of Lorne, which he considered unfair to the Church and unworthy of their exalted positions. About this period, besides, Dr. Story became editor of a new magazine, entitled the *Scottish Church*, which, while it was published chiefly in the interests of Church defence, contained also a great deal of excellent literary material.

The above sketch will serve to show what an active and industrious life as pastor, man of letters, ecclesiastical leader, the late minister of Rosneath has lived. We have not left ourselves space to speak of his work in connection with the Church Service Society. He was the inaugurator of that society, and has always been one of its most influential members. How much the Church owes to his action in this direction, we need scarcely to point out. On Sunday 5th June, 1887, Dr. Story bid farewell to the congregation of Rosneath, and the dynasty which had endured in the parish for seventy years came to an end. To those who had known Rosneath under the Storys there must be for evermore a certain sadness in the lovely Peninsula. Dr. Story's flock, like his friends, are proud, no doubt, of his promotion to the Chair of Church History in the University of Glasgow, a position of greater dignity and of larger influence than that of a parish minister. Still they will miss him from the pulpit of the parish church, he and the members of his family from the manse, from their own homes, from the waysides by the shores of the quiet loch with its encircling mountains. Dr. Story and his father alike laboured with their might, which was that of men of more than common force of character, for the diffusion among their people of the Christian spirit, and of larger views of the love of God that passeth knowledge. Their names, like that of their earliest predecessor, St. Modan, will be remembered by dwellers in Rosneath of generations yet unborn, as those of true workers for the cause of Christ and the Kingdom of God.

The Parish Church was crowded on Sunday at the noonday service, many visitors having come long distances to hear the farewell sermon of a beloved teacher. Dr. Story preached from Joshua vii. 10, with his usual brilliancy and vigour. There was a peculiar force and meaning in the whole discourse, and though no particular reference was made to the changed relations under which it had been prepared, no one who heard it could mistake the lessons it was intended to convey. The pent up feelings of many in the congregation found vent in tears; and the preacher himself was more than once nearly overcome with emotion as he said farewell in the following words: "Casting about in my own mind for a subject on which it might be suitable that I should speak to you to-day, it seemed to me that I could not do better than simply take the one which came in the ordinary course of our reading in the Old Testament, and which, when we look into it, teaches us the spirit in which all the changes and disciplines of life ought to be met, as you know a change is impending here, of which, to tell the truth, I cannot speak. The thought that the tie which has connected you and me for so many years is now broken, and that I shall never again stand here as minister of this parish touches me too deeply to be spoken about, all the more that I know it is not a matter of indifference to you—to some of you a matter of much concern and regret. For much encouraging friendship, for many acts of kindness received to the very last, I have to thank you. For many faults and failings in the past seven and twenty years, I have to crave your pardon. For whatever has been true in my preaching here I ask your abiding remembrance. Do not forget that those great verities of our most holy faith which I have tried to set forth as indeed the good news of God—the good news of a divine Fatherhood that embraces all mankind in the love which passes human understanding, of a divine forgiveness that blots out all our sins; of a divine righteousness which demands that we should be righteous too, and cannot be deceived by any observance of the letter while the spirit is neglected, by any religious profession without honest practice and sincere character; of a divine will that seeks the salvation of every human soul. And all this summed up and recalled to us in the life and words and works of the eternal Son of God, who lived and died that He might teach us to *know the Father*, and to cleanse our hearts and minds of bondage and fear by believing in His love. After all it matters little what is the outward history or destiny of this or any church, if its members bear living witness to these truths. Believing that witness, it is in its place a pillar and ground of the truth. It is faithful to the Master. It abides in the light of Him who said, ' He that loveth not knoweth not God, for God is love.' There are those who, walking in the slavery of fear, and the bondage of human systems, cannot understand this; but there are always some—one here and another there—who have been able to lay hold of it, and to whom it is the light of life. Let me hope that no change which may await this church—come how it will—shall ever find another or a lesser gospel preached within these walls, or no answering witness borne to it in some lives—be they ever so few—purified and ennobled by child-like love of God, and self-forgetful good will to men.

"The years that have passed over us have seen many a mournful change. How many have been taken from us! the beloved! the unforgotten! They have brought too much happiness, and many a good and perfect gift. May the coming years be yet fuller to you of outward prosperity and inward peace. Forsake not the assembling of yourselves together. Maintain the beauty of God's house, and the reverence and seemliness of its services. Keep His commandments, and be always mindful of His poor. With this I say farewell. When in the days to come you assemble here for worship, think sometimes, not unkindly, of one whose thoughts on the Lord's Day at the house of prayer will never be far from this dear and familiar place. I commend you all unto God and to the word of His grace, which is able to build you up and to give you an inheritance among them all which are sanctified, and to whom be all glory in the Church world without end. Amen."

During Dr. Story's ministry, the Kirk Session had lost several of its old and valued members, who had officiated as elders in his father's lifetime. On the vacancy being declared, a congregational committee was formed, the Rev. J. Webster of Row being moderator, and in August a new minister was elected, the Rev. Alfred Warr, M.A., who was educated at Edinburgh University, and had for some time acted as assistant in St. Cuthbert's Church. Its well known minister, the Rev. Dr. MacGregor, bore testimony to Mr. Warr's zeal in the work of parochial visitation, and he has since then diligently fulfilled his duties as minister of Rosneath. The Kirk Session at present consists of Mr. John M'Lean, postmaster, Mr. William Stewart, for over twenty years parish schoolmaster, Surgeon-General

Bidie, C.I.E., Mr. Alexander Airth, Mr. Finlay M'Callum, and Mr. David Silver.

Seventy-two years forms a long epoch of time for two ministers, father and son, to be connected with a parish, and of the members of the Presbytery of Dunbarton, it need scarcely be said, not one of Mr. Story's contemporaries is alive. Of those members who sat in the Presbytery when his son succeeded to the parish of Rosneath, there survive but four members, the Rev. Dr. Macintosh, long minister of Buchanan, the popular and genial Rev. John Lindsay, of Helensburgh, a valued friend of Mr. Story's, the Rev. Duncan Campbell, long minister of Luss, and the Rev. James Dewar, of Arrochar. Of the more immediate friends and neighbours of the beloved minister of Rosneath, allusion has already been made to the Rev. Dr. Macleod Campbell, whose name and works are now known all over the whole civilised world, and to the Rev. Dr. Wylie, over fifty years minister of Carluke, one of the most kindly and delightful of companions, ever cheerful, and zealous in Christian work, with a most courteous and attractive personality. Also a man dearly beloved by his parishioners, and long the affectionate friend of the minister of Rosneath, was the Rev. John Laurie Fogo, over fifty years minister of Row. He was well known by high and low on the banks of the Gareloch, and always took part in the school examinations at Rosneath, besides frequently officiating at the Communion season, and attending both physically and spiritually to the wants of the sick, for he was well skilled in medicine. But none of his brethren in the ministry was more beloved by pastor and people than the late Rev. William Dunn, for nearly fifty years minister at Cardross, who died at the close of 1885. A man of striking simplicity and gentleness of manner, full of devotion to his Master's work, exuberant in large-hearted benevolence and intense in his sympathies for those in anguish or sorrow, Mr. Dunn left a name which assuredly will long be held in affectionate remembrance. His tribute, in the funeral sermon he preached, to his beloved friend Mr. Story, may be fitly quoted here : " And over a man of finer, more graceful mould and form, over a more genial friend and companion, over one whose face and presence threw more light, and cheerfulness, and vivacity into a social circle, over a kinder and more loving heart, over one with larger and wider sympathies—sympathies with all humanity, with all creatures and created things, enjoying with a keener relish everything enjoyable on earth, with a quicker ear and eye to all sweet sounds and sights of beauty, with a merrier laugh and a more exquisite sense of humour, and a readier tear, over one who took into his bosom so many and so diverse persons, of all variety of temperament, of all sects and denominations, and had room and space for each, and a special nook for all unfortunates and outcasts, cast adrift on life's voyage, over a man who had seen more of human life in all its aspects, in the hall and in the cottage, and who had such a store of anecdotes and illustrations gathered from books and men, the grave of a country churchyard never closed."

The old church, whose ruins stand in the churchyard, beside the

Clachan Burn, is by no means a venerable structure, having been built about the year 1770 on the site of a much more ornate edifice. The father of Miss M'Dougal, who, with her sister, for well on to half a century, has occupied the small, red-tiled cottage near the Clachan Burn, remembered the old church, which was pulled down when he was about seven years old. His recollections were necessarily vague; all that seemed to have impressed him was its cruciform shape, and row of stone images round the pulpit, with the ornamental basin for holy water at one side of the main entrance door. Also on the right hand side of the doorway were five or six "jougs," as they were termed, iron manacles for detaining wrong-doers by the neck, which were supposed to have a deterrent effect upon evil disposed persons. It is believed that old Dr. Drummond, who must have had unusually decided Protestant proclivities, persuaded the Duke of Argyll to pull down the edifice dedicated to the Virgin Mary, although for his Grace's convenience there was a special gallery and staircase in the church. However, one relic of the old church still survives in the shape of the interesting and peculiar belfry, which still surmounts the existing ruin in the churchyard—the bell having been transferred to the present parish church, where it does duty every Sabbath. A considerable portion of the wall on the side of the church next the manse, with the west gable wall, surmounted by the picturesque old belfry, still stands in the centre of the churchyard, the outside overgrown with clustering masses of old ivy, and several tombstones are erected against the

THE OLD CHURCH, ROSNEATH

walls. The two windows in the wall, and the door in the gable, are all of the simplest style, and the architecture was evidently of the very plainest and least ornate description, befitting the name by which it was designated by John, Duke of Argyll, namely, "The Barn." Still, there is a charm about the relic of a byegone century, whose roofless walls and ivy-mantled stones speak with thrilling, though inaudible, accents to those who can recall the happy days when the old church rung with the soul-moving strains of many a grand and pathetic psalm or paraphrase. Mute they are now, save when of a soft summer's evening, from the summit of the old belfry, the mavis may be heard pouring forth its liquid, trilling notes, until the warm air is resonant of song, as the strain is echoed by his fellows from their sylvan retreat.

The service in the old church was, both summer and winter, from 12 to 3, there being no interval allowed, and all were expected to remain, for Mr. Story was a strict disciplinarian, and had been known publicly to rebuke several who had sought to slip away unnoticed when a pause took place. There was first a psalm, then a long full prayer; after it reading the Bible, followed by an exposition of the passage, another psalm, and a shorter prayer—very often the Lord's Prayer—then the sermon, after it prayer again, and the service was brought to a close by the concluding psalm. After this two of the elders went round with the collecting ladles, being a small box, with a slit in it, affixed to the end of a long handle, there being, contrary to the usual custom, no plates at the door of the church. This being over, the benediction was pronounced, and the congregation were free to disperse. Previous to the ordinary church service, the Sabbath School was held at eleven o'clock, conducted by Mr. Dodds, and the children came into church and remained along with their parents till three o'clock. Mr. Dodds was one of the old school, and did not approve of too lengthened abstention from mental effort, so he generally set the young people a pleasant holiday task to learn the 119th Psalm.

Inside the church, when it was used for public worship, everything was of the plainest description. The seats were of rough deals, and the floor was long only of earth, while a gallery ran round three sides of the interior—the pulpit standing between the two windows next the manse. Opposite the pulpit was the Duke of Argyll's pew, alongside which was that of Mr. Campbell of Peatoun, and of Lord John Campbell, who also lived at Ardencaple Castle on the opposite shore of the loch. When the sacrament was dispensed, there was one long table running down the passage, from door to door, the minister and elders occupying one end. The crowds who assembled to hear celebrated preachers, such as Edward Irving, were fain to fill the church-yard, and listen to the great pulpit orator from the "tent." The walls of the building were plain and white-washed, and grew green through damp and mould, and altogether the church had a forlorn appearance, although it was regarded with affection by many of the old forefathers of the parish. There are not a few living who can recall the long earnest homilies of Mr. Story, who kept up the old fashion of the double discourse or sermon, and sometimes sorely tried the patience of the volatile and less serious members of the congregation. Shortly before the old minister's death, the heritors had decided to erect a new church, which now stands nearly opposite the manse. A portion of the field in front was taken for the purpose, and the public carriage road, which passed the side of the wood bordering the manse grounds and in front of the house, was turned into a mere walk for pedestrians. The new church was commenced in 1853, and finished in the end of that year,—a plain building in the early English style, from the plans of Mr. Cousin, architect, Edinburgh. Since then two additions have been made to the edifice, in the shape of wings, affording a good deal more accommodation, and enabling an organ to be inserted, which is worked by water power from the burn. The interior has now a pleasing appearance, though it is rather dark, owing to the introduction of two large stained glass windows—one erected many years ago by Mrs. Oliphant, the well known authoress, a frequent visitor to the parish, in memory of a daughter, and the other at the opposite end, to the memory of Dr. Macleod Campbell. Near the latter is a smaller window of stained glass, in memory of his son John, of the Bombay Civil Service, who died in 1888 at sea, on his way home, after more than twenty years' service, and mourned by a wide circle of friends. On the walls of the church are several monuments in marble and brass—the principal one being at the west end of the church, on the wall, to the Rev. Robert Story, referred to before. Close beside it, on the wall, there is a brass tablet, above the manse seat, dedicated to his widow, Helen Boyle Dunlop, who was born in 1805 and died in 1882—a token of respect and affection by her son and daughter. On the opposite wall is a brass tablet in memory of Lieutenant Carey, who died in 1885. On the wall of the wing in which the organ stands there are two touching memorial marble slabs, one of them is dedicated by his brother officers and friends to the memory of John Campbell, a native of the parish, commander of the steamship *Britannia*, who, "while bravely doing his duty was swept overboard and lost during a severe hurricane in the North Atlantic on the 22nd December, 1865, at the early age of 26 years." The other tablet is in memory of a boy of much promise, Gordon S. Carnachan, son of Dr. Carnachan of Clynder, who was drowned while boating with a young companion, son of Captain Archibald Campbell, Clynder, who also met the same fate. This painful occurrence took place on 22nd September, 1884. Adjoining them is the tablet to the memory of Mr. and Mrs. Stewart of Clynder House, long resident there. In the nave of the church there is a tablet to the memory of the late Robert Crawford Cumming, a kindly and genial man who formerly owned the estate of Barremman, and died in 1876; also of his widow, died in 1890. In the wing opposite to the organ are two memorial brasses, one to Mary Campbell, widow of John M'Leod Campbell, D.D., who died in 1881; the other in memory of James Bernard Richardson, a young cavalry officer, whose father has lived many years at Hartfield in the

Peninsula, and who was killed while bravely discharging his duty in the Soudan, on 22nd March, 1885.

The church was intended by Mr. Story to have been inaugurated for public worship by the famous Scotch preacher, the Rev. John Caird, formerly of Park Church, Glasgow, now Principal of its ancient University. But the late well known, and very able minister of St. James' Church, Glasgow, Dr. John Muir, happened to be doing duty for him on the 4th of September, 1853, and, on arriving the previous night at the manse, Dr. Muir was highly displeased on hearing that he was to officiate in the old mouldy "barn" in the churchyard. The genial and humorous doctor was determined to have his way, and conduct worship in the new church, in spite of the opposition alike of the minister, the session-clerk, the greatly respected Mr. John Dodds, for fifty years parish schoolmaster, and last, but certainly not least, John Sinclair, the good beadle and church-officer. The latter was even more emphatic than the session-clerk, who pleaded, "we can't clean the church on Sabbath morning," worthy John simply asserting, "The thing was clean oot o' the question." "Can you speak Gaelic?" suddenly rejoined the doctor turning to the resisting John, at the same time speaking in the dialect of the land of the "mountain and the flood—land of brown heath and shaggy wood." An instantaneous change came over the old highlander when his beloved Gaelic greeted his ears, and ere long the obstacles were all surmounted, and the sacred edifice rendered quite fit for the large congregation who assembled. Worthy John was subsequently overheard muttering to himself, as if half repenting of his somewhat pusillanimous compliance with the demand of the imperious divine from Glasgow: "That auld man, I never heard the likes o' him, he wad rule even the minister himsel'." The good doctor preached a powerful discourse from the text, "Behold I make all things new," delivered in his own eloquent and impressive way, coloured with the inimitable pathos and wit which gained Dr. Muir so many devoted followers. In his prayer he did not omit to invoke the Divine blessing upon "this neat and commodious edifice."

Rosneath churchyard is one which furnishes a good example of how easily the resting places of the dead may be kept in order. There used to be a low, half-ruined dyke, covered with turf, which ran round the spot, and some fine old plane trees were placed at intervals within the wall. It was thought better to remove these, though some of the parishioners mourned their destruction, and the wall was rebuilt, and the old church put into more decent condition, ivy being carefully trained up its mouldering walls. An old enclosed grave of Dr. Drummond, with very high railings, was altered by the two large stones being removed from their position against the wall of the church, and laid flat upon the ground. Inside the ruin, and fixed with iron rivets into the window, is an interesting memorial stone, with curious scroll work, similar to what is seen on the ancient Town Crosses in many parts of Scotland. This stone, some years ago, was dug up in the churchyard, and is, doubtless, of great antiquity. A notice of it will be found subsequently, which is taken from the proceedings of the Society of Antiquaries. The mantling ivy is covering a good part of the ruined walls of the church, giving it a more venerable appearance than its actual age, and it forms a decided addition to the picturesqueness of the spot. On being removed from the old belfry the church bell was fixed in its appropriate place in the new edifice, and its soft, pleasing tone, is heard every Lord's day, and also, according to an old custom, at midnight on the last day of the year. The old bell is now getting considerably worn, as it was cast towards the close of the 17th century in Holland. It bears the appropriate inscription :—"Soli Dei gloria—Johannes Burgerhuys me fecit." As the soft mellow tones of the old bell, indicating the birth of a new year, are wafted across the peaceful waters of the Gareloch, the response is heard from the steeple of the Row Church, but with a more resonant sound, the omen, as it were, of a year of joyous anticipation.

Probably, in ancient times, there was another church or burying place at Portkiln, near Kilcreggan, on the Loch Long side of the Peninsula, though all traces of the sacred fabric have disappeared. Its site was believed to be on the sea shore, nearly opposite Gourock, below the modern dwelling-house of Portkiln, and it was said to have been dedicated to the Virgin Mary. *Port Kill*, in Gaelic, means a landing place, near the church or burying-place, *Port-na-Keel* or *Kill*. The English word "Cell," the Gaelic "Keel," and Irish "Kill," much resemble one another, and all signify a place for interment. The most ancient mode of inhumation, no doubt, was that of simple interment in the earth. Urn burial followed the introduction of the funeral pyre, and was extensively practised amongst the Greeks and Romans, with costly accompanying rites. The cinerary urn also became common in Britain, and frequently was contained in large stone cists, or chests, six feet long by two broad, where the calcined bones of the dead were found. Spear and arrow heads of stone or flint were frequently found in the chests or in the vicinity of the grave, indicating that a warrior's dust had here found its last resting place. About half a century ago, some men were trenching the ground near the site of the old church at Kilcreggan, and they came upon several old stone cists or coffins. The local factor ordered them to be covered up, and they were left undisturbed, otherwise, probably, further investigation might have brought to light some additional traces of the church. It is believed by many that it was an ancient custom to bring the dead from a distance to Kilcreggan for interment in the old Rosneath burying ground, as being considered consecrated earth, and that the track taken was from the landing place at Portkiln, in an oblique direction, over the shoulder of the high ground at the back of the old mill, near the Free Church, until Rosneath churchyard was gained. Indeed, one of the old residents of the Clachan village can remember her father describing how dead bodies were brought by Highlanders from Arrochar, on a sort of bier carried by two men, there being then no proper road beside Loch Long for wheeled vehicles. In a similar way the bodies of the deceased were conveyed from Arran and Ayrshire to the Clachan place of interment.

Tradition also speaks of the famous John Balfour of Burley, one of the murderers of Archbishop Sharp, being buried in Rosneath churchyard. It would appear that during the persecuting period of the later Stewart Kings, a good many Presbyterians found shelter on the shores of the Gareloch, and colour would seem to be given to this by the names and histories of various local families. One of those was Chalmers of Gadgirth, a noted leader of the Covenanters, who during the troubles in the Western Lowlands had come to Rosneath to enjoy the favour of the powerful Argyll family. Balfour's share in the murder of the unhappy Archbishop is well known. He ordered Sharp to come out of his carriage on Magus Muir, and upon the miserable man refusing, fired a pistol at him, while others stabbed him until death ensued. Burley was afterwards wounded at Bothwell Bridge, a battle so disastrous to the Covenanters, and made his escape to Holland, where, for a time, he found refuge. According to the historian of the Scottish worthies, he obtained liberty from the Prince of Orange for the purpose of returning to Scotland, to arouse vengeance against those who persecuted the true defenders of the Protestant faith, but perished on the ocean. Local tradition affirms that he found an asylum at Rosneath under the assumed name of Andrew Salter, and that his descendants continued there for generations, and were always considered of more gentle kin than the farmers of the district. The last of the race died about the year 1810, and a small stone with the letters A. S., rudely traced and barely discernible in the corner of the churchyard, used to be pointed out as indicating the last resting-place of the terrible Burley.

Although the Rosneath churchyard is undoubtedly of great antiquity, for it must be remembered that, even in the charter of the twelfth century, the building was designated the Church of St. Nicholas—and the whole Peninsula was styled the Virgin's promontory—still there are no ancient monuments existing. Most of the older head-stones bear Celtic names inscribed on them, indicating the large number of Highland families formerly located here. Campbells, M'Arthurs, M'Farlanes, M'Colls, M'Kellars, M'Lellans, M'Aulays, form the majority of the names on the stones, though Turners, Chalmers, and Ritchies, seem to have long lived in Rosneath. Inside the walls of the old church are several graves, the most notable being that of the Rev. Dr. Macleod Campbell, born 1800, died 1872, and his widow,—a handsome Iona cross of grey granite. Old Mr. John Dodds, for fifty years the parish schoolmaster, and his widow, are buried close by. The former minister's grave, the Rev. Dr. George Drummond, for fifty-two years minister, who died in 1819, is close to the wall of the church. The stones covering Dr. Drummond's grave and that of his widow now lie flat on the ground. Very near them are two large flat slabs to the memory of Major H. G. Johnston, of the York Hussars, grandson of the Earl of Delaware, who died at Greenock in 1809. His widow, who also is buried here, was daughter of Lord Frederick Campbell, which accounts for the intimation on her husband's tombstone, that he lay there by special permission of George Duke of Argyll. Near this is the Peatoun family grave, two large flat stones, indicating that underneath rest the bodies of Donald Campbell of Peatoun, who died in 1812, at the age of ninety, and his widow, Isobel Drummond. Also, there is a plain granite obelisk to the memory of John Douglas Campbell of Peatoun, long resident in the Clachan House, a man of singular beauty of character and guileless life, greatly beloved by all, who died in 1881, and his brother, Dr. George Campbell, an eminent surgeon of Montreal, died 1882, and their sister Caroline, died 1891. A little way off are two tombstones marking the graves of the Campbells, long tenants of the farm of Mamore, a fine race, the last of the family resident at Mamore being Colin Campbell, who died in 1874, aged 69, a grand old specimen of a Highland farmer. His massive head and white locks long formed a conspicuous feature in the Parish Church. Others of the same name, Malcolm and Murdoch Campbell, tenants of the Little Aiden farm, are buried close by. More to the east, near the gate of the church yard, is the burying-place of the Cumming family, long possessors of the Barremman estate. Patrick Cumming died 1770, and Mary M'Farlane, his wife, are buried here, and, later on, the last proprietor of the estate, the genial and kindly Robert Crawford Cumming, died 1876, and his widow, Sophia Connell, in 1890. Several old stones, much covered with moss and lichens so as to be barely decipherable, are scattered about, one certifying that it belongs to Archibald and Janet Ritchie, another, James Ritchie, died 1763, and another to John Hunter, farmer, Meikle Oven, died

1772. One of the older stones is that of J. Chalmers, farmer, Kilcreggen, died 1789, and two still older certify that this is the burying-place of Hugh Reily, 1765, and a flat stone near the wall bears the initials D. R. and date 1720. An ancient looking stone bears to be in memory of Janet Liston, "Spouis" to John Ramsay, servant to John, Duke of "Argyel," 1744. Another venerable-looking stone is evidently in memory of a shoemaker, for plainly delineated on its face are a boot, an old-fashioned high-heeled shoe, and the curved knife used in cutting leather. A little way off is a small slab, with the initials P. W.—H. M., 1721.

The grave of old Mr. Story and his widow is close to the wall of the churchyard next the Manse, and is marked by a marble Iona cross with an appropriate inscription. A white rose bush grows on the grave, and sheds its leaves over the resting-place of the loved pastor, whose voice so long sounded in the mouldering ruin close by. Mr. Lorne Campbell is buried beside him, a man of integrity and sterling worth, long the local representative of the Duke of Argyll. Eminent as a practical farmer and agriculturist, and thoroughly trained in the management of large estates, and possessed of much force of character, Mr. Campbell, to the last, retained the unbounded confidence of the noble family of Argyll. Inside the low parapet wall of the grave are two large flat stones, much grown over with moss, and scarcely decipherable as to their inscriptions. On the upright headstone are recorded the names of Colin Campbell, died 1806, at the patriarchal age of 94; his wife, Ann, died 1834, and their son

Lorne, Chamberlain of Argyll, and factor on Rosneath estate, born 1791, and died 1859. A little way off is the large flat grey stone covering the resting-place of the Rev. James Anderson, who was ordained minister of Rosneath on 25th July, 1722, and died on the 28th day of June, 1744, in the 50th year of his age. West of this tomb is another massive flat slab, broken and much moss-grown, which covers the grave of another minister of Rosneath, the Rev. J. Kennedy. The inscription is in Latin, commencing, J. Kennedy, *apud Roseneath pastoris*, et V.D.M., 1765. Beyond this is a venerable flat stone in memory of Catherine Anne Campbell, died 1786, and her son Archibald; a similar one adjoining, to the memory of Alexander M'Phail, died 1788, aged 24. The following curious inscription occurs on a stone: "Here lies (in the grave's cold but hospitable bosom) the remains of Margery Cumming, who departed this life the 3rd June, 1801, aged 39 years. She was pleasant in life and pleasant at her end." The stone was placed by her husband, Donald M'Farlane. East of this, an old stone, with an inscription nearly all illegible except the date, 1716. The grave of a faithful servant, by name Margaret M'Phail, adjoins this; she was forty years in the families of Professor Muirhead, Glasgow, and of Mr. R. P. Wood, died 1862. Near the west end of the church is the head-stone over the grave of James Chalmers, farmer, Barbour, died 1768. An old family tomb, against the ruined fabric of the church, is that of the much respected Robert Campbell, who long resided in the Clachan House, where so many of the same name have lived. This grave has a deserted and ancient appearance, being canopied over with sombre yew trees and mantling ivy. Close beside it is the elegant monument, of a design much in vogue in the early part of the last century, erected over the remains of more than one member of the Argyll family. A classical stone pedestal is surmounted by a pyramid of correct and graceful architectural lines, but there is not a trace of any inscription. It is understood, however, that this monument is to the venerable tenant of old Campsail House, known as "Lady Carrick," from her having married Captain Campbell of Carrick. This lady, Jean, daughter of Archibald, ninth Earl of Argyll, the unfortunate nobleman who, following the fate of his illustrious father, was executed in Edinburgh in 1685, was married in 1725 to John Campbell of Carrick. Adjoining this grave is another, much overgrown with ivy and moss, understood to be the resting-place of the Reverend E. T. Bury, a clergyman of the Church of England, who was the second husband of Lady Charlotte Campbell, daughter of John, fifth Duke of Argyll. This lady was distinguished as an authoress. Her mother, Miss Gunning, was one of the famous beauties of the Court of George III. One of the old inhabitants of the Clachan well remembers the funeral, which was attended by several of the lady members and friends of the Argyll family,—the first time she had ever seen ladies at a funeral. The venerable narrator of the funeral was told the day before by old Malcolm M'Wattie, the gravedigger, " ye'll see a strange sicht on the morn, a minister walking through the kirk-yard readin' oot o' a book, wi' his sark on the tap o' his claes." A little way off is the burying ground of Mr. Dugald Campbell of Campbell's villas, well remembered for a racy humour, ever ready to come to the front on the occasion of public gatherings in the Clachan schoolhouse. His son John, one of the well known commanders of the Anchor Line, was drowned in the Atlantic, and his grandson Archibald also was cut off in early youth by a similar death in the Gareloch in 1884. The grave of the Robertsons of Strouel Lodge is at the west end of the church, under the belfry, William Robertson, who built the Lodge, died in 1858, aged 70; his widow, a much loved lady, Jane, daughter of Mr. Campbell of Ormidale, died 1872; and George Robertson, the last of the family in that line, born 1818, died 1887. Near this is the grave of the old ferryman of Coulport, Archibald Marquis, to whom allusion has already been made, in some respects a man of great energy and character, who died in 1890, aged 86. Near it is a very old stone with a death head and cross bones and hour glass sculptured on it.

Beyond this again is the large enclosed grave of an old family of Turners, who, for many generations, were farmers at Duchlage in the last and the present century. The names, Duncan, Archibald, Coll, and Malcolm, occur on the upright slab. Beyond is another enclosed tomb of an English clergyman, Reverend William Nelson Clarke, D.C.L., Ch. Ch., Oxon., who died in 1855, and an inscription in Latin, somewhat difficult to decipher, in which the words, *Nisi in cruce*, occur. Two plain old stones beyond record the death of Andrew M'Adam, died 1789 and Neil Fletcher, the respected old

fisherman near the Ferry Inn, who died in 1856, and his widow, Isobel Shearer, died 1886, aged 98—a most interesting and remarkable old Scotch character. Near the churchyard wall there is an old stone to the memory of Archibald Niven, who sailed boats and did all sorts of work, including teaching, in olden times, and died 1735. On the reverse of the slab are sculptured a rudely done cherub's head and wings, a male and a female figure, a coffin, a coat of arms, and representation of scales on the right hand, and the inscription:—
"Here lyes the corps of Archibald Niven, who died 1735, to whose memory this stone is inscribed." Mr. and Mrs. Stewart of Clynder House, old and respected residents in the parish, rest near this. A little way off is the grave of a greatly respected old native of Rosneath, John Sinclair, the old grave-digger and beadle, who died 1871, aged 78 years, and a neat mural slab is raised to his memory on the outside wall of the new church. A curious inscription is placed upon the upright old stone marking the grave, to the west of the church, of one of the numerous M'Farlanes of the Peninsula:—"Here lyes the body of John M'Farlane, son of John M'Farlane, farmer in Mukle Reheine, who died December 15, 1795," and on the back of the stone the rude lines:—

> " My glass is run, and thin is running,
> Remember death for judgment is cumming."

The last tomb which may be noticed is one near the extreme southwest corner of the churchyard to the memory of a faithful black servant, who is well remembered by a good many who live near

Rosneath. The inscription is understood to have been written by old Mr. Story.

"In memory of Robert Story, a native of Western Africa, in early life torn from home and sold in Rio di Janiero as a slave, then for his good fidelity he was set free by his master, whom loving, he followed to this country, and who retains the most grateful remembrance of his faithful services. In this parish he dwelt for many years, an example to all servants for honesty, sobriety, and truthfulness, ever reverent to his superiors, obliging to his equals, kind and courteous to all. His most blameless life, after severe suffering, meekly endured through faith in a Redeemer's love, was closed in peace and hope in the 30th year of his age on 4th August, 1848."

The above are the most noticeable tombs in the old churchyard, either from their greater age or from being in memory of some of the best known and respected inhabitants of the peninsula. The secluded, peaceful situation of this solemn spot, and its great antiquity, renders it a most appropriate resting place for the departed forefathers of Rosneath—

"Each in his narrow cell for ever laid."

During Mr. Story's ministry at Rosneath, and up to the memorable period of the Disruption of the Church of Scotland in May, 1843, there was little overt expression of dissent in the parish. The wave of ecclesiastical excitement which passed over Scotland at that time stirred up to unwonted agitation the placid waters of the Gareloch district, with the result that in due time a Free Church was established at Rosneath. At a meeting, held shortly after the Disruption, on the 18th of May, attended, amongst others, by Lorne Campbell, the well-known Chamberlain to the Duke of Argyll; James Campbell of Barbour, Shore Cottage; James Harrower, Campsail; Donald Turner, Clachan; Malcolm Chalmers, Mill Rahane; Archibald Turner, Peatoun; and John Orr, Meikle Rahane, it was resolved to set up a place of worship in connection with the Free Church. Two of these, Mr. James Campbell and Mr. Orr, were elders in the Parish Church—the former of whom still survives, in a green old age, highly respected for his piety and worth. The congregation assembled for the first time for worship in the then schoolhouse at Knockderry, and on alternate Sundays there and at the old Saw Mill, at the foot of the Mill Brae, near Campsail. On 23rd August a meeting was held to elect as Deacons Messrs. Lorne Campbell, Archd. Turner, James Harrower, Donald Turner, John M'Callum, and Malcolm Chalmers, and on the 13th October the Free Presbytery of Dunbarton met in the Saw Mill to moderate in a call to the Rev. John Grant of Pettie, who was inducted on the 7th of November. At the close of the service, the Rev. Dr. M'Farlane of Greenock laid the foundation stone of the existing edifice, which has ever since accommodated the Free Church congregation of both sides of the Peninsula. The two wings of the church were added about the year 1858, and though the architecture is of modest, unpretentious character, it is well suited to its surroundings amidst the fir woods of the Mill Brae.

Before the alteration the entire cost of the church was £404 15s. 4d., but the whole of the cutting of stones and a good deal of the labour was given free.

The success which attended the Free Church of Rosneath, especially in its early days, was largely due to the commanding influence and strong personality of Mr. Lorne Campbell, the chamberlain. He was a man of fine presence, of much benevolence and kindliness of heart, of powerful will, and he possessed the art of swaying men in an eminent degree. He was held in the highest esteem by the Argyll family, and his word was law throughout the Peninsula. His financial assistance was invaluable in erecting the church, which was opened for public worship on 28th April, 1844. Mr. Campbell, at his death in 1859, left £1000 to the Sustentation Fund of the Free Church of Scotland, to be invested by that Committee as they should see proper, the annual proceeds thereof to be paid to the minister of the Rosneath Free Church. He also built the existing school at Kilcreggan, and handed it as a gift to the Free Church of Rosneath, and left £500 to the Education Committee of the Free Church for behoof of the teacher. This school, after doing excellent work, was, upon the passing of the Scotch Education Act in 1873, handed over to the School Board, and the endowment was appropriated by the Endowed Education Commissioners, for the purpose of bursaries and scholarships.

The Rev. Mr. Grant continued as minister until 1855, when, owing to his delicacy of constitution, he had to travel abroad, and ultimately had to get a permanent assistant. The last of those who officiated in that capacity was the Rev. John M'Ewan, the present respected minister of the congregation. Mr. Grant's memory was long cherished as a man of simple, unostentatious piety, and a faithful pastor whose visits were highly appreciated by his people. As a preacher, he was effective and eloquent, rarely referring to his notes, and giving forth a sound and stimulating Bible message. In 1856 the Rev. John M'Ewan was chosen as minister over the congregation, a choice that has been evidently justified by his successful career. Mr. M'Ewan was born in Glasgow, and educated in the High School there, and thereafter became a clerk in the office of Messrs. A. A. Laird & Co., shippers. His gifts as a preacher are considerable, and he is a clear expositor of Scripture, his views being of an unswerving orthodoxy and characterised by much culture and vigour. The volume from which we have already quoted about the ministers of the Gareloch district has the following appropriate remarks concerning Mr. M'Ewan:—"He entered upon his duties at Rosneath with a zeal and earnestness that have never flagged during his incumbency of now over three decades." Like Goldsmith's village preacher, he considers himself "passing rich" on the annual quota distributed from the Church's Sustentation Fund, supplemented by whatever local balances the congregational exchequer yields, and has "never changed, nor sought to change his place." The two Storys, Dr. Shanks, Dr. Corbett, Mr. Young, and Mr. Warren have passed to their rest, or to a higher sphere of usefulness during these one and thirty years, while the minister of the Free Church remains, his hair—now quite abundant—blanched to the whiteness of the snow wreath, but otherwise he is as springy and vigorous as ever. His earlier discourses attracted the attention and commendation of the Rev. Dr. Candlish, who at this period, and for several consecutive years, was a summer resident at Kilcreggan. These sermons were eminently evangelical in tone, intensely earnest, and vigorously and impressively delivered." Mr. M'Ewan is seen to excellent advantage at his prayer meetings, conducted sometimes in a house at Kilcreggan, and frequently at the house of his respected elder, Mr. James Campbell, at Strouel. His addresses are pointed and full of fervour, and are listened to by the attached worshippers with an earnestness all the more striking from the habitual indifference to such gatherings exhibited by those who have fallen in with the prevailing laxity of the times. Besides Dr. Candlish, Dr. Buchanan, and other leaders of the Free Church who have preached in Rosneath Free Church, it has resounded to the eloquence of noble missionaries like Dr. Wilson of Bombay, and the Protestant patriot Gavazzi. On one occasion the somewhat eccentric Rev. Dr. Nathanael Paterson, Free St. Andrew's, Glasgow, author of the "Manse Garden," was preaching for Mr. M'Ewan. The latter observed his reverend friend sticking two pins through the manuscript of his sermon and into the leaves of the Bible to prevent his notes slipping out of their place. The worthy Doctor, observing Mr. M'Ewan's anxiety regarding the leaves of the sacred volume, remarked quietly, "Aye man, the Bible has got mony a waur dab than that!" Mr. M'Ewan is a diligent reader, and vigorous defender of the faith, diligent in the duties of his sacred calling, and will be encountered in remote corners of the Peninsula, faithful in his visitations to the members of his flock. In addition to his regular work as minister, Mr. M'Ewan has ever taken a deep interest in the educational work of the parish, has been a member of the School Board from its commencement, and for the last five years has filled the position of Chairman of the Board.

Mention has already been made of Craigrownie Parish Church, the foundation stone of which was laid on the 31st of July, 1852, by Mr. Abercromby of Craigrownie, and it was completed in the same year at a cost of over £1100. The architecture is of early English Gothic, with chancel nave and transepts, and the church originally was seated for 350, but increased accommodation was gained by an addition in 1889. It has a fine commanding situation on the high ground overlooking the waters of Loch Long and the Firth of Clyde, and an excellent manse stands in the vicinity of the church. The Rev. George Campbell, now the minister of Eastwood, near Glasgow, was ordained to the charge, and did good service in organising the work of the church. Shortly before he left the Communion was dispensed in the church for the first time, the officiating elders being Mr. John Dodds, schoolmaster, Rosneath, and Mr. John Lindsay, long the respected parish schoolmaster of Row, both of whom have passed away. The first elders were Mr. Adam Stewart, and Mr. James

Carsewell, and it was a great advantage to the summer visitors on that side of the Peninsula having regular Sabbath services.

Mr. Campbell remained little more than a year as minister of Craigrownie, and the choice of the congregation then fell upon the Rev. David Shanks. He was a native of Monkland, educated there and subsequently at Glasgow University, where he specially distinguished himself as a student in Hebrew, which he sedulously cultivated throughout his life. After leaving the University, Mr. Shanks for a short period was assistant to the revered Rev. Dr. Jamieson, of St. Paul's, Glasgow. Licensed in 1854, he was about twenty-five years old when he was ordained as minister of Craigrownie. In 1864 the church was raised to the status of a *quoad sacra* parish church, and Mr. Shanks, while diligently fulfilling his ministerial duties, also was appointed Clerk of the Dunbarton Presbytery on the death of Dr. Pearson of Strathblane. He was for years a member of the Rosneath School Board, in whose affairs he took deep interest. The University of Glasgow in 1885, recognising his eminence as a master of Oriental languages, conferred upon Mr. Shanks the degree of Doctor of Divinity. In June following a gratifying pecuniary presentation was made to him, shortly after which, owing to failing health, he made a trip to the East. Unfortunately, Mr. Shanks never regained his health, and he died in March, 1887, in the fifty-ninth year of his age, sincerely mourned by his attached congregation. In his funeral sermon, the Rev. Dr. Dykes of Ayr, bore warm testimony to the ability of his departed friend. "The ability of your late minister qualified him for a much more extended sphere of work than he ever attained. He was absolutely destitute of the showy elements of pulpit appearances, which so often secure to the preacher success, or, at least, temporary success. While many men who had not half his mental power rise to positions of eminence, he was therefore known and appreciated within a comparatively limited range. But to those who loved the thoughtful treatment of religious truth, his sermons were instinct with interest and instruction. His buoyant spirit, which so often brought the sense of pleasure into the homes which he visited, remained in some measure with him after the burden of illness was weighing him down; and those who had known him long were pained to see how, with evident difficulty, he was striving as long as he could, to do his work in cheerfulness and with patience."

The successor of Dr. Shanks is the Rev. Kenneth A. Macleay, B.D., a student of St. Andrews, who at that time was assistant at Wallacetown, near Ayr. The Rev. Principal Cuningham of St. Andrews, in introducing Mr. Macleay to the congregation, took occasion to refer to the excellence of his attainments, especially in his philosophical studies. Craigrownie church is well situated for the increasing requirements of the large summer population which is attracted to the picturesque shores of Loch Long. As far back as 1868, however, it was felt that the considerable villa population in the immediate vicinity of Kilcreggan pier would derive much advantage if they had a place of worship for those in communion with the Church of Scotland. A movement for subscriptions to erect a chapel was accordingly started, when a number of gentlemen, chiefly connected with Glasgow, who frequented Kilcreggan in summer, raised sufficient funds to build the present iron church. The Duke of Argyll had kindly granted a site for the chapel, which stands at the foot of the steep brae leading up from Kilcreggan pier, and opposite to the old ferry house. The church was opened for public worship on 30th May, 1869, when the services were conducted by the Rev. R. H. Story, the parish minister, and the Rev. Mr. Stephen of Renfrew. In his sermon, Mr. Story referred to the tradition that, previous to the Reformation, a church had existed almost upon this very site, and the name of the district, *Kilcraigan*, or Kilcreggan as it is now called, indicated the church of the Rock. The sum of £498 was taken in the church collection that day, a commendable commencement of the necessary funds. The first minister was the Rev. Robert S. Warren, at that time assistant to the Rev. Dr. Wylie of Carluke, the beloved friend of the Story family, who was introduced to his charge on the 18th July by the well-known Rev. George Matheson, now minister of St. Bernards, Edinburgh. Mr. Warren's popular and kindly gifts soon drew in a congregation to the new chapel, and much regret was expressed when, in June, 1872, he was called to Stranraer. On the 12th September, 1872, the Presbytery of Dunbarton met in the chapel to conduct the ordination services of the Rev. John Stevenson, B.D., who had been elected in June, and on the following Sabbath the new minister was introduced by the Rev. Dr. Graham of Kilbarchan. Mr. Stevenson is a native of

Ayrshire, and finished his education in Glasgow University, gaining honours in the arts and theological courses. After license by the Presbytery of Hamilton, he was first assistant in Kilbarchan Parish Church, and afterwards in Stevenston Parish Church, until his translation to Kilcreggan. Mr. Stevenson's retiring disposition and dislike to the somewhat effusively oratorical style adopted by some young preachers, cause his gifts to be well appreciated by those who like a quiet style of pulpit oratory. He has been content to remain in his present rather secluded position, where, while attending to his pastoral duties, he has time to gratify the tastes of his studious temperament. There is another small place of worship connected with the Church of Scotland, namely the iron chapel, built a number of years ago on the shores of Loch Long, near Peatoun. The chapel is only open for a short time in summer, but it fills its place in affording Gospel ministrations for those visitors who are unable to take the long walk of several miles to Craigrownie.

The other place of worship on the Loch Long side of the Peninsula is the United Presbyterian Church of Kilcreggan, situated about midway between Cove and Kilcreggan piers. With commendable liberality the Duke of Argyll granted a free site on ground near the shore, and in the first instance a wooden building was erected, which was opened for worship on 20th June, 1858, by the well-known Rev. Dr. King of Greyfriars, Glasgow. In 1862 Dr. King left for London, and on 17th June of the same year the Rev. Mr. Corbett was inducted to the charge. Mr. Corbett continued minister until 25th

April, 1869, when he preached his farewell sermon, and left a considerable and attached congregation. The old wooden structure had served its purpose, and the foundation stone of the handsome stone structure, in which the worshippers now assemble, was laid by the Rev. Mr. Corbett on 10th August, 1867. Upon Mr. Corbett's removal to Manchester in 1869, his successor was appointed in the person of the Rev. Forrest F. Young, afterwards of Wark-on-Tyne, who was ordained as second minister. On 14th June, 1869, the present church was opened for public worship—a commodious edifice, which was designed by Mr. Hugh Barclay, architect, Glasgow, holding 600, and erected at a cost, including price of site, of £3,098. In the same year the manse was built at a cost of £1,069, and furnished by the managers of the church at a subsequent period, when there was no regular minister, and the charge was temporarily filled during the summer months. Amongst those who thus occupied the pulpit were well known ministers, such as Doctors Logan Aikman, James Brown of Paisley, Joseph Brown, J. M'Fadyen, Goodrich of Glasgow. On the 28th August, 1883, the Rev. Robert M'Lean, M.A., of the U.P. Church, Millport, was inducted to the vacant church, and remained until 17th December, 1891, when he demitted his charge to go to Liverpool, to the great regret of his flock. His ministrations were highly appreciated, as a preacher he was much in request, and his talents and energy were apparent in whatever he undertook. His successor, the Rev. Armstrong Black, had for years filled a charge in Edinburgh, and was held in esteem by an attached congregation.

CHAPTER V.

Traditions, Natural History, and Folk Lore.

In the statistical account of Scotland, published under the auspices of Sir John Sinclair in the year 1792, the details regarding the parish of Rosneath were furnished by the Rev. George Drummond, so long its minister. It was meagre in its facts, and written without any attempt to embellish the baldness of the narrative. The parish apparently could sufficiently supply its inhabitants with provisions, if they were not obliged to sell their produce for ready money in order to pay their rents. The land rent of the parish amounted to about £1,000 sterling. The population of the Peninsula, according to Dr. Webster, was 521; amongst them were 7 weavers, 3 smiths, 4 shoemakers, 5 tailors, 96 herring fishermen, 5 Seceders, 14 Cameronians. The annual rent of a cottage and yard was from ten shillings to twenty shillings. The fish commonly caught were cod, mackerel, skate, flounders, and salmon—the latter fish sold from 1d. to 3d. per pound. One salmon fishery, with piece of ground attached, let for £30 a year. A small lake on the upper moor of the parish abounded with perch.

There were no villages in the Peninsula, but 98 dwelling-houses, all detached, scattered over its surface. There had been a decrease in the population since the previous returns, owing to the proprietor taking some farms into his own possession, and thereby displacing several families who formerly lived on them. The church was rebuilt in 1780 and the manse in 1770. The average stipend of the parish, including the glebe, was £110, which was paid by the three heritors, the Duke, Campbell of Peatoun, and Cumming of Barremman. The educational wants of the population were met by a schoolmaster, who enjoyed the modest salary of £8 9s., while, in addition, the fees and perquisites amounted to £8 7s. In winter the number of scholars was 38, and £18 the annual amount raised for support of the poor of the parish. The provisions which were in use in the parish were of the usual kind customary in rural districts of Scotland. The cost was small compared with prices of the present day. Beef and veal 5d. the pound, mutton 4d. to 6d. the pound. A good hen cost 1s., a chicken 4d.; butter was 9d. to 1s. the pound; oats sold for 13s. the boll. The wages of a common labourer, without victuals, were 10d. to 1s.; joiner, 2s. a day; mason, 2s.; and a tailor, 8d. a day and his meat. The common fuel used by the cottagers was peat, only a few families using coal, which cost 5s. per cart. Though there were no regular ale-houses or taverns, yet, in the language of the minister, there were "plenty of whisky houses," and the morals of the natives suffered in consequence. Almost no cottagers were employed in agriculture, unless by the

Duke of Argyll. It spoke well for the residents, however, that for upwards of twenty years no person residing in the parish had been imprisoned, except one poor man, for a short time, for a small debt.

Salmon and sea-trout were common in the Gareloch, and the herring were regular in their visits, and taken in abundance. There were also oysters and abundance of mussels in the Gareloch, and the tunny fish had been captured in the loch of the great length of 9 feet. At one time it was believed that the soil of the Rosneath Peninsula had the remarkable peculiarity of being so abhorrent to rats that none of those unpleasant animals would frequent it. The Glasgow and Greenock skippers were in the habit of shipping earth as ballast from Rosneath so as to secure immunity from the plague of rats, and it was currently alleged that a sagacious West Indian planter had actually imported a quantity of the earth of the Peninsula in the hope of exterminating the creatures, which were destroying his sugar canes.

When the rebellion of 1715 under the Earl of Mar took place, the parish minister caused the Clachan bell to be rung, and gathered fifty stout parishioners together, and marched at their head to join the Duke of Argyll, who fought on the side of the Government. When they drew near to Stirling, they were by chance met by the Duke himself, who was much astonished when he encountered the party and was informed of their errand. He remarked that the men of Rosneath were more suitable for handling the plough and the oar, than the sword or spear, but commended them for their patriotism, and retained some of them for service on the boats on the Forth, which supported the army on shore.

Rosneath is greatly changed in many ways since 1839, when the Rev. Robert Story wrote his short but interesting sketch of the parish for the then *Statistical Account of Dunbartonshire*. He then commented upon the mildness of the climate and the healthfulness of the parish as indicated by the remarkable longevity of the population, and in spite of the fact that a considerable part of the surface of the parish consisted of marshy grounds. The prevalent diseases then were rheumatic and pulmonary affections, which was accounted for by the moistness of the climate and the nature and situation of the cottages. Fevers rarely occurred, and were almost in all instances traceable to infection brought from outside the parish. During the visitation of Asiatic cholera there were two cases, both of which terminated fatally, and but little assistance was given by the terror-stricken inhabitants; the minister himself having had personally to wait upon both the patients, and superintend their interment.

The waters of Loch Long and the Gareloch were in these days singularly pellucid and free from pollution, which is more than can be said of their present condition. The great increase of population which has taken place and consequent discharge of drainage into the Loch, and the numerous steamers and yachts which frequent its waters would account for the difference. There is a considerable stream in both Lochs, in the Gareloch especially; between the Row Point and Rosneath the current runs at the rate of three and a half miles an hour. There is excellent holding ground and deep water for vessels in the Gareloch, and when trade is dull as many as a dozen large steamers have been anchored at various points in the Loch. The passage at the "Narrows" used to be a good deal deeper; it is now not above six fathoms, and off Barremman pier it increases to sixteen fathoms, while the deepest part of the Loch is about midway between Strouel bay and the Shandon side, where it attains a depth of twenty-five fathoms. In former years the Loch was much used by the early Kings of Scotland as a station for the royal navies, and about seventy years ago a 74 gun ship-of-war lay for a long time at anchor between Row and Rosneath Castle point. Not far from this the fine old wooden ship, H.M.S. *Empress*, now lies at anchor, having been granted by the Admiralty for the purpose of a Training-ship for boys, the bulk of whom enter the merchant service, and many of them, eventually, the Royal Navy. This beneficent institution has done great good, and at the present time about 400 boys are under instruction in the ship, under the energetic superintendence of Captain Deverell, R.N. There is an Executive Committee of well-known Glasgow gentlemen who manage the affairs of the Training-ship, which comes under the Industrial Schools Act of 1866. The boys are eligible above eleven and under fourteen years of age, and are admitted under a magistrate's warrant for any of the following causes :—Begging or receiving alms ; found wandering and having no settled home or visible mode of subsistence ; found destitute, either being an orphan or having a parent undergoing imprisonment, or being charged with an offence punishable by an imprisonment or a less punishment and under twelve years of age, and also boys refractory in a poorhouse or pauper school, and under fourteen years of age. The boys are carefully instructed in various branches under an efficient staff of teachers, and are taught certain trades, shoe-making, tailoring, and carpenter work, etc., and thoroughly instructed in seamanship. They are divided into 22 messes of 18 boys in each, with a captain and second captain to keep order. Careful religious instruction is also imparted, and the boys assemble to worship morning and evening, when a pleasing effect is heard on shore as the strains of the hymn are wafted across the waters of the Loch. During summer, all the most advanced boys are sent away in the brig *Cumbria*, attached as a tender to the *Empress*, and learn the duties of practical seamanship. Government defrays the principal expense of the training-ship, but subscriptions to a good amount are received from the public, and a small sum is contributed from the public rates for a certain class of boys. The previous Training-ship, the *Cumberland*, was moored in the same waters for seventeen years, and maliciously set on fire by four boys in February, 1889. All who witnessed the grand spectacle of the conflagration of the gallant old ship in the early hours before dawn, will never forget the sight. The whole scenery of the Gareloch shores was lit up with lurid red fire, each rocky promontory and verdant height bathed with crimson tint, and great streams of flame surging up to heaven from the doomed ship. Happily no lives were lost, owing to the promptitude and coolness of the Captain, aided by the teachers on board, but a favourite dog of the captain's was unfortunately suffocated in one of the cabins.

Fifty years ago the waters of the Gareloch abounded in salmon, shoals of herring, and numerous other fish, which found a ready market in Greenock and Glasgow. The herring were wont to appear in the Gareloch sooner than in any of the neighbouring inlets of the sea, and were reckoned equal to those of the far-famed Loch Fyne. Flights of gulls and other aquatic birds indicated the welcome arrival of the herring shoals, and the fishermen on the Loch side were on the alert with their boats. The herrings come to the Loch in autumn and winter, and even in May and June sometimes there are abundance of fish. Mr. James Campbell of Strouel has fished in the loch for over sixty years, and can give graphic descriptions of how he used to start in the early dawn, after gathering sufficient bait at low water, often in bitter cold weather, and get a good boat-load of fish. In these days the cost of hiring men was less than half what it now is, and a pretty good living could be made. There were various stations on the Gareloch with stake-nets, where large quantities of salmon were got, yielding a considerable revenue to the proprietors. In the 12th century, Amalec, the Earl of Lennox, granted to the monks of Paisley a right to all the salmon-fishing in the Gareloch, reserving to himself and heirs every fourth salmon. Cod-fishing also used to be prosecuted with much success in the Gareloch, and one old fisherman, thirty years ago, used to catch sometimes, in an afternoon, with the line and mussel bait, ten or eleven stone of fish of different sorts, cod predominating; many of them ten, twelve, and sixteen pounds weight. On one occasion he took with the line a cod twenty-three pounds weight, in the loch opposite Strouel Bay. But now, different causes prevent the fish coming up the lochs, the beam trawlers being one special element. Mussel bait is now difficult to get in any quantity, whereas, in former years, there were immense deposits of mussels in the Strouel Bay and near the "Narrows" of the loch. As many as ten and twelve large fishing-boats would be seen gathering mussels at low tide, and would carry away, each of them, tons of splendid mussels. And even now there is much reason for the Board of Fishery interfering, to protect the small remains of the mussel beds on the Gareloch and the contiguous arms of the sea. It is a pity to see men coming in boats and tearing up the immature mussel scalps, to sell the shell-fish in Glasgow and elsewhere, in a condition quite unfit for removal.

Seventy years ago the herring-fishing was a great source of profit and occupation to many who resided on the shores of the Gareloch. The owners of fishing-boats resided all up the lochside, from Row on to Faslane Bay, Gareloch-head, Rahane, Mamore, Crossowen, Clynder, Campsail Bay, Kilcreggan, and on to Coulport, where the Marquis family followed this occupation for well on to a century. Mr. Campbell can remember the time when over 100 fishing-boats would be in the loch at one time, a good number coming from ports on the East coast, and elsewhere. Now—such is the change from various causes

—there is only one solitary fishing-boat from the Gareloch which regularly prosecutes the herring-fishing outside the loch. The boats were large two-masted ones, half-decked, and they went to all the lochs on the West coast in the season, three men to each boat. In the Gareloch, the herring mostly abounded in the upper end, and the boats anchored close together and shot their nets. The herrings were so plentiful that it was no unusual thing for one boat to get as many as ten thousand herrings in a night, and the fish would sell at sixpence a hundred. The buyers came from Greenock, and often their custom was to go from boat to boat in the evening, before fishing commenced, and distribute bottles of whisky to the crews, a bottle to each boat, on the understanding that they got the night's take next day at their own price, the price being made up by agreement among the buyers. Most of the fishermen came from the Highlands, and engaged for the season, from June to November, at wages from £1 to £2 a month. During the rest of the year a good many found engagements with the farmers on shore. About 1827, the herring-fishing began to fall off, and in a few years very few boats went out, as the fish ceased to frequent the loch in anything like the former quantity. Gradually the boats were hauled up high and dry, or sold, and the herring-fishing practically became a thing of the past. Still, occasionally the fish return in great numbers, and twenty-five years ago there were large shoals in the loch. Salmon were tolerably abundant, and there were stake nets at different stations on the Gareloch where many fish were got. On the Loch Long side there was a small thatched house, near Peatoun, where Mr. Campbell lived, and had bag nets for catching salmon, fixed by heavy anchors to the bottom, yielding a fair supply.

As has been already observed, there is but little record of events of any historical interest connecting Rosneath with the stream of Scottish history. In the Loch Lomond expedition, in 1715, directed against the MacGregors, who had taken forcible possession of the island of Inch Murrin, and performed various acts of rebellion, amongst the gentlemen of the county who offered their services appear two Rosneath proprietors, John Campbell of Mamore, and John Campbell of Peetoune, as the name was spelt. This John Campbell of Mamore was a public spirited man, and an order appears authorised by the county authorities, under date 17th October, 1715, by which he was to be paid 240 pounds Scots for furnishing the "shyre" with ammunition and drums, and for defraying certain expenses. The MacGregors had long given trouble under the famous Rob Roy, who, as is well known, lived in the Inversnaid district on Loch Lomond, and thence made excursions for the purpose of levying black mail. This expedition seems to have been a formidable affair, and to have excited much attention at the time, partly, no doubt, on account of the exaggerated stories of the prowess of the renowned Highland freebooter. On the 11th of October, 1715, a considerable force of armed men from the ships of war then lying off Dunbarton, with two large screw guns and other appurtenances of war, were drawn up the rapid stream Leven into Loch Lomond. They were joined by the men of Kilpatrick, Rosneath, Row and Cardross, and after them on horseback, the Honourable Master John Campbell of Mamore, uncle of the Duke of Argyle, attended by a fine train of the gentlemen of the shire, amongst them Archibald M'Aulay of Ardincaple, Aulay M'Aulay, his eldest son, George Napier of Kilmahew, Walter Graham of Kilmardinny, James Hamilton of Barnes, and others richly mounted and well armed. At Luss they were joined by the Colquhouns. On the 13th October they effected a landing at Inversnaid, and drew up on the mountain side, and made a fine appearance; so narrates the quaint account of the expedition drawn up by one present, their flags flying and drums beating with all the ardour of war. The enemy, however, discreetly kept out of sight, or could only be descried far up on the summits of the lofty rocks, therefore they were obliged to content themselves with carrying off the boats of the Macgregors, with any fittings and stores on which they could lay their hands.

In Mr. Story's account of the parish, he speaks highly of the character of the natives of the Peninsula, they were well conducted, sensible, and judicious in the management of their affairs, sturdy and industrious, and exemplary in their attendance on religious ordinances. Many of the families had regular daily worship, and were diligent readers of the Scriptures, whilst occasionally there were remarkable examples of the transforming power of God. Even at that time the periodical influx of strangers for the summer months, although in some respects advantageous, was not regarded without serious misgivings in its moral and religious bearings. In such a country district agriculture and fishing were the principal employments of the people, and the Duke of Argyll gave a good deal of work in various ways, amongst others in opening up limestone and slate quarries. It was found, however, that lime could more easily and cheaply be obtained from the North of Ireland, and the slate quarries did not pay. A few years previously much judicious planting had been carried out; the Gallowhill, which is a hill opposite Greenock, used to be a mere heath and furze cover for game, but was then covered to its summit with an extensive and luxuriant forest of firs, which subsequently the proprietor cut down.

Sixty years ago there were hardly any of the fine villas which now form such a feature in the Peninsula, and the population congregated in the small villages or groups of cottages at the Clachan, Kilcreggan, Barbour, and Rahane. The cottages were contiguous and self-contained, and in the very smallest there were always two apartments. There were no turnpike roads, but good carriage drives and farm roads, mostly kept in order by the tenants, and one highway, stretching from near Kilcreggan all along the upper part of the parish over to Peatoun, and there meeting the road from Cove across the hill to Rahane, gave access to the farms on the high ground. The oldest road in the Peninsula is the one which extends over from Coulport, across the upper moor, then down upon Rahane, where it joins the shore road leading to Rosneath and Row ferries. The road used formerly to start from Letter farm, then up to the moor, along the top of which it kept for a considerable distance, then took a slant down above Barremman House, crossing the field between the present avenue and the wood above, and came out upon the shore road at Hattonburn. This latter part of the road has long been closed as a carriage road, and also from the brow of the moor above Rahane down to Coulport, but pedestrians going along it will be repaid by a series of singularly fine views of the receding heath-clad slopes and promontories of Loch Long. For hundreds of years it was the great road to the Argyleshire Highlands, across the Ferry between Ardentinny and Coulport, and then over to Row, for the droves of sheep and cattle going to markets in Dunbarton and Stirling shires. Steamers began regularly to appear in the Gareloch and adjoining waters before 1830, but the open packet boat or wherry still made the passage from Rosneath and Kilcreggan to the surrounding ports, and soon after, the daily penny post, subsidiary to Helensburgh, gave postal facilities. The carrier crossed the ferry with his bag and went along the shore to Clynder, then up to the hill farms, but frequently letters would lie days at the primitive post-office before being called for.

In those days education was in a very different state from what it is now, but at Rosneath the different branches of both commercial and classical instruction were taught by the efficient parish schoolmaster. The old school-house still stands facing the churchyard, the room at the left as you enter being the one where the children were taught, but the existing school-house at the end of the Clachan village was built about 1835. The salary was considered good in those days, amounting to nearly £80 per annum, with the fees, 2s. 6d. for reading, 3s. for writing, and 3s. 6d. for arithmetic. There was also a school in the parish at Knockderry, Loch Long, the teacher of which had a salary of £35 a year guaranteed to him by Mr. Lorne Campbell, the Duke's chamberlain. Though the parents paid 5s. per quarter for each child, yet the fees fell short of the sum guaranteed on account of the limited numbers attending, still it was a boon to the neighbourhood. There was also a small girls school established by the late Duchess of Argyll, chiefly for the purpose of instructing the girls in sewing, which for a number of years was carried on in the neat one-storeyed cottage at the end of the yew tree avenue. Now there is a School Board, and large well-appointed schools at Rosneath and Kilcreggan, and also, for a portion of the year, at Peatoun. There was also a good subscription library in those days, consisting of several hundred volumes in various departments of literature, and a juvenile library for the use of those who attended the Sabbath School. Neither friendly society nor savings bank existed at that time in the parish, and the farmers and their servants had to send to Greenock to lodge deposits. Reference has been made to the changes since the date of the former account, when there were about 96 herring-fishermen, and the whole effective male population were largely engaged in this calling. The farms were in a poor condition, imperfectly cultivated, and of such small dimensions as rather to merit the name of crofts. As farming was rather a precarious calling, the fishing fraternity hung together considerably, and on the division of funds by each boat's crew, there was a scene of drinking and treating, not over conducive to sobriety and morality.

Smuggling was quite an institution in Rosneath in the early part of the century, and many are the stirring reminiscences of some old natives in regard to this violation of the excise laws, which in those days was considered a venial offence. The form of the parish rendered it highly suitable for such operations, which were carried on by some of the younger fishermen, who found a ready market for their illicit produce in Greenock, Port-Glasgow, and other towns. Several of the burns on the Rosneath side, near Strouel and Clynder, were haunts of the smugglers, the one running into Strouel Bay in particular; and several of those who knew the Loch sixty years ago, are able to narrate their experience. At that time the revenue cutters kept a sharp look out for smugglers, although they were as a rule much more lenient in their operations than the regular Dunbarton excisemen. On one occasion the crew of a revenue cutter landed on the Peatoun shore, and all but took red-handed a number of smugglers engaged at their trade. Soon the news spread, and the natives emerged from their crofts, both men, women, and boys, and a goodly array confronted the revenue men as they were carrying off the spoil. Thus armed they encountered the revenue officers, who demanded a passage through, but were, owing to the force of numbers, compelled to yield up the booty they had. Shortly after regaining their vessel, the exulting crowd of Rosneath natives were standing triumphantly surveying the vessel, when all of a sudden the latter sent several cannon shots amongst the astonished crowd of spectators. Fortunately no one was hurt, but they beat a rapid retreat, and kept well out of sight the next time the cutter made her appearance on a voyage of investigation.

At Rosneath, in former days, marriage ceremonies were accompanied by more elaborate festivities than at present, and sometimes they were rather boisterous. Crowds assembled at the ceremony, and, on the intermediate days before the kirking, the young couple and their attendants, preceded by a bag-piper, perambulated the parish, from house to house, visiting their friends. The ceremonies were closed by the whole party, after divine service on Sabbath, adjourning for refreshments to the nearest tavern. Baptisms were too often desecrated by the accompanying ceremonies, and, after the service in church, the friends and relatives proceeded to the inn, and indulged in copious libations of ardent spirits. Even the funerals sometimes partook of the character of orgies, four services of spirits, with accompanying viands, being considered becoming honour to the departed. On the farms round the Gareloch some curious old customs lingered on till about sixty years ago. There was the cutting of the last sheaf, the "maiden," as it was called here and elsewhere in Scotland, and this sheaf, usually adorned with ribbons, was hung up in the farmhouse, and allowed to remain for months, sometimes even for years.

Before the days of the coaches and steamers, it was difficult often to keep up communications between the Peninsula and the mainland. Sometimes the Dukes of Argyll would send their baggage on to Inveraray by one or two men carrying a pack or portmanteau strapped on to their shoulders, and they would take the ferry from Coulport across to Ardentinny, and thence to the Duke's principal Castle. Mr. J. Campbell, Strouel, well remembers, more than fifty years ago, one bitter cold November night, bringing the wife of Mr. Proudfoot, the minister of Arrochar, all the way from the Ferry Inn to her own house, in his father's cart, there being no other way of transit. And I am informed by the well known chairman of the Glasgow School Board that, when his father tenanted the small house at Altmore, near Barremman, fifty-six years ago, on one occasion of illness the only doctor at Helensburgh had to be summoned in a small boat which chanced to be within hail. The first regular doctor only settled in the Peninsula a good many years subsequently.

Kilcreggan and Cove have for some years enjoyed an excellent water supply, a state of affairs which was much needed, owing to the inadequacy of the water afforded by the surface wells and burns of the district in dry seasons. Considering that the population on that side of the Peninsula swells to over 2000 in the summer, the Commissioners of Police, who were also the local authority, decided to arrange for a water supply ample for years to come. After long consideration, it was decided to get the water from a small loch above Coulport, named Lochan Ghlass Lavigh, or the "Grey Lake." This loch gathers the drainage of 210 acres, a sufficient quantity of water, if stored, to meet the requirements of a far larger population than ever Kilcreggan possesses. The loch has a surface of 20 acres, and is over 50 feet deep, and it was arranged that the water should be drawn off at 10 feet deep, so that there would be a supply of 42 million gallons available for the population of the district. A stand tower was erected some little way into the loch, with three inlet pipes, so that the water could be drawn off at different levels. The loch being about 540 feet above the sea level, the proposal was to carry the water down 150 feet, where water filters and a clear water tank were erected. The water would rise to any part of the houses which might be built upon the road, the highest level of which was 322 feet above the sea. The clear water tank holds 165,000 gallons, being about four days' supply. In all there were over 13 miles of pipes from Coulport on the north, to Port Kiln on the south, and the total cost of the works was about £9,000. The Duke of Argyll, the superior of the land, gave the water and all the necessary land, in addition to a handsome subscription.

On 26th November, 1881, the first sod was cut in connection with the water works, on a spot not far from Kilcreggan pier, by Provost Clark, chairman of the Water Committee, before a large assemblage of the residents of the district, the local clergy, and friends from Glasgow. The Provost gave a slight sketch of the initiation and progress of the scheme for supplying the district with water, and alluded to the privations which the inhabitants sometimes felt owing to the extreme dryness of recent seasons. Subsequently the Provost entertained the company at his residence, and speeches were made and toasts duly honoured in connection with the important undertaking. On 20th July, 1882, the Duke of Argyll performed the opening ceremony of turning on the new water supply, in the presence of a large assembly, in very unpropitious weather. A grand marquee was erected for the accommodation of the company, and the proceedings began by Mr. M'Cracken, the Burgh Clerk, reading an address to the Duke from the Magistrates and Commissioners of the Burgh, thanking His Grace for coming personally to inaugurate the water works. The Rev. Mr. Shanks, minister of Craigrownie, then asked the blessing of the Almighty on the works now happily completed. Thereafter the Duke drank a sample of the water from a silver cup which was presented to him, remarking to the assemblage :—" It's just a wee drumlie to-day, but it's quite sweet tasted,"—an announcement received with cheering and laughter.

Rosneath, happily, seems always to have been exempt from any serious crimes, if we except the remarkable double murder committed early in the past century, by one who would have succeeded to the old estate of Peatoun. This remarkable crime attracted great attention at the time, and an account of it was shortly afterwards published, but is now rarely to be met with. John Smith was born in Greenock, the son of Robert Smith, a rich merchant there, and was early discovered to be of a sullen, revengeful, malicious disposition. Some years after his father's death, his mother, Elizabeth Stirrat, was married to John Campbell, brother-german to the Laird of

Rachean, in the parish of Rosneath. When John Smith came of age he got his patrimony into his own hands and for a time carried on a successful clandestine trade with Ireland. After some years he rented the farm of Mamore near Peatoun, where his mother lived. Subsequently he married Margaret Campbell, the daughter of the laird of Peatoun, in the year 1721. On the very day of the marriage, he set his affections on Janet Wilson, one of the girls who attended upon his bride, though he did not reveal this to the former until January 1725, when he dissuaded her from marrying a gentleman who sought her hand. Still something excited the unfortunate bride's suspicions, who observed in hearing of the company, that "if she was dead that night, she did not doubt that John Smith would court Janet Wilson the next day." Soon after this Smith gave Janet a ring, and said "that he loved his son and her the best of any in the world, and that if his wife were dead, and she remained, he would marry none other but her." In April, 1725, John Smith gave Janet Wilson a book, in which was a letter written on one side with common ink, on the other with his blood, in which he told her she need never fear want, as he would give her the half of his substance, and he desired her to bury this letter as it was written with his blood, and this she faithfully carried out. They kept up a correspondence by slipping letters into their hands when they met, as it were accidentally. On 24th May, 1725, they met at Clynder, and Smith swore upon the Bible, which he took from his pocket, that he would give her a thousand merks for refusing to marry a man who had sought her hand, and that he would marry her when his wife was dead. It seems that he was unable to raise the sum which he had promised out of his own means, and the only method he had of getting the money was by murdering his sister Katharine, whose portion was to fall in to him if she died without children.

On Wednesday, 15th December, 1725, the body of Katharine Smith was found dead in a pool of water not very far from Peatoun, near a place which she often frequented on her way over the moor. The body was carried to Mamore, her brother John's house, and on the day of her funeral he consulted a lawyer about the recovery of the sum of money which was to fall to him in event of her death without issue. As yet there were no suspicions of her having met with her death by foul means. Meanwhile the murderer had accomplished but part of his horrible oath, and his wife being alive, he could not marry Janet Wilson until the former was out of the way. On the 3rd of September, 1726, after John Smith had taken breakfast with his wife, he and she were seen to go together towards the mill of Rachean, or Rahane, but on different sides of the glen. She went to the miller's house, and after a little got up saying she had to meet her husband near the place where her body was afterwards found, and was never again seen alive. Shortly afterwards, John Smith went home, dressed himself and mounted his horse, and as he rode by the mill of Rahane he asked if his wife had been there, and then rode on to the market of Drumford, three miles off. When there a Highlander stared fixedly at him, and told a friend that John Smith had either committed, or was about to commit, some evil deed. He came home about four in the afternoon, and a little way from home the servant met him and told him her mistress had not come in since the morning, and she supposed she was in a neighbour's house. He replied that she was not there, for he had enquired as he went by, adding, he was afraid she might have fallen and hurt herself. Search was then made in the fields near Mamore, her husband being observed to be looking in a place where it was told him it was impossible his wife could be. After leaving this spot he again returned to it, and he desired one of the searchers, a young woman, to look narrowly into some bushes there. She did so, and told him she saw a woman's head, when he replied, "Oh, that's my dear," and ran about apparently in a distracted state. The body was carried to the barn at Mamore, and the murderer desired his servants and others who were in the house to meet there and have family worship as usual. The Bible opened at the Psalms, and it was observed that he changed the Psalm wherein occurred threatenings against bloody men to another. The poor murdered woman was buried at Rosneath churchyard on the following Monday.

Some days afterwards suspicions appeared to have fallen against John Smith, and the rumours grew so pointed that the Hon. John Campbell of Mamore, being a Justice of Peace, was obliged to notice them, and apprehended the murderer in the churchyard of Rosneath, on the 3rd of November, where he was attending a funeral. On being seized, he appealed to God the searcher of hearts, and protested his innocence, continuing to do so until the Sabbath, when he confessed the murder. It appears that Smith attended church that day when the minister discoursed about the shocking murders that had been committed in the parish, and it was noticed that the murderer himself was the least affected person in the congregation. Certain papers, however, had been found at his residence at Peatoun, gravely incriminating Smith, and he thereafter made confession to the minister and one of the justices who visited him. He was committed to jail at Dunbarton, and his trial came off on the 13th December, being that very day twelve months on which he murdered his sister. He confessed his crimes before the jury, and received the sentence of death with the greatest unconcern, being appointed for execution on 20th January, 1727. Upon the 25th December he was brought to church, where he listened in an unconcerned manner to the service, though he showed emotion at night in his cell to those who visited him. A day or two after he made a determined effort to escape from prison, having managed to free himself from his irons, and had well nigh succeeded in his daring attempt. When he was convinced there was no further chance of escape from his doom, he showed more penitence, and expressed his hope in the mercy of God. He confessed that he had premeditated both the murders a considerable time before he accomplished them, and that when he had allured them to the place where the crimes took place, his heart misgave him, until he provoked them to say something that might irritate him. His sister he threw into a pool of water, and she recovering herself and crying, "Lord preserve me," he went down into the water, and by holding up her heels kept her head under water till she died. As to his wife, he confessed that after he had decoyed her into the thicket, the provocation he made her give him was that she would keep a part of a web of cloth for the use of her family, the whole of which he said he would sell. Whereupon he threw her into the pool with such force that she received some cuts on her head upon a rock on the other side, and thinking it would not favour his design of concealing the murder to leave her there, he took her up into his arms, and carried her some little distance to the place where afterwards her body was found.

Upon the day before his execution John Smith was confronted with Janet Wilson, and they both agreed in this, that the oath taken at Clynder, was to bind him to pay the 1,000 merks if she should live unmarried, waiting till he was able to become her husband, and to this she consented. Next day he was attended to the place of his execution by the Rev. Mr. Bayne, minister of Bonhill, Rev. Mr. Sydserf, minister of Dunbarton, and by Rev. Mr. Anderson, minister of Rosneath, who, after they had given most suitable exhortations to him and to all present, prayed to God fervently for the murderer. He himself was much affected, and earnestly begged God for forgiveness of his crimes, both of which he owned with all their aggravations, and lamented his profaning the Lord's table when his hands were reeking with the blood of his sister. He seemed very penitent and spoke solemnly to the spectators, entreating them not to encourage themselves in secret sins, in the hope of their not being discovered, for he had no peace of mind after the murder of his sister. Further, he commented upon the truth of that passage, "The bloody and deceitful man shall not live out half his days," which was truly fulfilled in his case, as he had scarcely arrived at the third portion of the time allottted by the Scriptures as the term of a man's life, and it was added that the whole scene had a very edifying effect upon the spectators of the execution.

There is still living in the Clachan village, Miss Macdougal, whose father was for ten years with the son of John Smith, who subsequently, through his mother, succeeded to the estate of Peatoun. Her father had often heard the stories connected with the mysterious murders, and it would appear that the death of Smith's sister was witnessed from a distance by a man, who having been pursued for sheep-stealing, had taken refuge in a thick rowan tree. This man described the unfortunate woman's death, how she and her brother had an altercation, whereupon he twisted her long hair round his arm and tried to throw her down, but she being a very strong woman, made a violent resistance. In Miss Macdougal's father's time the Ferry Inn was kept by people called M'Arthur; this was over a hundred years ago, and much drinking went on, although in the immediate neighbourhood there were two other public houses, one in the Clachan village, and the other an old thatched cottage in the field opposite the Manse. Her mother remembered when old John Campbell, Crossowen, was married in the church to Janet Colquhoun, and that day there was a marriage, a funeral, and a baptism. The bride carried the baby, who was the late Mr. Kerr of Springfield, and her mother even remembered the blue ribbons adorning the bride's shoes. After the ceremony, which was performed by Dr. Drummond, the parish minister, the company all adjourned to the public house, near the manse, and copious refreshments were served, and dancing continued to a late hour—a collection having first been made for the bellman. Old Mrs. Macdougal had a cousin, Archibald Marquis, whose family for about a hundred years kept the ferry at Coulport, on Loch Long, who had many traditions of the olden times at Rosneath. He had heard details of the visit of the young Pretender, Prince Charles Edward, after the disastrous Battle of Culloden, who slept a night at Knockderry, near Cove. Marquis had heard the story from the old tenant's daughter, who was a Campbell, and lived to the great age of 103. Prince Charles wanted Campbell to ferry him across to Stronhoulen on Loch Long side, and while the wife was getting breakfast ready she overheard the proposal, and was in great apprehension lest they should be deprived of their farm for assisting the outlaw in his flight. So she fell upon the expedient of filling her husband's brogues with boiling water and thus scalding his feet, which effectually prevented him from conveying the Prince to his destination. Miss Macdougal's father remembered the old church quite well, the one prior to the existing ruined fabric, a very handsomely decorated building, of cruciform shape, with a row of images round the pulpit, a fine font for holy water, and the staircase leading up to the family pew of the Duke of Argyll.

Old Mr. Macdougal was of an hospitable turn of mind, and was fond of entertaining the natives on their holiday occasions, and when they assembled for their favourite shinty sports. On New Year's day there was generally a great shinty match played in the "barn" park, when Mr. Lorne Campbell and his men came, with a piper, the laird of Barremman and his piper, and Archibald Marquis, accompanied by a piper, and the company indulged in various games. After the games were over, Lorne Campbell, Barremman, and others, came to Macdougal's and got refreshments of whisky and oat cakes. On the first day of the year there was always a dinner at the old Clachan House, where the Campbells of Peatoun lived for many years as tenants of the farm, and sometimes the attractions at Macdougal's and at the Ferry Inn, kept the company so long that the dinner would suffer. The shinty match was the great festival of the year, and hundreds assembled, old and young, with music and banners, to see the play, and a dance at the inn finished the proceedings, prolonged till dawn of the following day.

Both Dr. Story and Dr. James Dodds, formerly of Glasgow, now minister of Corstorphine, near Edinburgh, and natives of the parish, can recall many of the primitive ways of the inhabitants, and the look of the old church when it was used for public worship. They remembered the old "tent," as it was called, used on occasions of communion, and also the old box, where the watchers remained all night on the look out for "resurrection men," as they were termed in those days; also the high wall which surrounded the tomb of old Dr. Drummond, and the fine row of trees which formed a special feature of the old churchyard. Dr. Dodds can remember the Sabbath mornings of fifty years ago, and the people from the farms on Loch Long side streaming down the brae above the Clachan, the women bathing their feet in the burn, and putting on their shoes and stockings before entering the church. He recollects the pretty sort of bower or summer house in the beautiful wooded manse glen, near a clear deep pool of water, where Miss Helen Campbell of the Clachan House used to spend a good deal of her time. In his early days only three houses on the Loch side regularly took in loaf bread, which was brought from Helensburgh and across the ferry by the well-known "Gibbie" Macleod. In the other parishes the wholesome oat cakes constituted the principal, if not only, substitute for the "staff of life," and the boys and girls got a good supply with them when they went to school, for consumption at the meal hour. Butcher meat was supplied to the Clachan, Kilcreggan and Cove, for upwards of forty years, by Mr. M'Phun's van from Gareloch-head, which still makes its peregrination round the Peninsula as far as Coulport, and then crosses the moor down upon Rahane, although there are now local butchers at the different centres of population on both sides of the parish.

There used to be a famous echo in Rosneath, according to Dr. Bird, a writer upon acoustics, who, in one of his treatises, mentions "that somewhere in the 'Isle,' when a person at a proper distance played eight or ten notes on a trumpet, they were correctly repeated, but a third lower; after a short silence, another repetition was heard on a yet lower tone; and after another short interval, they were repeated a third time lower still." Mr. Story, more than half a century ago, tried in vain to discover where this remarkable echo was, and notes that the transmission of sound across the ferry at Rosneath varies considerably according to the degree of humidity in the air. He did, however, one day, in hailing a steamer at anchor off the small island, only visible at low tide, nearly opposite Strouel Bay, the words here repeated distinctly, giving an echo of nine syllables.

Mention has been made of some eminent men connected with the parish whose names were long held in repute. Dr. Anderson, the well-known founder of the Andersonian Institution of Glasgow, was the son of a former minister of Rosneath, and was born in the manse. He was a man of eminent talent and varied attainments, and will long be remembered as having first realised the idea of bringing within reach of the labouring classes the philosophy and science of the Universities. Mathew Stewart, one of the most distinguished of Scotch mathematical scholars, and well known as the father of the celebrated Professor Dugald Stewart, was for some years minister of Rosneath. He was a man of eccentric habits and great absence of mind, and was wont to walk up and down for hours in absorbed meditation in the venerable yew tree avenue. The famous Dr. Alexander Carlyle, the minister of Inveresk, visited Rosneath on his way to Inveraray in the month of August 1758. In his Journal Dr. Carlyle records how he rode all the way from home to Inveraray, having been invited there by the Milton family, who seemed regularly to visit that Highland town. He passed the first night at Shettleston, near Glasgow, where he stayed with his friend, Robin Boyle. The Journal goes on to state, " from Glasgow I went all night to Rosneath, where in a small house near the Castle, lived my friend, Miss Jean Campbell of Carrick, with her mother, who was a sister of General John Campbell of Mamore, afterwards Duke of Argyll, and father of the present Duke. Next day, after passing Loch Long, I went over Argyll's Bowling-green, called so on account of the roughness of the road." The doctor goes on to describe his reception at Inveraray, where he was most politely received by the Duke, his two cousins, and his brother, Lord Frederick, who were there. His Grace was sorry he could not offer Dr. Carlyle lodgings, but hoped he would see him every day at breakfast, dinner, and supper. "The Duke," adds Dr. Carlyle, "had the talent of conversing with his guests so as to distinguish men of knowledge and talents without neglecting those who valued themselves more on their birth and their rent rolls than on personal merit. After the ladies were withdrawn and he had drunk his bottle of claret, he retired to an easy chair set hard by the fireplace; drawing a black silk nightcap over his eyes he slept, or seemed to sleep, for an hour and a half." After his sleep the Duke made tea for himself at a small table set on one side, and then played whist with the ladies of the party, and at supper, which was served at nine, his Grace drank another bottle of claret and could not be got to bed till one in the morning. The politic doctor mentions especially the excellence of the viands and the wines, and stayed over the Sunday and preached to his Grace, who always attended the Church at Inveraray. He was told by the ladies that he had pleased the Duke, at which he was much gratified, because without his Grace's influence no preferment could be obtained in Scotland. The old mansion house which Dr. Carlyle visited at Rosneath, then belonging to the Campbells of Carrick, is the one whose foundations only exist in the immediate vicinity of the celebrated silver firs at Campsail.

Another Carlyle, still more renowned than the imposing and eloquent minister of Inveresk, seems to have visited Rosneath in August 1817. In Froude's "Reminiscences" the visit is thus recorded: "Brown and I did very well on our separate branch of pilgrimage; pleasant walk and talk down to the west margin of the Loch incomparable among lakes or lochs, yet known to me; past Smollett's pillar; emerge on the view of Greenock, on Helensburgh, and across to Rosneath Manse, where with a Rev. Mr. Story, not yet quite inducted, whose life has since been published, and who was an acquaintance of Brown's, we were warmly welcomed and were entertained for a couple of days. Story I never saw again, but he, acquainted in Haddington neighbourhood, saw some time after incidentally, a certain bright figure, to whom I am obliged to him at this moment for speaking favourably of me. Talent plenty, fine vein of satire in him, something like this. I suppose they had been talking of Irving, whom both of them knew and liked well. Her probably, at that time, I had still never seen, but she told me long afterwards." . . . "Those old three days at Rosneath are all very vivid to me, and marked in white. The quiet blue mountain masses, giant Cobbler overhanging bright seas, bright skies, Rosneath new mansion (still unfurnished and standing as it did) its grand old oaks, and a certain hand-fast, middle-aged, practical and most polite Mr. Campbell (the Argyll factor then) and his two sisters, excellent lean old ladies with their wild Highland accent, wire drawn but genuine good manners and good principles, and not least their astonishment and shrill interjections at once of love and fear over the talk they contrived to get out of me one evening, and perhaps another when we went across to tea; all this is still pretty to me to remember. They are all dead, the good souls, Campbell himself, the Duke told me, died only lately, very old; but they were to my rustic eyes of a superior furnished stratum of society, and the thought that I too might perhaps be "one and somewhat" (*ein und etwas*) among my fellow-creatures by and bye, was secretly very welcome at their hands."

There may be records of other famous men who have visited Rosneath scattered throughout some of the numerous books of reminiscences which from time to time appear. The many charms which the Peninsula possesses as a residence, have attracted crowds of persons for a longer or shorter period. Her Gracious Majesty the

Queen, with Prince Albert, once visited Rosneath, though the Royal yacht only lay for a night in Campsail Bay, and in her journal, the Queen records how she admired the youthful Marquis of Lorne, then in his boyhood. The Queen did not seem to have landed at the Castle on this occasion and has never since visited Rosneath, though she has been the guest of the Duke at Inveraray. Her Royal Highness the Princess Louise, however, with the Marquis of Lorne, has resided in the Castle on more than one occasion, and greatly enjoyed the quiet life, rambling through the woods and along the shore, and visiting the old estate servants in their cottages. Shortly after their marriage the Princess and the Marquis visited the Castle, and were received, on landing at the point, by the principal tenants, the magistrates of Kilcreggan and Cove, and a few of the resident gentry. As the Castle for many years past has been let to different families, chiefly for the shooting season, the Argyll family have not resided in it at all, but they are much attached to Rosneath, and would fain return to the home where their father and mother long resided, and where they spent a great many of their happy days of childhood.

In Rosneath are to be found a considerable number of birds, more or less familiar to the West of Scotland. The extensive woods in the vicinity of the Castle, and elsewhere throughout the Peninsula, offer good cover for the feathered songsters, and the range of moorland insures an ample stock of game birds for the purpose of sporting. Both grouse and black game are tolerably plentiful, the Argyll moors generally affording several hundred brace in the season. These birds will be seen in considerable numbers in the early morning, when the fields of grain in the vicinity of the moors are about ready for the reaper, enjoying their repast. Though their food is chiefly the young heather shoots and certain Alpine plants, yet they seem to get something to eat in the stubble and even turnip fields. In autumn and winter the woodcock are found, having arrived in numbers from other countries in their annual migrations. Of late years, two instances of the woodcock nesting in Rosneath were noted by the son of Mr. George Clark, the well known gamekeeper to the Duke for over thirty years. In one nest, which was at the foot of a rhododendron bush near the shore, there were four eggs ; the other nest observed was in a hollow in the ground amongst the bracken, near the Green Isle point. Snipe will be found to a fair extent in the marshy ground in the moors, and also about the drains in the higher fields. Pheasants and partridges are tolerably plentiful, the former bird frequenting the woods of Campsail and around the Castle, and the familiar chirp of the partridge is heard amid the ample fields of turnips.

The birds of prey are not so numerous of late years, as the keepers are addicted to destroy these in their zeal for game preservation. Sparrow-hawks may be seen flying around the farm yards ready to pounce upon any runaway chicken, and sometimes even will dart upon a covey of partridges and carry off their prey. This hawk breeds in the high fir trees in the Castle woods, also in the rocks. The kestrel also is met with, and constructs its nest in the cliffs and rocky ground, sometimes at the foot of a rowan tree where the ground falls rapidly away to a burn. There are plenty of owls in the old woods about Campsail and the Clachan glen, and their melancholy cry, with weird effect, is to be heard on moonlight nights. Occasionally the snowy owl has been seen, and Mr. Howie, tenant of the Clachan farm, shot one of this large and handsome species in his yard some years ago. This is not a common bird, but it has been found in various parts of the West of Scotland in the vicinity of the Clyde, near Ben Lomond, in Ayrshire and Renfrewshire. It is a frequent visitor to the Outer Hebrides and in the Lewis. That destructive bird of prey, the hooded crow, is encountered in the Peninsula, its nest being generally in some secluded glen, on a fir or rowan tree, composed of sticks lined with wool and heather. This most omnivorous crow preys upon the eggs of almost every variety of bird, and therefore is in great disfavour with keepers. Shell-fish of various sorts, snails, crabs, and mussels, are its favourite food, the crabs being carried to a height and dropped upon the rocks, so as to dislodge the occupant from its shell. However, when driven to straits for food, the hooded crow will feed upon the berries of the rowan and other shrubs. Although the rook frequents the Peninsula often in numbers, it does not seem to find the trees congenial for nesting, for the only place where there are a few nests, is upon Knockderry farm. A good many jackdaws, however, have established themselves in the woods, near the Castle, and their short quick cries resound amid the high fir trees as you pass along.

Eagles are rarely seen in Rosneath, but in 1890 a fine specimen of the golden eagle, *aquila chrysaetos*, was captured in the small wood at the back of the glebe. The eagle was observed by Mr. M. Campbell flying near the ground, between the glebe and the Clachan brae, finally alighting on a field in the glebe, Noticing that it seemed rather feeble in its flight, he ran after the bird, which then flew into the wood on to a bed of thick bracken. Seeing that it was entangled in the bracken, Mr. Campbell rushed forward, while the eagle tried to rise, but being hampered by the trap, still attached to one leg, in which it had been caught, its captor was enabled to grasp it strongly by the throat, and, in spite of its violent struggles, conveyed it to his house. Then it was seen that two of its claws had been caught in the trap, which was only attached to the leg by a portion of cartilage, and probably had been for several day's fixed to the bird's leg. The trap weighed about two pounds, and on being detached from its foot still retained the claws in its iron grasp. After its capture, the bird was kept some time, and a good many of the residents went to see the feathered monarch of the moor. It showed no anger or fear when approached, and took with avidity and impartiality either flesh, fowl, or game. It had a majestic appearance, standing on a stone with its splendid plumage extended, and its singular bushy bunch of feathers something like a hood, which it elevated or depressed according to its mood. The wings measured almost eight feet from tip to tip, and the beak and legs had a fine golden colour. Subsequently the eagle was sent for exhibition to a shop in Glasgow, where it lived for more than a year, and then seemed to pine and died.

Of the usual summer visitants which delight us with their song, there are a considerable variety. There are not many larks, but they may be heard on the fields above Kilcreggan, and sometimes on the moor. It is to be regretted that the numbers of this delightful songster seem to be diminishing, for it is difficult to surpass the beauty of its melody, as rising in circling flight from the heather, the bird pours out its music in liquid notes, as it trills its upward way. The mavis is found in great numbers all over the Peninsula, and in the wood near the Clachan their clear warbling notes are heard from "morn till dewy eve;" sometimes a single bird perched upon the picturesque old belfry of the ruined church will sing of an evening by the hour. Equally common is the blackbird, who finds congenial shelter amid the thick boughs of the yew tree avenue, and in the dense rhododendron groves in the Castle woods. Although these two familiar songsters chiefly frequent groves in the vicinity of inhabited houses, yet Gray, in his well known work on the *Birds of the West of Scotland*, mentions having seen both thrushes and blackbirds in the remote rocky islands of the Hebrides, and even far up on the heights of Ailsa Craig. The goldfinch is an occasional visitant, this bird not being so common in the west, though still plentiful in Dumfriesshire. Bullfinches and chaffinches are abundant enough, especially the latter, whose quick lively note and bright plumage make him a welcome visitant to our hedges and groves. The chaffinch is found nearly all over Scotland, seemingly equally at home amid the rocks of Islay and Skye as in the gardens of Dowanhill, and it is difficult to see anything more beautiful in its way than the nest of this favourite little bird, with its exquisitely arranged outer covering of moss and lichens, and its soft interior lining of down, hairs, and feathers. The greenfinch may occasionally be seen during a hot summer day near some of the streamlets which flow into the Loch. The linnet's note resounds lightly from the oak or beech trees, and in late summer the familiar strain of the yellow hammer is heard along all the roads, and its nest may often be met with on the ground cleverly concealed in the long tufts of grass near the roots of birches or whins. Everywhere will be found the pert little robin, with his red breast and bright round black eye, and his pleasing little song is heard when the rest of the minstrels of the grove are silent. The black-cap warbler will be found still lingering in the woods when other migratory birds have flown away, probably enjoying the ruddy rowan berries, so plentifully distributed all over the district. In spring the cuckoo makes its regular appearance, its well known call resounding from every glen and hillside, and some poor little robin or hedge sparrow has, in due time, to do duty as foster-mother to the rapacious young cuckoo which has dislodged the legitimate occupants of the nest. As is well known, the cuckoo deposits its egg furtively in the nest of some other bird, and the unwelcome stranger, in due time, proves too strong for the other nestlings, who are ejected by the intruder as soon as it finds itself sufficiently powerful.

It is needless to say that every summer finds the swallow an everreturning guest to our Peninsula, and they will be seen circling in their graceful flight round most of the farm houses and many of the villas on both sides of the loch. After the middle of September groups of those sweetly twittering little birds will be observed sitting on the telegraph wires near the churchyard, generally the sign that in a few days they will have winged their way to summer climes. Swifts also will be seen nearly every year, their aerial gyratious, far above the flight of the swallow, being of especial interest to witness. Another migrant which also takes its departure ere the early frosts of winter have begun to chill the air, is the corncrake, which utters its familiar rasping cry often far into the summer night, and re-commences its note in the morning. Curious it is to watch the wary bird rapidly running through a field of young grain or of hay, uttering its cry at short intervals, causing you to suppose that there is not one but several birds in the field. The starling is a regular resident bird in the Peninsula, and sometimes considerable flights of them will be observed, especially in the vicinity of the fields near Rosneath Castle. There are some old ash trees near the Castle point which seem to be a favourite perch for these birds, and they sit there for hours, chattering when any one passes by, or sometimes uttering a peculiar low whistling note. The numerous old ash trees, many of them having hollows in their trunks, have a special charm to the starlings for nesting purposes, and they return year after year to the same hole. For years a pair of starlings made their nest in a deep hole in the trunk of a rowan tree on the glebe, quite close to the ground.

Wood-pigeons abound in Rosneath, the numerous plantations of firs affording them ample shelter. This bird is a great foe to the farmer, and its destructive powers are chiefly exercised in the consumption of grain, and it will devour bushels of the leaf of white clover. Its rapid flight and wary habits make it difficult to shoot, and when other food is not available it will devour the turnip bulbs. In autumn and winter the wood-pigeon will feed upon gooseberries, beech nuts, hawthorn, holly, and rowan berries, and various roots of smaller plants. The melodious note of the cushat has a soft sound, and its plaintive cooings will be heard all through the woods in the district. Magpies are found, but only occasionally, and thin chattering note heard from some of the high trees near Campsail Bay, but their destructive practices in plundering pheasants and partridges nests make them peculiarly liable to the vengeance of keepers. Also in the same vicinity may sometimes be seen the handsome jay with its curious blue patch on its wing, but it is becoming more rare in its visits. Fieldfares visit the Peninsula at times, and may be observed on the beach about high water mark picking up some of the small marine animals brought up by the tide. The dipper, or water-ouzel, is not common, but a pair used to be seen in the small burn which runs into Campsail Bay, skimming from stone to stone in rapid flight. It is a beautiful bird, with its dark plumage and snowy breast, and the male bird has a sweet clear trill, which may be heard amid the wimple of many a Highland burn. The nest is often close to a tiny waterfall, and is bedewed with spray, the eggs of a delicate white tint and beautiful shape being only too easily seen by the chance passer by. Among the whins on the verge of the moor, and about the Gallowhill, will be heard at even the peculiar clicking note of the stonechat, or lower down amongst the brambles, and sometimes in the tall coarse weeds of the high fields, its monotonous and rather eerie note startles the pedestrian as he hurries along some unfrequented path over the moor as nightfall is coming on. Of the smaller summer visitants, the whitethroats and garden-warblers will be seen perched on the hedgerows and keeping up their short serenades at the breeding time, and the sweet clear notes of the tiny wren are familiar sounds. Various descriptions of the species of tits are to be met, the great tit with his singular note, which has been likened to a file upon a saw, as he rapidly flits from branch to branch, the pretty little blue tit with his blue head and yellow breast, and the cole tit, whose favourite haunts are the fir plantations. The hardy little wren, with his sharp clear song, is to be heard when other songsters are silent, while the beautiful nest he builds is a marvel of industry and skill. Gray speaks of the variety of materials which the wren uses in his nest; one he saw being of green moss firmly interwoven, another of beech leaves, another of dried ferns, another of fine white straws, a fifth of slender larch twigs, and a sixth entirely of lichens. The tiny bird lays often ten and twelve eggs, and hard work it must be to supply the wants of her numerous nestlings and not to miss one in the dark recesses of the nest. Not so common a visitor is the golden crested wren, which is also very partial to the fir plantations, where it delights in picking the insects off the fir trees and searching minutely for its food. There are other small birds of the wagtail species, which the naturalist will encounter in his rambles, and their pretty plumage will be observed as they rapidly turn in the air and flit from stone to stone in the clear running burns.

Of water and shore birds there are a good many varieties, and the bay of Campsail abounds at certain times with aquatic birds. The stately heron, with his slow and powerful flight, is to be seen all along the shores, especially on the Gareloch side, or perched upon some partially submerged stone watching for fish. He stands erect and rigid, quite motionless, until some fish ventures near, when instantly the long bill darts into the water and emerges with its finny prey. On being disturbed he rises slowly and with some effort, but very soon sails away with measured flappings of his long grey wings. Several descriptions of gulls will be seen in Campsail Bay, especially when the tide is out, when their movements may be best studied. Evidently there is some special attraction at low-tide in the shore of this bay, as it is a favourite feeding place for those birds. Black-headed gulls and common gulls are generally there, and their graceful movements and cheery cries give life to the placid bay, while the birds at times will forsake their haunts to pick up the worms in the newly-ploughed fields. Here also will be heard the curious, long-drawn, shrill, quavering note of the curlew, which is an invariable visitor on the shores and moors of Rosneath. When disturbed near its nest, the watchful bird and its companions set up an interminable querulous screaming, and it has another sort of note, sharper and quicker, when it is wheeling in the air near its nest in the breeding season. The wigeon is another aquatic visitor to be met in numbers, the male bird displaying his bright plumage to advantage in the fine summer mornings. Dunlins and dottrels are less common, the former bird sometimes going in great flights with their silver-lined wings gleaming in the sunlight. Wild ducks are abundant both on the shore, and will be found inland, for they are very partial to the ripe grain, and even will feed upon potatoes. Occasionally wild geese frequent the Loch shores, going in small flocks in the winter months, and water hens may sometimes be seen about the Green Isle point, or on a marshy place in the woods there. A common bird on the shore is the redshank, foraging for its food among the small pools left by the receding tide, and being very wary and vigilant is not easy to approach. Sandpipers are abundant all along the shores, skimming rapidly along the surface of the water close to the beach, and then lighting on a small boulder and keeping up a succession of shrill pipings as they do on the wing. A favourite place for their nests is the turf bank bordering the shore at Green Isle point, and sometimes at the foot of tufts of brushwood plants. Plovers are also common, and their pleasant cheery note salutes you as you may be wandering along the unfrequented moor or the fields on the Home farm towards the point of the Peninsula.

It is pleasant to watch their quick circling flight, and to listen to the familiar note of this interesting bird, which seems to enjoy its life greatly, and which deserves a better fate than to provide eggs annually in rapidly declining numbers for the dinner tables of Glasgow epicures. Solan geese, cormorants, and the larger species of sea birds are hardly ever seen in the waters washing the Peninsula, but in the open channel on the Kilcreggan side the goosander, and other divers will be regularly noticed.

This list of the birds of Rosneath by no means pretends to be perfect, or to exhaust the list of our occasional feathered visitors to the shores and uplands of the Peninsula. For such as desire to make a study of ornithology there are considerable advantages in Rosneath, on account of its being well wooded, and not quite so liable to the inroads of the professional bird-catcher. The woods and moors are well preserved, but the proprietors will always be found willing to give facilities for genuine students of natural history, who may be trusted not to abuse the privileges granted. In his rambles along the shores or up the numerous small streams which precipitate themselves into the Loch by a series of cascades, the naturalist will find many sights to delight him and add to his store of knowledge. The woods give favourite shelter to a good many squirrels, who may be seen clambering up the lofty trees or springing lightly from branch to branch. Here, too, occasionally may be seen the graceful roe-deer, bounding along between the thickets of rhododendrons. A good number of these deer have for years had their abode in the woods near the Castle and the Clachan glen, and sometimes they appear in winter in the gardens about the village, to the destruction of the roses and ivy leaves, of which they are fond. Graceful creatures they are, and they have for very many years frequented the woods and moors of the Peninsula, but their numbers are not increasing, and they will soon be extinct. Hares are seldom seen now, though they are still shot on the moors, and they are getting scarcer every year, but rabbits flourish in ever-increasing numbers. The farmers both shoot and snare large numbers, but they abound all along the shore, and can be seen in dozens in the early mornings feeding in the grass parks or scampering across the lawn.

Of botanical specimens there are not many beyond the ordinary plants to be found in the Peninsula, the common variety of ferns abounding, and both the oak and beech species can be got in the glen. Primroses, blue bells, wild hyacinths, and the usual wildflowers abound, and upon the Castle point cowslips grow in profusion. Fuchsias grow to the size of trees almost, and honeysuckle scents the air, and the holly and the rowan in their season are decked with their scarlet berries. Lovers of woodland scenes will meet with much that will afford them delight, and there are many sweet secluded spots in the glens abounding in mosses and tender creepers that spread over rocks and trunks of trees.

All the local names in the Peninsula are of Gaelic derivation; the name Rosneath has been treated before and its meaning given. In Chalmers' *Caledonia* we read that the name has been derived from the British *Rhosneth*, signifying the promontory or peninsula of the small dingle or hollow, or from the British *Rhosnoeth*, the naked or bare promontory or peninsula. Kilcreggan or Kilcraigan, the burying place of the rock. Knockderry, the stormy knoll. Peatoun, or Peatburn, in Gaelic, *Alt-na-mone*. Barbour should be in Gaelic, *Bran-na-bruach*, above the bank. Mamore, from *Mam*, a knoll, *more*, great, also Mambeg, the little knoll. Rahane or Rahian, John's promontory, in English. Crossowen is Ewen's Cross. Strouel, from *strulag*, a spout. Fernicarry, near Garelochhead, where the Campbell family lived, mentioned in Mr. Story's memoir of Isabella, is supposed to have been in full Feorlin-na-Carrie. In the title deeds of the farm, it is written Feorlin Carrie, the first part of the name meaning a portion of land, while Carrie may have been an enclosure for taking fish, of which structures there are still some found on the Clyde shores, built so as to receive the tide, which receding, left the fish inside.

The author has been favoured by the venerable and greatly respected Rev. Dr. Smith, so long minister of the parish of Cathcart, with some most interesting details regarding his reminiscences of Rosneath, extending as far back as the year 1811. Old Mrs. Cumming of Barremman was the sister of Dr. Smith's mother, and he was a frequent visitor at the old mansion-house. At that time the only access to the Peninsula, unless by the road round the Loch, was by boat, and he went from Glasgow to Helensburgh by carrier's cart, and then walked to Row and crossed the Ferry. Very soon after, however, the *Comet* steamer was built by Henry Bell, and Dr. Smith sailed in her, and well remembered her owner sitting on the deck, a lively, cheery man, talking with pride about the success of his vessel. He was also the first who introduced one horse cabs; before his time all hackney carriages were drawn by a pair of horses. At that time the Clachan of Rosneath consisted of the small row of thatched houses, with the school-house facing the churchyard, and there were only the three farm-houses, humble thatched buildings, of Strouel, Clynder, and Crossowen, until you came to Barremman House and farm. The latter estate also included the farm of Ailey on the Cove shore of the Peninsula, and it was a small estate, a good deal in moorland, with no plantations of wood. The old laird was rather a character, had served long in the *Bellerophon*, and fought under Lord Howe in the famous engagement of 1st June, 1794, where he was wounded in the leg and carried the bullet to his grave. Dr. Smith subsequently, in 1829, built Altmore, the small house beyond Barremman, looking towards the entrance of the Loch, for his mother. Soon afterwards the prettily situated Glengair, immediately adjoining on the other side of the burn, was erected by Mr. Campbell, on a building lease from the Duke of Argyll, and it is now occupied by his niece, Miss Eliza Campbell. Dr. Smith's grandmother lived in Helensburgh, and therefore he was a frequent visitor to the Gareloch.

At that time, the new Castle opposite Ardencaple was occupied chiefly by Lady Augusta Clavering, a sister of the Duke of Argyll, while what remained of the old Castle, which was destroyed by fire, was occupied by Mr. Smith of Jordanhill. His residence consisted mostly of the old kitchen and servants' accommodation, but it formed a comfortable abode on the verge of the shore near the point. He was well known as a man of scientific acquirements, and as the author of the *Voyages and Shipwreck of St. Paul*, a work prized by Bible students, and which brought him considerable reputation. In those days, people lived in a primitive style, the dinner hour being two o'clock, and it was on very rare occasions that wine was seen on the table, except at the houses of the titled and wealthy. Peatoun House was occupied by Mrs. Campbell, and her nephew, George Drummond, lived with her, who was an officer in the 60th Rifles, and fought at Waterloo. He was a fine horseman, but in other respects not an estimable character, and having married, sailed with his wife to foreign parts, but the vessel was never afterwards heard of. He was also nephew to old Dr. Drummond, the parish minister, who used to come to Barremman to visit the laird; an infirm, old man, who generally had some one with him to help his tottering steps. The Monday dinner of the elders after Communion Sabbath, always took place at the manse, and was also graced by the presence of Lady Augusta Clavering, who used to be escorted back to the Castle by Mr. Lorne Campbell. On the Tuesday, the ministers who officiated were always entertained at breakfast at Barremman, where the usual dainties which grace the morning meal in Scotland were spread in profusion. The old-fashioned hospitality, for which Scottish country gentlemen were famous, was well sustained at the

Clachan House on Sundays, luncheon being provided between the two diets of worship for the visitors at the different houses. Old Mr. Story introduced the custom of having the two services amalgamated, a good deal to prevent the somewhat unseemly feasting and drinking which used to prevail at the public houses in the intervals between worship. Mr. Story used often to come up to Barremman, and enjoyed going out to fish in the Loch with the young people in the house, and Dr. Smith can well remember the present Duke of Argyll, as a little child, along with his brother, coming in state, with several nurses in attendance, to visit at Barremman.

The society of Rosneath was but limited in those days, and when Mr. Angus and his two nieces came to live at "the Chateau," which he built, they were considered quite an acquisition. The families lived plainly, household bread was a rarity, scones and oat cakes being chiefly used, and butcher meat was got, perhaps once a week, from Helensburgh. Peats were largely used for fuel, being carried from the moor on what was known as "cars," drawn by horses, a sort of sledge, with two long poles resting on the horse's back, no wheels, and two or three upright boards at the back against which the load rested. The farm servants got brose and "sowans," and were well content with their lot, although their wages and those of domestic servants were but small. The young people used to go out early in the morning to fish in the Loch, and invariably brought in a good haul of several dozens of whiting, haddocks, skate, rock cod, and other varieties. Dr. Smith also, as a boy, knew well about the smuggling which was so extensively carried on in the "Island," as Rosneath was almost universally termed, and in particular, can remember two favourite spots for this illicit trade being carried on. One place where there was a secret still was in the moor up at Barremman, near where it marched with the Duke's estate, the other being in the burn above Hattonburn, and not far from the old road which went from thence across the field, and then past the Mansion House over to Coulport. He can distinctly recall the smugglers constructing a long flue, with holes at intervals, so that the smoke from the fire might not emerge in too great a volume, and attract the attention of the revenue cutter in the Loch.

Such a subject as the Peatoun murder would be well calculated to impress the boyish mind, and Dr. Smith went over to see the scene where the dreadful crime was perpetrated. His recollection of the spot was a precipice of rock in the burn near Peatoun House, with a deep pool of water below, into which the murderer precipitated his victim. Old Mrs. Cumming, who lived to be 95, must have been a child at the time of the crime, and could probably retain some dim recollection of the event. The murderer, it seemed, had breakfasted at Barremman on the fatal day and then proceeded to market near Dunbarton, so that the crime must have been committed in the evening. The tradition was that when suspicion began to be aroused against John Smith as being accessory to the murder of his wife, on a particular Sabbath, not long afterwards, the minister of Rosneath took occasion to preach a sermon in which special reference was made to the crime of murder. Officers from Dunbarton were in readiness, and they took special notice of the murderer during the delivery of the sermon. His agitation became so uncontrollable as to arouse general observation, and, after the service, he was quietly apprehended and judicially examined.

The family at Fernicarry was well known to Dr. Smith, the father, a jovial burly Highlander, the saintly and beautiful Isabella and her sister Mary, and thus the Mamore family and the party from Barremman used to meet together on the Sundays on their way to church. A very usual mode of travel, for those from a distance, was for five or six to occupy a cart; a plank of wood across the middle of the cart, accommodating two or three, and others on bags of straw behind. The old head of the house at Fernicarry was an officer in the Argyllshire Fusiliers, a man of some consequence in his day. He had placed an inscription over the door of the house, being the date of building it, in Roman capital letters, MDCCCV. This puzzled the neighbours considerably, who were ignorant of the signification of the letters, until one more sagacious than his fellows read it to be, Maister Donald Campbell, Cowal, Captain Volunteers.

The old laird of Barremman took his young nephew on one occasion an excursion to Inveraray, the two making the expedition on foot, going by Coulport Ferry, thence by Loch Eck to Strachur, and across Loch Fyne. Glenfinnart was then occupied by Lord Dunmore, and the ferry at Ardentinny was worked by the Marquis family. Young Smith, being a minister's son, was known to some of the clergy in the district, and Mr. Cumming knew many of the farmers, so that they were hospitably entertained on the way. He remembers the happy evening spent at his father's friend's hospitable manse at Lochgoilhead, the neighbouring laird, Campbell of Drumsynie being one of the party, and they were sorry when their expedition ended by their being ferried across by the farmer on Loch Longside over to Portincaple.

An interesting reminiscence of Dr. Smith's is his description of an old Highlander, a pensioner of the Argyll family, who was very decrepit, and used to be carried about in a sort of box on wheels, sometimes drawn by a dog. He was famous from having fought at the Battle of Culloden, and it was a delight to young Smith and his companions to hear the veteran detail his experiences of the celebrated fight, and the sympathies of his auditors were generally with the "young Chevalier." Every year the old man made a peregrination from Inveraray, where he lived, to Rosneath, meeting with good cheer on the way at the numerous friendly farm houses. Thus an interesting link is supplied from one still alive,—and, to the joy of his many friends, hale and hearty—who had spoken with one of those who took part in that historic battle, when the last hope of an ancient family reigning on the throne of Great Britain was for ever extinguished.

CHAPTER VI.

Historical, Archæological, and Miscellaneous.

THE subject matter of this chapter will be found of varied interest, and has been arranged under appropriate headings, so that reference will be facilitated. So much supplementary information had been sent to the author, that in place of trying to incorporate it with the narrative in preceding chapters, he thought it best to insert the details as follows :—

ANCIENT STONE FOUND IN CHURCHYARD.

The following extract is from the proceedings of the Society of Antiquaries, a description by Dr. Story of the stone dug up in 1880. "It is sculptured on both sides and both edges ; on the one side the work is more worn and undecipherable than on the other. The stone is oblong, slightly rounded and abraded at top and bottom; its length, 6 feet, breadth, 1 foot 11 inches, thickness, 6 inches, and seems to be of a hard sandstone not found in the parish, so far as I know. It was discovered about 4 feet below the surface of the churchyard and to the west of the church of Rosneath. The churchyard is a very old one, and the pre-Reformation church now no more, stood in the centre of it, eastward from where this stone was found."

The editor adds the following note :—"The rubbings show that the monument is a shaped slab about 5 feet long, 20 inches wide, and

5 inches thick, ornamented on both faces, and on both edges with patterns of interlaced work. On the obverse it presents a cross of the whole length of the slab, the centre filled with a spiral pattern, and the shaft and summit with patterns of interlaced work. The reverse also bears a cross of the whole length of the slab; the ornament is much more defaced, but seems to consist entirely of interlaced work and fret. The edge of the stone has its ornaments also of interlaced work. The monument thus differs entirely in the character of its ornaments from the crosses and slabs decorated with foliagenous scrolls, which are so common in the West Highlands. Its style is earlier and corresponds with the purely Celtic ornamentation of the erect and shaped slabs of the western area of Scotland."

The Marquis of Lorne has kindly favoured the author with the following notes regarding the decorations on the old stone dug up in the churchyard :—

"Many of the patterns on 'Iona' stones are simply direct copies of the patterns seen on stones along the Adriatic coast and in Lombardy. The simple scrolls of leaves, the intertwined vertical or horizontal leaf scroll are often identical. So is a good deal of the interlaced knotted ornaments, although the Culdee Church's later artists developed the 'krest' into further intricacies. Many Irish and Scottish monks worked in Lombardy. As for example Columbanus, who founded the monastery of Bobbio in Lombardy (near Alessandria) whence the Ambrosian Library at Milan has many Celtic MSS. The Church of San Ambrojio at Milan shows many fine examples of so-called 'Celtic' ornament. In its present state it is supposed to date from the ninth century. Another characteristic 'Celtic' habit in decoration was to make the tails of animals, especially griffins, descend the scroll, becoming leaf work. This is seen at Milan, and the griffin is precisely that found on the West Highland crosses and tombstones."

THE OLD COMMUNION CUPS AT ROSNEATH CHURCH.

The author is indebted to the Rev. Thomas Burns, M.A., one who has written a valuable work on old Scottish Communion plate, for the following details of the above:—" They are about the oldest in Scotland, and it would be interesting to know who was the donor of them. Their type is thoroughly characteristic of the age. They were made in Edinburgh by a famous goldsmith, John Mosman, who was admitted to the Incorporation of Goldsmiths in 1575. The cups were made in 1585-6. Mosman was Deacon in that year, and they bear his Deacon's punch. They stand $8\frac{3}{4}$ inches high, and have a depth of bowl of $3\frac{3}{4}$ inches. They are most valuable on account of their antiquity, apart from their historical associations."

THE ARGYLL FAMILY AND THEIR CONNECTION WITH ROSNEATH.

An account has been already given of how the Campbells first became connected with the Peninsula, and how the lands of Rosneath were conveyed by a royal gift to Colin, first Earl of Argyll, in 1489. It was but a comparatively small portion of the estate, as it now exists, that was so conveyed. Rosneath was constantly used as a residence by the family, and one or two letters are here given, written from the castle. This one seems to have been written in 1633 :—

"For my loving cousing the Lard of Glenorquhay.

"Loving cusin,—Man propons but God dispons. I intended to heave gone presentlie to Inuerraray, bot I had ane letter within thir two or three days from the Thesaurar Traquair, desyring me to be in Edinburgh so soon as I could, quhiche hes altered my resolution that my familie cannot stur till it pleas God I returne. I will asoor you your foster longs very much to see you, and doethe not dar to tell he had rather be thair nor her, and I asoor you he shall heave his choice, bot as you may see be this letter of his grandfather's, the Earl of Morton, thit he intends to be in Scotland so shortlie, his mother desyrs if it pleas God to heaue her childring togither till that tym, to draw her father her; and if wee hear any contrair advertis-

ROSNEATH OLD CASTLE (Now Destroyed)

ment of his dyet you shall immediatelie heaue him (as Archie calles it) home. So remembring my service to your lady I rest your loving cusin
"LORNE.

"Rosneithe last May."

"To my much respectit and guid friend the Laird of Glenurquhy.

"Luefein friend,—I haife sent this bearar to know how yea and my sone are in healthe, and to shaw you that all friendis heare are weall. I heair my sone begines to wearye of the Irishe langwadge. I intreatt you to cause holde hime to the speakeing of itt, for since he hes bestowed so long tyme and paines in the getting of it, I sould be sory he lost it now with leasines in not speaking of it; bot this I know, yea wilbe more cairfull as in everything that concernes him, so that I will fully leaffe him to your awin caire; only prayeing the Lord to giffe ane blessing to all the meanes of his educatioune, and so I shall still remain your most assurett friend
"MARGARET DOUGLAS.

"Rosnethe, the 14 of December 1637."

"For my loving Cusin the Laird Glenorquhy.

"Loving Cusin,—Since it hath pleased God to call my father to his eternall rest, I doutt not bot you kno als weall as I can desyr you what is fitting for your self to doe, onli in this I desyr you to suffer your foster with you to wear murning, and so ever make use of me as your most affectionat cusin to my power.
"ARGYLL.

"Rosneithe, 4 September, 1638."

The Rosneath estate has gradually become consolidated under the Argyll family until, with exception of the two small properties of Peatoun and Barremman, the entire Peninsula is owned by the Duke. It is not easy to trace the exact dates when their possessions in Rosneath were acquired, but, through the courtesy of their present owner, a few details are given from his Grace's title deeds.

THE RAHANE ESTATE.

There is an extract disposition by Archibald Campbell of Rachean, with certain consents in favour of John, Duke of Argyll, in liferent, and to John, then Marquis of Lorne, his eldest son, of the lands of Rachean, Knockderry, Cursnoch, and Blairnachtraw, dated 11, 12, and 18 May, 1764. An instrument of Resignation of the lands of Rachane and others, and charter under the great seal, dated 6 August, 1764. An instrument of Sasine in favour of John, the second Duke, in liferent, and John, third Duke, in fee, of the lands of Cursnoch and Blairnachtraw, date 19 October, 1764. Extract Disposition and Taillie by John, Duke of Argyll, of Rachane, in favour of himself and his heir, July, 1789.

THE KILCREGGAN ESTATE.

Disposition granted by Dugald M'Kellar of Kilblaan in favour of Patrick M'Kellar, date 15th September, 1696. Charter of Confirmation by Archibald, Earl of Argyll, to Patrick M'Kellar, date 11th September, 1750. Precept of clare constat by the commissioners for John, Duke of Argyll, in favour of Malcolm M'Kellar, October 1711. Articles of Sale between said Malcolm M'Kellar and John Campbell, 29th January, 1752. Extract Disposition by Malcolm M'Kellar with consent of his wife, in favour of Archibald, Duke of Argyll, dated 2nd November, 1752. Missive from John Fisher, Tacksman of said lands, obliging himself to assign his tack to the Duke, 19th October, 1751.

THE ESTATE OF RAHEAN AND KNOCKDERRY.

I.—RACHEAN.

Charter of Sale by Walter Leckie of that ilk to Donald Campbell, 4th November, 1580. Instrument of Sasine given by Donald Campbell in favour of John Campbell, his son, October 1598. Decreet of Adjudication at the instance of Donald Campbell, second son of Archibald Campbell of Rachean, against John Campbell, eldest son of said Archibald Campbell, January 1680. Disposition by said Donald Campbell to Archibald Campbell, his son, February, 1694.

II.—KNOCKDERRY AND BARBOUR.

Charter by Cuthbert Cunninghame to said Donald Campbell, June 1586. Decree of Adjudication at instance of Donald Campbell, against his brother, John Campbell, March, 1683. Adjudication by John, Marquis of Athole, and others, as Commissioners of the Duchess of Lennox, in favour of said Donald Campbell, March 1683. Precept of clare constat by James, Marquis of Montrose, to Archibald Campbell of Rachane, as heir to said Donald Campbell, his father, May, 1705. Disposition by the said Marquis in favour of the said Archibald Campbell of the superiority of the said lands, May 1705.

III.—RAHANE AND KNOCKDERRY.

Charter of Adjudication in favour of said Archibald Campbell, April, 1708. Precept from Chancery in favour of said Archibald Campbell, May, 1764.

IV.—CURSNOCH AND BLAIRNACHTRA.

Charter by Archibald Earl of Argyll, in favour of Colin Campbell of Ardkinlas, May, 1669. Procuratory of Resignation by said Colin Campbell in favour of Archibald Campbell of Rachane, in life-rent, and John Campbell, his son, in fee, May, 1669. Resignation by said Earl in favour of Archibald Campbell, in life-rent, and John Campbell, in fee, May, 1669. Precept of clare constat by John, Duke of Argyll, infefting Archibald Campbell as heir to said John Campbell, his granduncle, December 1761. Adjudication granted by Archibald Earl of Argyll, in favour of Donald Campbell, 1680. Precept of clare constat by said John Campbell, December 1761.

LANDS OF DUCHLASS, NOW DUCHLAGE.

Charter under the great seal of the five merk land of old extent of Duchlass, in favour of Colin Campbell of Carrick, March 1597, and instrument of sasine thereon. Instrument of sasine upon a precept furth of Chancery, following on retour of the special service of John Campbell of Carrick, as heir of the said Colin Campbell, his grandfather, May 1665. Retour of the special service of Captain John Campbell of Carrick, as heir to said John Campbell, his grandfather, October 1722, duly retoured to Chancery. Precept from Chancery thereon, for infefting the said John Campbell, November 1722. Instrument of resignation in favour of said Duke of Argyll, on procuratory in trust conveyance, by the said John Campbell, in 1742, dated November 1746.

In his learned work respecting *The Gael of Alban or Highlanders of Scotland*, Colonel Robertson, F.S.A., traces the rise of the powerful Clan Campbell. It appears that the earliest spelling of the name is *Cambel*, in the Ragman Rolls of 1292 to 1296, and also *Kambel*. He considers that the idea of the derivation of the name from the Gaelic cam-beul, or crooked mouth, cannot be maintained. The first crown charter of the Argyll or MacCailean Mor branch of the name for lands in Argyllshire, was one by Robert the Bruce to his nephew, Sir Colin Cambel, dated at Arbroath, February 1316. Colonel Robertson also states that the whole of the Clan Campbell have also another designation in Gaelic, namely, the "Clan Diarmad na'n Torc," or Diarmid of the Wild Boar, an ancient and celebrated Pictish hero, which explains why the boar's head is a prominent part of the Campbell crest. The MacCailean Mor family rose to great influence and obliged several small clans to assume the name of Campbell. In 1420 to 1423, the ancestor of this branch of the family was designed "of Lochawe," and became first Lord Campbell. He was reputed one of the wealthiest of the barons of Scotland, his revenue, a very large one in those times, being stated at 1,500 merks.

From the Marquis of Lorne the author is favoured with the following details of interest in connection with the Argyll family, under date May, 1893.

"I hope you will quote 'Blind Harry's' account of the taking of the old castle by Wallace. I have written to Mr. Wyllie to ask him to send you a rubbing of the cypher of the Marquis of

Argyll, and of his wife, Margaret Douglas, which was carved on a stone of the Castle (Rosneath) burned in 1806, and which stone is now at Inveraray. Rosneath Castle was the halfway-house to the Lowlands, when the family travelled south from Inveraray, and feudatories held lands for the service of providing a galley or two for the crossing from Loch Goil to Rosneath, or from the Holy Loch to Rosneath.

"My own recollections are of no value, being so recent. One of the most vivid is that of seeing (I was too young to think much of hearing) Mr. Story preaching in the church at the end of the yew avenue. His fine countenance, the large and kindly brown eyes lighting the benevolent face under the great waves of snow-white hair, was one children and men and women all liked. A very worthy helpmate in the guidance of the parish was Lorne Campbell, whose portrait, by Watson Gordon, at Inveraray, is excellent. I send some old lines on Rosneath I wrote some years ago, they are at your service."

THE PEATOUN ESTATE.

This beautiful estate on Loch Long has been for hundreds of years in possession of this branch of the Clan Campbell. The present possessor, Mr. Lorne Campbell, is resident chiefly in Montreal, Canada, where he was born. He succeeded to the estate of Peatoun, or as it is termed in the petition for authority to disentail presented to the Court of Session in 1882, *Peitoun*,—on the death of his respected father, Dr. George William Campbell. The latter resided in Montreal and practised as a doctor there for many years, and died in 1882 in Scotland, without having made up his title to the said lands and estate. Mr. Lorne Campbell was infeft therein, conform to extract degree of his special service, as nearest and lawful heir of tailzie and provision of the deceased John Douglas Campbell, his uncle. The estate came into possession of this branch of the family in virtue of a disposition and deed of entail, dated March, 1810, by Donald Campbell of Peitoun, in favour of himself in life rent, and Colin Campbell, sometime of the island of Grenada, then residing at

Clachan of Rosneath, eldest and lawful son of the deceased Reverend William Campbell, minister of Kilchrenan and Doilwich in the county of Argyll; whom failing to the Reverend Alexander Campbell, minister of Kilcolmonell, in county of Argyll, second son of said William Campbell; whom failing to Robert Campbell, chamberlain at Rosneath, third son of said William Campbell. In the petition the estate is styled "all and whole the five-merk land of old extent of Peitoun, commonly, or of old called Altermonie, or Alter Peitoun, as also all and whole the other five-merk land of old extent of Letter, commonly called Letterbeg, with houses, biggings, yards, orchards, woods, fishings, parts, pendicles, and whole other pertinents of the foresaid lands, whatsoever, all lying in the parish of Rosneath and shire of Dunbarton."

In the Blue Book Peatoun is stated at 710 acres, with a rental of £350. The present rental to Whitsunday 1892 may be stated:—

Peatoun and Letter, agricultural rental,	£257
Feu Duties, etc.,	182
Total,	£439

The oldest writ in possession of the Peatoun family is dated October 1598: it is the oldest branch of the Ardkinglas family.

THE BARREMMAN ESTATE.

This estate, now the property of Mr. Robert Thom of Canna, was for over one hundred and fifty years in the possession of the Cumming family. It was acquired by Walter Cumming, styled "Indweller in the Clachan of Rosneath," of date 13th March, 1706, under Disposition by Daniel Campbell, Collector of Newport, Glasgow, in return for a "certaine soume of money, as the full and adequate pryce of the lands aforesaid." The lands so disposed, comprised "all and haill the lands of Clandearg (Clynder) and Boreman, extending to a seven-merk land of old extent, with the yards, houses, orchards, parts, pendicles and universell pertinents of the same, lying in the Isle and Baronie of Rosneath, and Sheriffdom of Dumbrittaine."

The disposition of Barremman is full of the quaint legal phrases of the day, "Wherefore witt ye me" (be it known unto you), says the granter, and "grants assignation to the wrytes, maills and duties of said lands. In the name of God and men be it known to all by these grants, that upon the 29th day of November, 1706, and of the reign of our Soveraign, Ladie Anne, and by the grace of God Queen of Great Britain, France and Ireland, Defender of the faith, year in presence of His Grace, John, Duke of Argyll, me, nottar public and witness after named, compeared personally John Campbell of Knockriock, mort in Edinburgh, as procurator specially constitute for Daniel Campbell, Collector, Newport, Glasgow, by virtue of his patent letters of procuratory."

The Deed closes thus :—"These things were done within the said Duke his lodging, in the Abbey of Holyrood house, betwixt the hours of 10 and 11 forenoon, day, month, place, and year of God foresaid, in presence of Archibald, Earle of Ilay, Lord Charles Kerr, director of H.M. Chancery, Lord John Kerr, Colonell in H.M. Regiment of Horse guards, James Campbell, Jr., of Ardkinlas, and Captain Campbell of said Duke his Regiment of foot, witness called and required to the premises."

In the Blue Book Barremman estate is as follows :—Acres 597. Rental £288.

Present Rental, 1892—agricultural, etc.,	£576
Feu Duties,	466
Total,	£1,042

The feuing on the Barremman estate began in 1825, when Achnashie, then known as the "Chateau," was taken off by Mr. Angus, in which year Strouel Cottage, or Frith Cottage, was taken by John Howe. This was subsequently acquired by Mr. William Robertson of Greenock, who in 1829 built Strouel Lodge on a feu of some eight acres. Whitelea was taken off in 1829 by Mr. Stenhouse, and passed to its present owners, the Misses Wilson. In the following year the villas constructed by Mr. Monteith at Clynder, were gradually feued to some advantage, and substantial houses erected.

BIRDS OF ROSNEATH.

The author is indebted to Mr. Donald Clark, who has long resided at the Green Isle at the extremity of the Peninsula, for some notes on the birds of the district. His father, the late George Clark, head gamekeeper to the Duke of Argyll, was a notable man in many ways. He was a native of Inveraray, and a man of powerful frame and dauntless courage, who would face any number of poachers and put them to flight. Nothing would cause him to quail, and few were found daring enough to face an encounter with such an adversary. Mr. Clark removed to Rosneath nearly forty years ago, and continued in his position as head keeper till the day of his death. For the last twenty-five years of his life he had to lie flat on his back, owing to a serious injury he had sustained, and thus he was enabled to acquire stores of information on all sorts of subjects. Gaelic was one of his special studies, and he frequently made communications to the newspapers. Nothing came amiss to him, and he would discuss many erudite topics with some of the famous men who might be on a visit to the Castle. The Princess Louise had many a talk with Mr. Clark, and all who sought him were struck with the remarkable intelligence he displayed in his conversation upon the most diverse topics. There he lay upon his bed, and the remarkable flashing eye, and long locks, gave him the appearance of a seer. The Argyll family had much respect for Mr. Clark, and when he died they lost a faithful and valuable servant.

His son Donald has a turn for natural history, and being of an observant disposition has utilized his opportunities. He writes respecting the Heronry at the Green Isle point as follows :—

"The Heronry at the Green Isle I suppose to be of old date. I recollect when the wood on the side facing Green Isle point was much thicker than it is now, many of the trees having been separated by severe gales, within the last two decades. The herons no longer build, as they used to do, on the side facing Green Isle point, but have retired further back into the wood, as better suiting their love of solitude. They seem also to be fewer in number than they used to be. They invariably build in Scotch fir trees, which are here in great plenty, although not so densely massed as they were at one time in my recollection. The heron nests very early in spring, and the nest appears from below like a large mass of brushwood fixed among the branches without much appearance of neatness in construction. I have heard young ones cry in the month of March, which is earlier than most other birds hatch. At the time when incubation and the feeding of young goes on the whole wood used to seem alive with the discordant noises of the birds. They are very shy in their nature and can seldom be approached very closely. In feeding, unlike gulls, curlews, and most other shore birds, they are generally solitary and unsocial in their habits. It is an unusual thing to see more than two together wading for food, and often they are found in solitude. When there is a storm of wind they become more sociable, and at such times a whole battalion of herons may be found congregated together in some open glade close to the heronry, walking about on the grass and enjoying the shelter. *Starlings.*—The starling at the nesting time is seen perched on the back of a sheep helping itself to nesting material or searching for insects. The starling has a peculiar way of using his bill to dislodge an insect that may have burrowed in the sand or between two pebbles. He sticks his bill, fast shut, straight down, and when he has it down he suddenly opens it out to its full extent, thus exposing the insects' hiding place."

In the neighbouring parish of Row, in 1838, the minister mentions the following birds as regular visitants, many of which would doubtless make their way across to Rosneath. Peregrine falcon, sparrow hawk, kestrel, merlin, common buzzard, hen harrier, kite, spot-eared owl, barn owl, tawny owl, goat sucker, chimney swallow, martin, sand martin, common swift, spotted fly-catcher, missel thrush, fieldfare, song thrush, redwing, blackbird, moor blackbird, dipper, redbreast, redstart, black cap, white throat, wood wren, golden-crested wren, great tit, blue tit, cole tit, long tailed tit, hedge sparrow, pied wagtail, grey wagtail, yellow wagtail, shore pyet, sky lark, yellow bunting, corn bunting, house sparrow, chaffinch, mountain finch, siskin, goldfinch, brown linnet, green grossbeak, bulfinch, crossbill, starling, raven, carrion crow, hooded crow, rook, jackdaw, magpie, jay, common creeper, wren, cuckoo, ringdove, pheasant, black grouse, red grouse, partridge, heron, curlew, redshank, sandpiper, woodcock, snipe, jack snipe, dunlin, corncrake, gullinule, coot, oyster catcher, turnstone, water ouzel, green lapwing, golden plover, ringed plover, barnacle goose, sheldrake, wild duck, teal, widgeon, scaup, goosander, horned grebe, red throated driver, bill auk, gull, herring gull.

FISHING IN THE GARELOCH.

The following list of fishermen on the Loch between the years 1817 and 1830, who were all personally known to Mr. James Campbell, Strouel, shews how important a calling it was in these years:—

Row	Peter Brodie, with two men.
Faslane	Alexander M'Farlane and one man.
Do.	John M'Kinlay, with two men.
Do.	D. M'Vicar, with two men.
Gareloch-head	Peter M'Leod, with two men.
Do.	Malcolm M'Leod, with two men.
Do.	Peter Campbell, with two men.
Do.	Allan Campbell, with two men.
Do.	Charles Stewart, with two men.
Do.	James Stewart, with two men.
Do.	Robert Smith.
Rahane	John M'Arthur, with two men.
Mamore	Robert Campbell, with two men.
Do.	Archibald M'Glashan, with two men.
Rahane Ferry House	Allan M'Farlane, with two men.
Do.	John M'Farlane, with two men.

Rahane Ferry House	John Brodie, with two men.
Do.	Alexander M'Nicol, with two men.
Hattonburn	Donald M'Kay, with two men.
Crossowen	John Campbell, two boats and four men.
Do.	David Chalmers, with two men.
Clynder	John Angus, with two men.
Do.	Duncan M'Lellan, with two men.
Clachan of Rosneath	Archibald M'Kellar, with two men.
Do.	Malcolm M'Wattie, with one man.
Campsail	John M'Coll, with two men.
Do.	John M'Glashan, with two men.
Low Barracks near Castle	Donald M'Donald, with one man.
Upper do. do.	Dougald M'Kichan, with two men.
Home Farm do.	John M'Kellar, with two men.
Kilcreggan	John M'Farlane, three boats—nine men in all.
Do. Little Aiden	L. Campbell, with two men.
Do. Meikle Aiden	James Orr, with two men.
Cursnoch	Robert Chalmers, with two men.
Blairnachtra	Robert M'Arthur, with two men.
Barbour	Robert M'Cunn, with two men.
Do.	James Chalmers, with two men.
Do.	Malcolm Chalmers, with two men.
Do.	Archibald M'Nerran, with two men.
Letter	Donald M'Kellar, with one man.
Coulport	Archibald Marquis, with one man.
Do.	Alexander Marquis, with two men.

This long list shows what a busy scene the Loch must have presented in those days when the herring fishing constituted so large a portion of the industry of the Gareloch.

OLD MURDER TRIALS, ROSNEATH DISTRICT.

In Pitcairn's *Criminal Trials of Scotland*, there appears under date A.D. 1532, June 8, remission to Alexander John Carrickissone of Dunevaig and Glynnis, and three others, for their treasonable fire-raising and burning of the houses of the lands of Rosneithe, Leuenar, Craiginche, and sundry others within the realm, and with burnings, slaughters and hereschips of the lieges, inhabitants thereof, and for high treason to this date.

In the Circuit Court of Justiciary of our Sovereign Lady the Queen, Shire of Dunbarton, held and begun in the hall of the house of the Provost of the College Kirk of Dunbarton, on Monday the 18th day of the month of April, in the year of our Lord, 1547, in presence of the noble and potent Lord Archibald Earl of Argyll, Lord Campbell and Lorne, and Justice General of the kingdom of Scotland, compeared in judgment before said Justice General, Duncan M'Ferlane of Arrochar, and 58 other persons, as well as others indicated or arrested, and were accused by the ——— Rolls of being art and part in the cruel murder and slaughter of the late Robert Henry and William Henry his son, committed under silence of night in their houses of Ferslane and Little Bullernyk, on the second last day of the month of May, A.D. 1543, and for the robbery and away taking at the same time of 280 cows and cattle, old and young, 80 sheep, ewes and wedders, 24 goats, 20 horses and mares, 800 stones of cheese, 40 bolls of barley, along with the goods, utensils, and domicils which were in the houses on the said lands of Ferslane and Little Bullernyk, extenden to the value of 200 merks, which goods belonged to the late Patrick Maxwell of Newark.

THE PEATOUN MURDER.

This remarkable case has, more than once, been made the subject of dramatic narrative, on account of its harrowing interest. Lady Charlotte Bury introduced it into one of her novels, "Conduct is Fate," and a curious article upon it appeared in an old magazine, the *Scottish Monthly Magazine*, in July, 1836, under the heading of a "Tale of the Gairloch, from the Papers of Brigadier General F———." The tale opens with a description of the murderer at the market near Dunbarton, and how the General was warned by an old Highlander, "Have no dealings with a doomed man. He has either murdered his fellow being, or will do so before he is two days older. I read it on his brow like the broad mark of Cain," and thereupon the murderer mounted his horse and galloped madly from the moor. The author then goes to visit his old friend, the minister of Rosneath, and accompanies him to the funeral of the poor murdered woman who met her death shortly afterwards. A terrible scene takes place in the churchyard after the funeral, when the incriminating document, written in letters of blood, had been found, and suspicion was powerfully aroused against the guilty laird. The suspected man "sat motionless with folded arms, and his hat drawn over his face. A dim light was diffused through the church, the windows of which were almost closed by the thick foliage of the surrounding trees. There was something spectral in the noiseless tread with which the old men glided through the cool, shady, and empty building to occupy their official seats near the widower." The clergyman at length speaks and narrates how and where the paper had been found, a solemn engagement between John Campbell and Janet Campbell to marry each other, in the event of the death of the wife of the said John Campbell. "This flagitious contract, entered into with such horrid ceremonies, and deposited in such a fearful hiding-place, has been dragged into the light of day by the unwitting hands of playful innocence, at the very moment when we were depositing in the tomb the mangled remains of that wife, over whose last moments a cloud of mystery rests. John Campbell, speak and clear, or condemn yourself. Is there blood on your hands? The blood of that being whom you were pledged at the altar to cherish and defend? The blood of one who, by the mystic bond of matrimony, was bone of your bone and flesh of your flesh? The clergyman paused, and for some minutes a horrid silence pervaded the church. The whole frame of the accused was visibly convulsed. He essayed to rise, but reeled in the attempt, and clung by the nearest pew to support himself. He essayed to speak, but his voice could find no way. He grasped his throat, as if to press down the hysterical swelling which threatened to strangle him. He tore open his vest. His hat fell off, and we saw his dark locks rising from his brow as if instinct with life, his features distorted, and his complexion livid as if from suffocation. Unable to utter a word, he dashed himself again upon the seat from which he had arisen. Campbell at last faintly waved his hand, and hissed rather than spoke the words, "There is blood on my hands." At last he goes on to say, in half-whispered, hoarse accents, "It was during last autumn that, in pursuit of game, I crossed the moor that lies behind this church, and descended by that burn-side. I was standing not a gun-shot from the place where we now are, in the green field which stretches out to the sea. A slight shower had just passed away. The trees were touched with the colours of autumn, but the grass was still green, and sparkling with the recent rain-drops. The waters of the bay lay still and motionless amid the enriching woods, looking blue beneath the returning blue of the sky. The last thin wreaths of the rain-mist were passing away over the hills on the other side of the loch, and the sun had stamped a rainbow on them, through which the woods and heather looked like a vision of fairyland. I felt the beauty of earth, sea, and sky, as I never had felt them before. I was absorbed in contemplation of them. While I stood leaning on my fowling piece, lost to all impressions save those of sight, a female figure passed before me. She was tall and of a full luxurious form, but there was undulating grace in all her motions, and the springy elasticity of the roebuck in her step. Her light bonnet had fallen back and hung loosely from her neck, displaying redundant clustering ringlets of a brown colour, which was lighted up by a golden sparkle. Her white brow was high and commanding. She looked at me in passing; and what a paradise of beauty beamed from her countenance." In this highly-coloured imaginative strain the murderer continued his description of the fair being who captivated him, and who in turn yields him her heart. Then there comes the remorse he feels by and bye in allowing himself to be the victim of this love for another when he remembers his marriage vows. The unhappy man still persists in his infatuated course, and on one occasion proposes to his wife that she should embark with him on the dark waters of Loch Long for a pleasure sail, but the poor woman seemed to have become suspicious, and not without good cause. "She shrunk with horror from my proposal, and hastily left the shore. I ground my teeth together; Is the mark of Cain on my brow? I muttered to myself." He then spoke of how the girl whose heart he had won repented of her having signed the fatal bond, and wished to be released from its provisions. "One night is distinctly present to my soul. I was at midnight in the yew-tree walk, which leads from this church to the house of her father. She was with me. She wept and knelt as we stood by the church-yard wall, and implored me to destroy our unholy bond. She said for her soul's sake she dared not fulfil it, and that the bare thought of its existence was maddening to her. I could not speak; even she shrunk from my leprous association. I broke from her without a reply." He then roamed about the country side in an aimless, miserable frame of mind. "At length one day I left my horse at the Row, and crossed the ferry after sunset. I walked up and down in the dark shadow of the yew-tree walk. I was mad, if ever man was mad. I then took my way up the side of the Loch, and struck across the moor to my own dwelling;; it had long been no home for me. Passing the lake above my house, I saw something white a little way from the road-side. The moon was shining, but thin clouds passing over her face obscured the light, and the mist was creeping down the hills. I approached; it was my wife, sitting with her head bent and weeping. She had not heard my approach, and she looked up when my shadow darkened over her. She thought some heavier cloud was passing between her and the moon: it was her murderer. What need of words; I hurled her over the crag. I nerved myself to conceal and deny the deed. What will he who has the sin of blood-guiltiness on his soul not do and dare? I asked the servants when I returned to the house where their mistress was, with a clear and steady voice. I pretended to wait for her return; and then to avoid any suspicion that might arise from the omission of a habitual custom, I went through the mockery of family worship; while every moment I expected Almighty wrath would hurl a thunderbolt at the house. I sent the servants to seek for the missing one, and I gazed on her face when her mangled remains were borne into the house. Enough, you know my guilt, death is welcome; for it will relieve me from my suffering." He added in a voice of unutterable despair, "my suffering here." And shortly after this the narrative ended, showing that the author had followed, with some manifest deviations, the actual course of events in the case of this dreadful crime.

THE KILCREGGAN AND COVE WATER WORKS.

On occasion of the inauguration of the water supply for the district on 20th July, 1882, the Duke of Argyll made an interesting speech, in the course of which he gave some of his early reminiscences of the Rosneath Peninsula. After referring to the rainfall of the district His Grace went on to say, "I believe that in this parish we have an average rainfall of at least from fifty to sixty inches; nevertheless there are some peculiarities about the geographical position and the physical structure of this parish which renders it liable upon particular occasions to great want of water. You know that Rosneath is called by Sir Walter Scott the name by which it used to be called in ancient times, 'the Isle of Rosneath.' We all know that it is not strictly an island, but a Peninsula—a peninsula, however, of a somewhat peculiar character. It is a prolongation of the ridges of mountains which run to the head of Loch Long on the eastern side of that arm of the sea. It consists of one long ridge of hill with rapid slopes on the one side to Loch Long and the Firth of Clyde, and on the other side to the Gareloch. It has a very small quantity of level or hollow ground at the top, what engineers would call a very small catch basin; and the consequence is that there is a very small storage of water, and, although we may have fifty or sixty inches in average years, it runs off rapidly along the two sides of the mountain, and leaves us somewhat deficient in that element. Now, we know that a few years ago, we had some very dry summers. I do not think that we are likely to be affected in that way this season, but two or three years ago we had some very dry summers, and undoubtedly the inhabitants of this parish suffered very considerably for want of water. It was under these circumstances that the Chief Magistrate and Commissioners of this burgh conceived the idea of making a permanent supply of water to Kilcreggan. They communicated with me on the subject, and, I was very glad, indeed I have the greatest possible pleasure in doing what I could towards the promotion of so spirited an undertaking. I rejoice that it has been brought to a satisfactory conclusion, and that by the skill of our engineer, Mr. Brand, and by the energy of our contractor, Mr. Quin, both of whom are present on this occasion, we now have for the burgh of Kilcreggan an ample and constant supply of excellent water. It is now thirty-eight years since I came to take up my residence at Rosneath. At that time there was not a single house between Duchlage at the one end, and Kilcreggan at the other. When I say there was not a single house, I believe I am not strictly accurate, because there was one small cottage to the east of Cove, very near the present site of Craigrownie, which was occasionally inhabited by a gentleman from Glasgow; and I remember hearing during my earlier residence here that the climate was so favourable that those in charge of the Botanic Gardens, Glasgow, used to send their delicate plants to the garden near that cottage, in order to survive the winter at Rosneath. It was not, I think, until four or five years after this that I determined to open up this shore for feuing, and I am here to-day, after that long interval of time, an interval which has seen many go, and has seen some who were then children arrive at manhood,—I am here to-day to see a flourishing burgh, with an assessable rental of something like £13,000 a year, met together for the purpose of celebrating this great public undertaking, which will be one of great interest and value to a large, and I trust, increasing community. I know no part of Scotland where there is such a variety of beautiful views as the Peninsula and parish of Rosneath. The road across the top of the hill carries you from the magnificent prospect which is now before us—from Arran on the one side to the Bowling-green of Argyllshire on the other; that road takes you over a moor, at the top of which I have always maintained there is one of the most beautiful views which I have ever seen in any part of Europe. I now trust that the security which will be felt that there will be on all occasions, even in the driest and most occidental summers, an ample supply of water for the purpose of health and domestic use, and will induce a larger and larger number of people and families to commit their children to our healthful breezes and our beautiful scenery. I have only to point out the houses which have been erected around you, some of those houses almost fit for the mansions of large estates; sums have been expended by gentlemen upon their property, and they have laid out these sums with the confidence, under the stipulations that I have referred to, that they were coming to a quiet neighbourhood, and one which was not likely to be invaded by whisky shops of various kinds. I say, therefore, it is in the interests of you, gentlemen, who have laid out your money upon this property, to see that these stipulations are enforced, far more than it is my interest to see that they are enforced, because I have no doubt whatever that so far as my own money interests are concerned, I could get no end of land feued for the purpose of whisky shops. But I should think I would be breaking faith with you were I to enter into any such speculation. I wished, gentlemen, specially to refer to this, because, although it may be an open question with all of us whether there should be a respectable hotel or inn erected upon this shore, I wish to intimate to you distinctly that, so long as the law permits me to do so, I shall enforce every stipulation which is for your comfort or for your security from invasion, and to secure the shore from the erection of any kind of nuisance. And now, having said so much, I must warmly thank you for the kindness of your reception to-day. I am no longer permanently resident in Rosneath, but I am, and I hope I shall be, a frequent visitor. I regard it as one of my earliest, and one of my happiest homes, and I consider that there is no part of Scotland to be compared to it in the number and beauty, and variety of its views." His Grace concluded amidst loud cheers from those assembled.

Provost Clark, Kilcreggan, in the name of the other members of the Local Authority, returned thanks for a vote in favour of the Commissioners. He believed the scheme of water supply just inaugurated was an exceptionally good one, the engineering was skilful, and the workmanship thoroughly substantial. Though at first there might be grumblings as the tax-collector made his annual call, still in a good many cases a good many blessings would be mingled with the murmurings, and at the end of thirty years, in the year 1912, when the tax-collector would cease from troubling, and the next generation would succeed to the inheritance of the water supply, there would be sounds of quite a different import.

LETTER FROM MR. MACKENZIE OF CALDARVAN, CONVENER OF THE COUNTY OF DUNBARTON.

The author wrote to R. D. MacKenzie, Esq., of Caldarvan, a gentleman long and highly esteemed throughout the country, and whose great, great-grandfather was a Rosneath man, by name M'Kinnie, and received the following kind reply :—

"I am favoured with your note, and wish I could give you any information regarding the interesting and beautiful 'island' of Rosneath. My knowledge of it is confined to an occasional visit to the Clachan and its hospitable inmates; the first in 1828, when the family consisted of the old gentleman, Mr. R. Campbell, his two sisters, Betty and Ellen, and his five sons and three daughters. The only other dwellers that I remember were old Mrs. Campbell, Portkiln, her son Lorne, and her daughter, Mary M'Dougall, and old Mr. and Mrs. Cumming and their son. The old gentleman we knew as the 'Bullyruffian,' that being the name by which he spoke of the *Bellerophon*, in which he served so long, and during which he was as lost to his friends, that another heir to the estate had well-nigh completed a prescriptive title to it before he appeared to claim it. The only feus were Miss Angus's and Robertson's, and a house (Altmore) near Barremman, occupied by Mrs. Smith, Mrs. Cumming's sister and her daughters. Neil Fletcher occupied a wooden box beside his stake-nets, and Mr. Dodds, the schoolmaster, was courting the governess at the Clachan, Miss Macalister.

"My mother, who was an occasional visitor at Ardencaple, used to speak of the old castle on the shore, that was entered from near the roof, and of an untoward incident in the family of Lady Augusta Clavering, who, on the marriage of one of her daughters, Mrs.

Fletcher, told the clergyman when he asked for a certificate of proclamation that they had none, it had been forgotten. My uncle has, with glee, often told how he circumvented the minister, who, not having been asked to the ceremony, would have nothing to do with it.

"Colin Campbell, the laird of Peatoun, never visited the property. He generally paid a visit, yearly, to Sheriff Campbell at Dunbarton, and was a very nice man. The history of the family before his time I never understood, but he had a dread of the place, and would not be persuaded to visit Rosneath after his succession to the estate, although up to that time he often stayed with his uncle at the Clachan. The walk round the parish, the view from Tomnahurich, and the fishing for sea-trout in the eddies caused by the flowing tide on the west side of the Row Point, were the incidents that live in my recollection. They are all of the pleasantest, and I wish there were more of them.

"Yours very truly,

"R. D. MACKENZIE."

P.S.—"I notice you spell Roseneath with an *e*. In the course of last year I was asked as to the spelling by the County Assessor, and told him it should be 'Rosneath.' He desired to have from me as Convener of the County some warrant to change it, and I had no hesitation in saying that it should be so written."

"R. D. M."

OSSIAN AND THE CLYDE.

Dr. Hately Waddell, in his learned work, *Ossian and the Clyde*, seems to imply that the famous Gaelic hero and poet must have been familiar with some of the scenery of the Clyde which had inspired some of his grand lays, the island of Arran having clearly suggested some fine descriptive outbursts. Whether he ever set foot upon the Rosneath Peninsula may be open to question, but its rounded heath-clad heights and rock-fringed shores might well afford subjects for his muse. But when we go far back to the early ages of history, we must remember that the Frith of Clyde then, with the various lochs and inlets opening off it, was very different in appearance from what they now present to the beholder's eye. At that period the sea rolled round Dunbarton Rock, its dark blue waves reaching, perhaps, halfway up the Vale of Leven. The cliffs at the eastern side of the railway beyond Cardross, near the entrance to the tunnel at Dunbarton, clearly show that the sea once laved these fissured sides. Similarly, at the Gareloch, near Rosneath Castle, the conglomerated cliffs shew every indication of there having once been an old sea beach at their base. Dr. Waddell, in his work on Ossian, points out that marine deposits have been discovered all about Cardross and Ardmore Point, and that the acquired lands, near the former place, yearly increasing by the recession of the tide, are full of purest sea channel of all modern tints, and with similar varieties of shells. The Clyde estuary would in some places seem to be diminishing in breadth, although, as has been pointed out, in some parts of the Gareloch the soil near the beach has been gradually washed away by the tide. Long ages ago, says the learned author, there would be great changes in the Clyde estuary, "Erskine submerged, Dunbarton Rock a double-headed islet, and Cardross a tongue-land from Dunbartonshire. Ardmore and Rosneath Points, now rich with verdure and waving with trees, would then be invisible; Rosneath itself a mere circular Peninsula, tacked like an emerald by a link of rock to the solid land; Ardenslate and Hafton all but separated from Dunoon; Bute divided by Kilchattan Bay, at Kingarth; Portincross cut off from the shore, and Arran intersected by deep and rocky inlets, or scooped into wider bays. Loch Winnoch and Loch Lomond, at the date in question, would be inland seas—the Cart, the Gryffe, and Leven, as rivers, gone."

The author goes on to speculate upon the changes: "If so, and we have no reason to doubt it, then there was corresponding breadth and depth of water in the Gareloch, in the Holy Loch, and Loch Fyne. Certain it is that, in the glacial period, icebergs with their load of boulders, like crystal decanters with a cargo of pebbles, were afloat in the Gareloch. I have myself counted not fewer than 90 of these huge blocks in a mass together, the burden, doubtless, of some iceberg which had swung in from the south-east and grounded above Fernicarie. In those days the ridges between the Gareloch and Loch

Long would be a mere step, and the moor at Poltalloch, through which the Crinan Canal now runs, between Lochgilp-head, the Western Ocean would be quiet and deep water. Loch Long, for example, at no very remote period, must have been deep water a mile and more beyond the highway at Arrochar; where an alluvial deposit of vegetable matter, of which the strata can still be counted, lies plainly extended as a beautiful valley, from 15 to 36 inches deep of soil on the old bed of the sea."

THE SMITHS OF JORDANHILL.

Two distinguished members of this well-known Glasgow family resided for a number of years in the old Castle of Rosneath, now no longer in existence. Mr. James Smith, F.R.S., who was born in 1782, and died in 1867, at Jordanhill, and his residence at Rosneath closed in 1823, when he succeeded to the family estate. As a scientific discoverer and a diligent student in botany, geology, meteorology, and other physical sciences, Mr. Smith achieved very high distinction, and as an author of several works, showing much eruddition, his name adorns the ranks of literature. The great work on which his name rests is *The Voyage and Shipwreck of St. Paul, and Dissertation on the Life and Writings of St. Luke, and the Ships and Navigation of the Ancients.* This volume has gone through many editions, and has been received with unqualified approval not only in this country, but in America, and on the Continent of Europe. To quote only two testimonials from men of high eminence,—Dr. Whewell affirmed "that no finer piece of demonstrative writing has appeared since the time of Paley," and Professor Sedgewick wrote to Sir Charles Lyell, "It is one of the most remarkable critical works that ever was written—it is as clear as crystal, and as demonstrative as Euclid." Mr. Smith wrote other books and scientific treatises, and formed at Jordanhill a valuable library, more especially of works of discoveries by sea and land. For sixty years he was an enthusiastic yachtsman, and owned various crack vessels, the most notable perhaps being the *Orion*.

Mr. Archibald Smith, LL.D., F.R.S., son of the author of the *Voyage and Shipwreck of St. Paul*, had an honoured career, and his memory is affectionately cherished by all who knew him. Born in 1813, he died at the close of 1872, and many of his early years were passed in the old Castle of Rosneath. There he had lessons from the respected parish schoolmaster, Mr. John Dodds, who was always very proud of his youthful pupil. Throughout his life he was an enthusiastic lover of boats, and displayed much enterprise and daring in the voyages he carried out among the western coasts and islands of Scotland, sometimes in very diminutive craft. In 1828 he entered the University of Glasgow, and there soon showed his remarkable capacity for mathematical science, and amongst his brother students there were Tait, afterwards Archbishop of Canterbury, and Dr. Norman M'Leod, with both of whom he retained friendship through life. In 1832 he entered Trinity College, Cambridge, and in 1836 became Senior Wrangler, and first Smith's Prizeman, two coveted distinctions. Soon after this he entered upon the profession of the Chancery Bar, and gained considerable practice, and during his laborious career as a barrister, he found time for those deep mathematical and magnetic researches which gained him European fame, and nautical science received benefits, the practical importance of which can hardly be overstated. In the year 1865, the much prized gold medal of the Royal Society was awarded to Mr. Smith, and he was also elected by the Naval Scientific Committee of Russia, with the sanction of their highest authorities, a corresponding member, and the Emperor of Russia, in 1866, with a most complimentary letter, presented him with a gold compass, emblazoned with the Imperial Arms, and set with brilliants. Soon afterwards the British Government offered him a grant of £2,000, along with a highly appreciative letter from the First Lord of the Admiralty, not by way of recompence, but as a mark of the great sense the Government entertained of his distinguished services. He left many mourning friends who could testify to the warmth of his heart, his unassuming modesty, and the noble simplicity of his disposition.

OLD STEAMERS ON THE GARELOCH.

Some of the old inhabitants of the Gareloch side remember the days of the "green" and the "black" steamers, so called from their prevailing colour. The runs were fairly regular considering that the era of steam communication had not long commenced. Mr. John Kibble of Coulport can recall the time, fifty-five years ago, when the *Lochgoil*, Captain Grahame, used to land passengers at that, even now, but little frequented spot. In those days Coulport was visited chiefly by those who wished to cross to Ardentinny, and it was a romantic and secluded spot, abounding in bracken, heather and ferns, amongst the latter numerous specimens of the fine "royal fern" being encountered, though now the plundering propensities of tourists have completely eradicated this species.

An unhappy catastrophe occurred on 21st March, 1844, when the old steamer *Telegraph* blew up at noon off Helensburgh Pier, with a terrific explosion, scattering death and dismay around. Eighteen persons perished by the explosion, amongst them being Mr. Hedderwick, a member of a well known Glasgow family, and part owner of the vessel. The mid section of the steamer was blown to pieces, and some of the massive machinery thrown far up on to the beach. The water had been allowed to get too low in the boiler, and the plates got overheated, so that when cold water was suddenly introduced the whole burst with a report as if a large cannon had suddenly been discharged. This vessel was intended to work at high pressure, and to enable passengers to reach Greenock and the Gareloch in little longer time than they could do by rail.

Other Gareloch steamers were the *Clarence*, *Caledonia*, *Sultan*, *Waverley* and *Helensburgh*. The latter was of 125 gross tons, and had one side lever engine of 52 horse power, made by Robert Napier of Camlachie, latterly of Lancefield and Govan. She commenced the run as far back as 1834, and was the first steamer on the Clyde that had two eccentric rods, one for going ahead, the other astern. After doing service for a time on the Clyde, she was sold to Liverpool owners, and finally broken up at Birkenhead in 1845. The story of Henry Bell and the old *Comet*, the first steamer on the Clyde, commencing to ply as far back as 1812, has so often been told, that it need not be repeated here.

FEUING AT KILCREGGAN AND COVE.

An obliging correspondent, a native of the Peninsula, Mr. Robert Harvey, Cove, has given the author some interesting details of the feuing on Loch Long side, his information being largely derived from Mr. Jos. M'Adam, a very old inhabitant. He says, "Perhaps the only houses on the shore line at one time were the Ferry House, which stood at the foot of Mr. Richardson's road, and a few cottages at the head of where Cove Pier now stands. The Ferry House was occupied by one Peter M'Farlane, who was ferryman. One of the cottages built against the cliff at Cove Pier was then occupied by Mr. M'Lean, father of the respected post-master at Rosneath. The cottage had a large garden attached which extended over the green park, now on the low side of the road at Cove Pier. Just below the side of the garden, where the rocks dip suddenly into the Loch, is supposed to be the natural landing-place which Sir Walter Scott describes in the *Heart of Midlothian* as 'Caird's Cove.' Craigrownie cottage, built by a Mr. Thomas Forgan, was the first feu. It might almost be said that Mr. Thomas Forgan, Mr. John M'Ilroy, Mr. John Murchie, and later, Mr. Leckie, and Mr. Johnstone, really made Cove and Kilcreggan. Mr. Forgan, after building Craigrownie cottage, taking a strip of ground immediately beyond Cove Pier, and building Cove cottages, Rocklea, Seymour Lodge, Ferndean, etc. He also built Turf Hill cottages. Mr. M'Ilroy took off another strip of ground, running from where the Cove reading room now stands, down to, and including the Kirklea feu, and built a series of houses, all beautiful models of architecture—Baron Cliff, Craig Ailey, Glen Eden, etc. He also feued the ground on which Craigrownie Castle and Hartfield House, Mr. Richardson's, stand. Messrs. Forgan and M'Ilroy also built Cove Pier, I believe, in 1850. They also built a steamboat to ply on Loch Long called the *Ardentinny*. Mr. M'Ilroy was the first Provost. Mr. John Murchie built Rockburn, the first house in Kilcreggan, and a Mr. Darley built Seaview."

The present magistrates for the Burgh of Cove and Kilcreggan are: Chief Magistrate, Mr. Peter Donaldson, assisted as Junior Magistrates by Messrs. Hugh F. Murchie and Robert M'Neilage. Mr. Cayzer, M.P. was appointed County Councillor for the Burgh, and Mr. John Kinloch by the Parochial Board.

OLD ROADS IN ROSNEATH.

There is little doubt that the existing roads in the parish, with the exception of the one over the moor, and down upon Coulport, were brought into their present condition during this century. Before that they were mere rough tracks, little suitable for wheeled vehicles, and paths across the moor led from each of the farms in the Peninsula to the church and clachan village. The author has been favoured by the Rev. Mr. Calderwood, minister of Gareloch-head, with the following memorandum as to a road along the Gareloch and Loch Long, gathered from an old stone on the road-side beyond Whistlefield :—

> THIS ROAD WAS MADE
> FROM
> THE CASTLE OF ROSNETH
> TO TENNE CLAUCH
> IN THE YEAR 1777 BY HIS
> GRACE
> JOHN, DUKE OF ARGYLE
> ERECTED BY
> DONALD FRASER.

Mr. Calderwood adds, "The position of the stone is in the dyke, exactly opposite Arddarroch gate. I have given the lines and the spelling exactly as they occur. I am not at all sure, however, about the third figure in the date. It is very indistinct, and looks as if it had been tampered with. It might be 1707, or 1777, or 1787. I find that the word 'Tenne Clauch' on the inscription at Arddarroch is for 'Tighni-Cloich,' the name of an old inn which once stood at the cross-roads in Arrochar, near where the present hotel now stands. The word means 'the house by the big stone,' probably some large boulder stone beside the house."

This road would probably be made about the same time as the one along Loch Long side, past Cove and Knockderry. A similar circular space in the road, like that at Barbour, will be noticed near Mambeg pier for turning a carriage.

APPENDIX.

Rosneath Church—Succession of Clergy as far as can be traced.

        MODAN.
- 1199. MICHAELE GILMODYNE.
- 1225. NEVINUS.
- 1350. RICHARD SMALL.
- 1458. WILLIAM.
- 1515. JOHN CLERK.
- 1545. JOHN SCLAITER.
- 1565. MALCOLM STEINSON.
- 1566. DAVID COLQUHOUN (Reformed).
- 1601. GEORGE M'GLEIS.
- 1618. GEORGE LINDSAY.
- 1646. EWAN CAMERON.
- 1650. NINIAN CAMPBELL.
- 1659-63. A. GATTIE (ejected for non-conformity to Episcopacy)
- 1665. ALEXANDER CAMERON.
- 1682. JAMES GARDINER (ejected as non-juror).
- 1689. ROBERT CAMPBELL.
- 1690. DUNCAN CAMPBELL.
- 1709. NEIL CAMPBELL (afterwards Principal of University of Glasgow).
- 1719. DANIEL M'LAURIN.
- 1722. JAMES ANDERSON (father of the founder of the Andersonian Institution).
- 1745. MATTHEW STEWART (afterwards Professor of Mathematics in Edinburgh; father of Dugald Stewart).
- 1748. ALEXANDER DUNCANSON.
- 1764. JOHN KENNEDY.
- 1766. GEORGE DRUMMOND, D.D.
- 1819. ROBERT STORY.
- 1860. ROBERT HERBERT STORY, D.D. (Professor of Church History, Glasgow University).
- 1887. ALFRED WARR, M.A.

In 1839, when Mr. Story wrote his account of the parish, the living was 210½ bolls of meal, 26¾ of bear, and £8 10s. in money, with an allowance from the Duke of Argyll, for communion elements, of £5. The teinds were exhausted. The glebe contained 6½ acres of rather poor land. Of this, 1½ acres are now feued at £13 an acre. By an arrangement made with the heritors, the minister now draws the rents of the sittings in the two additions to the church.

The manse was rebuilt in 1838 chiefly out of the stones of the former manse, and considerably improved and added to in Dr Story's time.

Ancient Church History and Saints, Rosneath.

The Breviary of Aberdeen, under date February 4, has six lessons on St. Modan. I. The venerable father Modan was the reverenced and most religious father of many monks. From the very beginning of his life he passed his days under the monastic rule and habit, in poverty, chastity, and obedience; as a faithful soldier and servant of Jesus Christ, continually warring against the devil, the flesh, and the fleeting world, with the armour of faith, virtue, and righteousness. Armed with these he followed Christ and His apostles in the preaching of the Word, with manifest signs following. II. Casting aside riches, royal descent, and earthly estate, he clothed himself with the lowly cowl that he might become the heir of Christ; in frugality and sparingness of food, subduing his lower nature, content with bread and water, never using wine or flesh, but only herbs and draughts from the spring. By thus appeasing his hunger and thirst he so brought his body under, that he became a warrior of religion and a model of life in the ways of truth, virtue, and holiness. III. To how many wanderers from the light of faith did the blessed Modan restore their lost sight? How many ears, deaf and stopped up through the obduracy of unbelief, did he open to hear the voice of the Divine commands? How many transgressors, long bound in the chains of sin, did he so awaken by the ministry of the word of life, that they repented and believed, and were moved by the power of God, working through him, to renounce their evil ways? IV. Rightly, therefore, on this man, holy and dear to God, was bestowed the name of Modanus, as if, *modos odens vanos*, hating evil and vain customs, or loving those that are angelic, for what he lacked of heavenly grace he obtained by his prayers. By the gravity of his manners, and the austerity of his life, all could see the purity and modesty of his character, and he so turned the external senses, which have been termed the windows of death, that he never experienced the irregular motions of sin. V. For truly he closed these windows with the bars of Divine fear and love, and by chastity banished sensuality from the hearts of many of the sons of iniquity. He cast down anger by patience, he extinguished envy by love, he prostrated pride before humility, he overcame sloth by diligence in watching and prayer, and subdued every vice by its opposite virtue. So much so that the whole Scotic race which dwelt on the west side of the river of Forth, or Scottish sea, and at Falkirk, became imbued with his doctrine. VI. Thus the aforesaid race of the Scots had been converted to the inviolate faith of Christ by the merits, miracles, and preachings of the blessed Modan, and the disciples, who accompanied him; the saint, worn out with excessive labours and Divine studies for the salvation of that race, and himself, was so exhausted that he could scarcely walk, although still active in mind and ready to preach. Wherefore he retired to more secret places near the ocean of Scotia, not far from Dunbarton and Lochgarloch, in a spot sequestered from man by the sea and surrounding mountains.

Brief references to Modan, the saint, are given by old ecclesiastical chroniclers, such as Boetius, Leslaeus, Dempster, and Camerarius.

Sir Walter Scott, in the sixth canto of the "Lay of the Last Minstrel," thus refers to the saint of Rosneath:—

> " Then each to ease his troubled breast,
> To some blest saint his prayers addressed,
> Some to Saint Modan made their vows,
> Some to Saint Mary of the Lowes."

Chalmers mentions that Gilmodyne, the parson of Rosneath, witnessed a charter of Alwyn, Earl of Lennox, granted some time between 1180 and 1199; also, Nevin, parson of Rosneath, witnessed a charter of Amelec, the son of Alwyn, and brother of Maldowen, Earl of Lennox, in the reign of Alexander II. The patronage of the parish clerkship of Rosneath belonged to the Earls of Lennox. Chalmers also mentions that it was supposed that there was a monastery of canons regular founded at Rosneath by the old Earls of Lennox, and dedicated to the Virgin Mary. Of such an establishment at Rosneath no evidence could be discovered anywhere, and there was no indication of such a monastery in the chartularies of Lennox or Dunbarton.

APPENDIX.

In that part of the old parish of Rosneath which forms the present parish of Row there were, before the Reformation, two chapels, one of which appears to have been dedicated to St. Brigid, the other to St. Michael. The date of its erection is not known, but as it is a little way back from the shores of Faslane Bay, and in close proximity to the remains of the ancient stronghold of the Earls of Lennox, who resided at Faslane Castle, it was possibly built for that powerful family. Attached to the chapel is an old burying-ground, which is now very rarely used for interments.

STATISTICS, ROSNEATH PARISH.

From " Political Arithmetic in Dunbartonshire, 1824," by John Wilson, Esq. of Thornly.

Length of Parish, 7 miles.   Breadth, 1½ miles.
Area—English acres, 8,056.   Scotch acres, 6,445.
Valuation in County Books, £1698 6s. 8d. Scots.
Rental in the year 1792,   -   £1,000 Sterling.
Do.   do.   1810,   -   1,940   do.
Do.   do.   1824,   -   2,750   do.

Population Table.

	1755	1792	1801	1811	1821
Inhabited Houses,			98	124	127	129
Number of Families,				132	145	158
,, Persons,	521	394	632	747	754
,, Males,			207	303	378	370
,, Females,			187	329	369	384
Families chiefly employed in Agriculture,					55	56
Do. in Trade, Manufactures, or Handicrafts,					18	19
All others not comprehended in these two classes,					72	83

Ecclesiastical State.

The Parish is situated in the Synod of Glasgow and Ayr, and Presbytery of Dunbarton. Statistical account published in 1792 by the Rev. George Drummond. Duke of Argyll, patron. :—

Stipend in year 1635—112 bolls of oatmeal, 16 bolls of bear, and £2 4s. 5½d.

		£	s.	d.
Do.	in year 1755,	70	4	10¾
Do.	as estimated by W. Chalmers in 1795,	148	1	3
Do.	do. agricultural survey in 1810,	199	15	0
Do.	per decreet, 23rd May, 1821, modified to 15 chalders victual=240 bolls—half meal, half barley, £292 10 9 Money, £8 6s. 8d.; Manse and Glebe, £50, 58 6 8	350	17	5

Poor.

Their number in 1792—13.

Collections at the Church door, dues of marriages, mortcloths, etc., - - - £10 10 0
Interest of £150, accumulated stock, - 7 10 0
                  £18 0 0

In the Agricultural Survey in 1810 the number of the Poor—12.
Collections at the Church door, etc., - £18 0 0
Interest of £150, stock and Session funds, 12 0 0
                  £30 0 0

Number of Poor in 1817—11.

Annual amount of Collections at Church door, - - - - - £20 0 0
Do. of voluntary contributions, - 10 0 0
Do. Session funds, exclusive of collections, - - - - - 2 15 0
                  32 15 0

Highest rate paid per annum to Paupers, £5; lowest, £1 1s.

School.

Number of Scholars in 1792—38. Schoolmaster's salary, £8 9 0
Schoolmaster's other emoluments, - - - - - 8 7 0
                  £16 16 0

Number of scholars in 1810—40.
Schoolmaster's emoluments—£40.
Number of proprietors—3; number of farmers—48.

APPENDIX.

The ancient church of Rosneth was said to have been dedicated to St. Nicholas. It stood near the present church, and in the earliest notices was called the Church of Neueth or Church of Rosneth.

In the reign of Robert II. the lands of Rosneth were granted by Mary, widowed Countess of Monteith, to John De Drommond, and, by him, given to Alexander De Menteith. Legally annexed to the Crown, along with the Castle of Dunbarton, 1455, but Colin, 1st Earl of Argyll, had charter of lands of Rosneth under Great Seal of January, 1489. The Castle of Rosneth had existed as a royal castle before the end of the 12th century.

THE END.